IMPECCABLE GUIDANCE TO 2,138 WINES

For professional advice on almost any wine purchase you will ever make, turn to this comprehensive, convenient resource. No matter where you are—in the finest restaurant or your local liquor store—this essential guide will provide you with the information you need to make the wine selections that are best for you.

CRAIG GOLDWYN is the publisher of *International Wine Review* and wine critic for *The Washington Post*.

RICHARD FIGIEL is the editor of *International Wine Review* and co-author of *A Dictionary of American Wine*.

What the critics say about *International Wine Review* and its wine judgings:

"Smashing. The best wine magazine in America!"
  Robert Lewis Thompson
  Washington Post

"Long overdue."
  Frank Prial
  New York Times

"First rate. Very conscientious."
  Richard Paul Hinkle
  San Francisco Examiner

"Historic...revolutionary."
  Leon Adams
  Author of The Wines of America

"The most objective and authoritative."
  John Meredith
  Denver Post

EDITORS
Richard Figiel
Craig Goldwyn

CONTRIBUTING EDITORS
John Binder
Carole Collier
Jerry D. Mead
Denman Moody Jr.
Judy Peterson-Nedry
Christina Reynolds
Sheldon & Pauline Wasserman

ASSISTANT EDITOR
Elizabeth Schwartz

Special thanks to the readers of *International Wine Review,* who feed us; to our stockholders, who have made it all happen; to the rest of our staff; and to the "Grand Crew."

Macintosh typesetting by
Cayuga Press, Ithaca, NY

International Wine Review is a registered trademark of the Beverage Testing Institute, Inc. If you would like to subscribe to *International Wine Review* and receive this kind of handy buying information every other month, use the subscription form in this book or write to International Wine Review, c/o New American Library, PO Box 999, Bergenfield, NJ 07621. Subscriptions cost $30 in the US and its possessions, $35 to Canada (in US currency, $40 in Canadian currency), $42.50 to overseas locations.

THE
WINE REVIEW
INTERNATIONAL
BUYER'S GUIDE

by the Editors of
INTERNATIONAL WINE REVIEW

A PLUME BOOK

NAL PENGUIN INC.

NEW YORK AND SCARBOROUGH, ONTARIO

LIBRARY OF
WINE INSTITUTE

Dedicated to the people who put
up with us and support us.

NAL PENGUIN BOOKS ARE AVAILABLE AT QUANTITY
DISCOUNTS WHEN USED TO PROMOTE PRODUCTS OR
SERVICES. FOR INFORMATION PLEASE WRITE TO
PREMIUM MARKETING DIVISION, NAL PENGUIN INC.,
1633 BROADWAY, NEW YORK, NEW YORK 10019.

 PLUME TRADEMARK REG. U. S. PAT. OFF. AND
FOREIGN COUNTRIES
REGISTERED TRADEMARK—MARCA REGISTRADA
HECHO EN HARRISBURG, VA., U.S.A.

SIGNET, SIGNET CLASSIC, MENTOR, ONYX, PLUME,
MERIDIAN AND NAL BOOKS are published *in the
United States* by NAL Penguin Inc., 1633 Broadway,
New York, New York 10019, and *in Canada* by The New
American Library of Canada Limited, 81 Mack
Avenue, Scarborough, Ontario M1L 1M8

**Library of Congress Cataloging-in-Publication
Data**

The International wine review buyer's guide.

  Includes index.
  1. Wine and wine making. I. International wine
review.
TP 548.I58 1987   641.2′22   87–1528
ISBN 0–452–25922–3

First Printing, April, 1987

1 2 3 4 5 6 7 8 9

PRINTED IN THE UNITED STATES OF AMERICA

CONTENTS

The wine reviews in this book are divided into five major sections, one each for the five major wine types: red, white, pink, sparkling, and fortified. Within each section, the wines are divided into chapters according to how the wines are labeled and where they are made. Some chapters are named after important grape varieties, and other chapters are named after places — this is because some wine regions name their wines after grape varieties and other regions name their wines after the region.

❦

HOW TO USE THIS BOOK

HOW TO USE THIS BOOK

Walking into a wine shop or picking up a restaurant wine list can be intimidating and bewildering, even when you're no stranger to the wine world. There are simply too many different kinds of wines from too many different regions and countries with too many exotic names for any one person to know about them all.

But that same bewildering diversity makes wine the most fascinating of beverages and, indeed, the most fascinating of all foods. The adventures waiting for your nose and your tongue are limitless. Like all great adventures, exploring the world of wine calls for a good guide, one that describes the terrain in detail and gives you sound advice from experts who have been there.

We hope you will put this book in your briefcase, purse, glove compartment, or back pocket, and use it to guide you in your shopping. It will no doubt help you uncover some great wines and some great bargains.

About the listings, ratings, and tasting notes

This book consists primarily of a listing of wines with brief tasting notes and ratings, condensed from reviews appearing in issues of *International Wine Review* magazine from September 1985 to January 1987. It is intended to serve as a handy buyer's guide for use when you buy wine, as a companion for tasting wines, and as a reference to back issues of *International Wine Review*.

International Wine Review is a magazine that reviews and rates wines from around the world six times a year. Each issue features analysis of trends, new developments, market information, and buying tips, accompanied by tasting notes and ratings on hundreds of wines.

In four issues per year, a team of experts

focuses on wines from the world's major regions in France, California, the Northwest, the East, Germany, Italy, Spain, Portugal, and others, plus a special column on Rare Wines. The contributors to these "Critic's Choice" issues are listed below as Contributing Editors.

The other two issues of *International Wine Review*'s annual publishing schedule are devoted to two prestigious wine judgings: the American Wine Competition and the Bordeaux Classic. They are the most rigorous, professionally run wine judgings in the world. Each wine is tasted "blind" by a panel of expert judges from the wine trade, whose independent scores are averaged. Descriptions of the wines are compiled from all the judges' tasting notes. When wines received no medals in these competitions, they are listed in this book without a star rating and usually without tasting notes.

Each wine listed in this book has the initials of the source for the review.

AWC — American Wine Competition. Each year *International Wine Review* sponsors a competition dubbed by the press and trade "the Superbowl of Wine." The first judging to invite entries from every winery in the US, the American Wine Competition rates the nation's top varietal wines made from Cabernet Sauvignon, Pinot Noir, Merlot, Chardonnay, and Riesling. Both the 1985 and 1986 competitions are included in this book.

BC — The Bordeaux Classic. Each year *International Wine Review* conducts a judging of wines from the most recently released vintage of Bordeaux. A panel of Bordeaux experts assembles at the International Wine Center in New York City for three days to evaluate the wines. The two most recent vintages judged, the 1982 and 1983 vintages, are included in this book.

Contributing Editors

The wine reviews in this book that were not taken from the Bordeaux Classic or American Wine Competition were written by *International Wine Review*'s distinguished staff of contributing editors. Their initials follow the tasting notes:

JB — John Binder has worked in many levels of the wine retail, wholesale, and importing trades since 1977 in New York, Washington, California, and Chicago. His specialty is German wines. He is also an accomplished harmonica player specializing in Chicago blues; truly a talented tongue.

CC — Carole Collier is the author of *505 Wine Questions Your Friends Can't Answer* and *Collier's Wine Line: Computer Guide to Wine and Food*, a computer program designed for consumer reference in wine shops. She lived in Europe for 10 years and frequently travels to European and American vineyards and to wine judgings on the East and West Coasts. Her specialty is French wines.

RF — Richard Figiel is editor of *International Wine Review*, and co-author of *A Dictionary of American Wine* and *A Price Guide to Good Wine*. He also cultivates a "grass-roots" relationship to wine with his own vineyard in New York's Finger Lakes area. His specialty is the wines of the eastern US.

CG — Craig Goldwyn is publisher of *International Wine Review*, wine columnist for the *Washington Post* and *Syracuse Post-Standard*, wine editor of *Restaurant Hospitality* magazine, and a contributor to Lichine's *Encyclopedia of Wines & Spirits*. He also teaches wine appreciation at Cornell University. His specialty is anything that pours.

JDM — **Jerry D. Mead** is the author of the longest-running and most widely circulated syndicated wine column on the West Coast. He was named the 1985 Wine Writer of the Year by the trade publication *Wines & Vines*. He is chairman of the judging panel and founder of the Orange County Fair Commercial Wine Competition. His specialty is California wines.

DM — **Denman Moody Jr.** published the highly respected newsletter *Moody's Wine Review* until it merged with *International Wine Review* in 1983. Vice president of E. F. Hutton in Houston, Texas, he has an extensive cellar of rare wines which he calls "one of my best investments." His specialty is the world's great wines, and he writes a column on rarities in *International Wine Review*..

JPN — **Judy Peterson-Nedry** is the wine columnist for *Oregon Magazine* and author of the book *Showcase Oregon Wineries*. She also writes a weekly wine column for Portland's *This Week Magazine*. Her specialty is the wines of the Northwest.

CR — **Christina Reynolds** has worked as a wine retailer and wholesaler but considers herself first and foremost a wine educator. Her specialty is uncovering fine wines and great bargains from off the beaten path.

S&PW — **Sheldon & Pauline Wasserman** are the authors of seven books on wine, including *The Noble Red Wines of Italy* and *Guide to Sparkling Wines* . In 1985 they won the Barbi-Colombini Journalistic Award for an article on Brunello di Montalcino in *International Wine Review*. They write a column in *International Wine Review* on the wines of Italy, Spain, and Portugal.

Reading the wine reviews

All the reviews in this book are arranged in the same sequence. The first part of each listing is the name of the producer or brand name by which the wine is known. It is followed by the vintage, and then the grape variety, if any is listed on the label, then any special lot number or special designation, then the viticultural region from which the wine comes, and finally, the price. All of this information is in **boldface** type. For most wines, this label information is followed by a description of the wine. Then, in parentheses, we have listed the initials of the contributing editor who wrote the review, or the initials of the wine judging from which notes were taken. After the initials there is a slash and the date of the issue of *International Wine Review* in which the review originally appeared. The last item in each review is the rating, on a four-star scale.

Here is a fictitious example:

Domaine Brouhaha 1983 Chardonnay, Private Reserve, Bill's Vineyard, Napa Valley, CA $18.50. Rich bouquet shows wisps of smoke and pine. Flavors of ripe fruit and toasty, vanilla-like oak, balanced with healthy acidity. A heavyweight. (AWC/Nov. '86) ★★★1/2 (★★★★)

In this example, the name of the winery is Domaine Brouhaha, and the wine is a 1983 vintage made from Chardonnay grapes. This particular wine is the "Private Reserve" made from grapes grown in "Bill's Vineyard" in Napa Valley, California. It is different from two other Chardonnays made by Domaine Brouhaha. One is a private reserve from Jim's Vineyard in Sonoma Valley, and the other is also from Jim's Vineyard, but not a private reserve. The description is excerpted from the tasting notes of the judges at the American Wine Competition, and the review originally appeared in the November 1986 issue of *International Wine Review*.

Ratings

Our contributing editors rate wines on a four-star scale. This scale is based on how much the reviewers *like the wines* rather than on any attempt to be objective. The publishers believe that wine cannot be judged objectively. Taste is a matter of taste.

The judges at the American Wine Competition and Bordeaux Classic score the wines on a numerical scale and medals are awarded based on their average score. In order to make the ratings in this book uniform, we have converted the medals to the four-star scale. Below are the definitions of the ratings showing how much the contributing editors liked each wine, or what medal it won.

★★★★—Like extremely or Platinum Medal
★★★1/2—Like very strongly or Gold Medal
★★★—Like strongly or Silver Medal
★★—Like slightly or Bronze Medal
★—Neither like nor dislike, a useful wine
(★)—Estimated peak score with aging
No Star—A wine with no star is a wine that won no medal in competition or a wine that the reviewer disliked.

Listing Order

Under each wine category such as Red Bordeaux or Chardonnay, wines are listed in the order of their rating, beginning with the highest-rated wines. All wines with the same rating (for example, all Chardonnays with ★★★ ratings) are listed alphabetically.

Prices

Unless otherwise stated, prices are typical of major markets for standard, 750-ml bottles *at the time the reviews were written* (check the dates following the tasting notes). The prices of some wines are likely to rise as time passes. Prices may also vary *significantly* from state to state and store to store.

About the index

All the wines reviewed in this book are listed alphabetically by producer in the index, with the page number on which each review appears. If you want to look up a particular wine, the index is the place to turn first.

Finding the wines you want

Many of the wines reviewed are limited in production, and complicated marketing agreements often make wines that are bestsellers in one city unavailable in another.

There are thousands of wines on the market in the US and Canada, making it impossible for even big stores to carry more than a fraction of them. Big stores in large metropolitan areas are likely to stock more recent vintages of more wines from more regions, while rural and small stores tend to have a limited selection and fewer new releases.

Many merchants are happy to special-order wines if they are available from their wholesale suppliers. If wines you want are not available in your area, try to shop when you visit other cities. You might also ask friends living in major cities to pick up a bottle or a case for you.

Finally, don't limit your search to four- or three-star wines; there are many other good wines and bargains listed on these pages. Read the tasting notes.

Subscribing to
International Wine Review

If you would like to subscribe to *International Wine Review* and receive this kind of handy buying information every other month, use the subscription form in this book or write to *International Wine Review,* PO Box 285-G, Ithaca, NY 14851 USA. One-year subscriptions cost $30 in the US and its possessions, $35 to Canada (in US currency, $40 in Canadian currency), $42.50 to overseas locations. ❏

DRINKABILITY
ODDS CHART

International Wine Review DRINKABILITY ODDS CHART

Here is the wine buyer's counterpart to the horseracing form, showing you the odds for finding an excellent bottle of wine from the last 11 vintages available from the world's key wine regions. As in horseracing, there are no guarantees in betting the bottles. In any great vintage there are some mediocre wines made, and in an average or even poor vintage there are often some very good wines made.

There is ultimately no substitute for ratings and tasting notes on individual wines. It is also wise to cultivate a relationship with a knowledgeable and reputable wine merchant whose recommendations are based on his or her own sampling, not on inventory or price.

Regular numbers show the odds for finding an excellent wine for current drinking. For wines that need more aging to reach their peak, ratings are printed in **_bold italics_** and reflect the wine's potential rather than current drinkability. Wines at or past their peak are rated for current drinkability.

ODDS FOR EXCELLENCE

1   **Stacked in your favor**
2   **Favorable**
3   **Even odds**
4   **Outside**
5   **Long shot**
X   **Sucker bet**

A   Except Pinot Noir and Gamay, which ripen early like most white varieties. (Refer to ratings for whites.)
B   Except Riesling, which ripens late like most red varieties. (Refer to ratings for reds.)
C   Better in Mosel.
D   Better in Pomerol and St. Emilion than Médoc.
E   Better in Chablis.
F   Production was very small.
G   Better in Vouvray.
H   Better in Rosso di Montalcino.
I   Not as good in Mendocino and Lake Counties.
J   It is too soon to be certain about these wines.

This chart will be updated in June 1987.

Readers may order wallet-size versions of this chart by sending $1 ($1.25 Canadian) to *International Wine Review,* PO Box 285, Ithaca, NY 14851. Custom printing and bulk prices on quantities of more than 100 available on request.

RED WINES	85J	84	83	82	81	80	79	78	77	76	75	GREATEST VINTAGES
BORDEAUX	1D	4	2	1	3	4	2	1	5	5	1	85,83,82,78,75,70,66,61,59,53,49,47
BURGUNDY	1	4	2	3	3	3	3	2	X	X	X	85,78,71,61,59,49,47,45,37,34,29,28
BEAUJOLAIS	1	2	3	X	X	X	X	X	X	X	X	85,78,76,71,67,61,59,53,49,45,29,28
COTE ROTIE, HERMITAGE (N. RHONE)	1	4	1	1	3	3	2	1	5	3	X	85,78,71,61,59,53,49,45,29
CHATEAUNEUF DU PAPE (S. RHONE)	2	3	2	2	3	3	2	1	X	4	X	78,61,59,53,49,45,29
BAROLO, BARBARESCO	2	4	3	1	4	3	3	2	X	3	X	82,78,71,61,58,47
GATTINARA, GHEMME, SPANNA	2	5	3	2	3	2	3	1	X	3	5	82,78,74,64,52
BRUNELLO	2	4	1	2H	4	3	3	3	2	X	1	83,75,70,64,61,55,45
VINO NOBILE	2	5	2	2	3	4	3	4	4	X	X	75,70,67,58
CHIANTI CLASSICO RISERVA	2	4	1	2	4	2	2	3	2	X	2	83,75,71,64,58,49,47
RIOJA	1	3	3	1	1	2	4	2	X	2	2	85,78,70,68,64,55,52
NAPA, SONOMA, MENDOCINO, LAKE — A	2	4	3	2	2	3	2	2	3	3	2	75,74,70,68,64,51,46
MONTEREY, S.L. OBISPO, S. BARBARA — A	2	3	4	2	2	2	3	2	3	3	4	80,77,74,70,68
AMADOR, SHENANDOAH, LODI ZINFANDEL	2	2	3	3	3	2	3	3	4	4	4	80,74
WASHINGTON, IDAHO — A	1	2	1	2	2	2	2	3	3	3	2	83,80,79,78,75
OREGON PINOT NOIR	1	3	1	2	3	3	3	5	4	4	3	85,83,79,76,75
ATLANTIC COAST CABERNET SAUVIGNON	4	2	1	2	4	2	4	X	X	X	X	83
VINTAGE PORTO	F	F	3	3	F	3	F	2	F	F	3	77,70,63,55,48,45,31,27,12,08,04

WHITE WINES	85	84	83	82	81	80	79	78	77	76	75	GREATEST VINTAGES
BORDEAUX	2	4	2	5	2	4	X	X	X	X	X	'75,71,62,61,59,55,53,49,45,37,29,28
BURGUNDY, MACON, CHABLIS	1	2	3	5	5	3	2	X	3	X	X	'85,78,71,69,67,66,62,55,53,52,49,47
VINTAGE FRENCH CHAMPAGNE	2	3	2	2	4E	5	2	2	F	3	2	'79,75,71,64,55,49,47,45,37,29,28,23
ALSACE	2	3	1	2	3	3F	X	X	X	X	X	'83,76,71,64,59,49,47,45
LOIRE	2G	2	1	4	4	X	X	X	X	X	X	'76,71,64,59,49,47,45
SAUTERNES, BARSAC	3	5	2	2	3	3	3	X	1	X	2	'76,67,62,59,55,53,50,47,45,37,29
RHEINGAU, MOSEL (QUAL, KAB., SPAT.)	1	4	1	3	3	3C	X	5	4	4	4	'85,83,75,71,64,59
RHEINGAU, MOSEL (AUSLESE, BA, TBA)	F	F	2	F	F	3	F	F	2	2	2	'76,75,71,67,59,53,49,45,37,34,21
CALIFORNIA DRY WHITES — B	2	3	3	3	4	4	4	X	5	X	X	'80,78,75,73
CALIFORNIA BOTRYTISED RIESLING	2	1	2	3	5	3	3	X	5	5	X	'78,73
WASHINGTON, IDAHO — B	1	2	2	2	4	4	5	5	X	X	X	'85,82,80,78
FINGER LAKES CHARD., RIESLING, SEYVAL	2	3	1	2	3	3	X	X	X	X	X	'82,83,80,78,75

INVESTING IN WINE

INVESTING IN WINE:
how liquid are your assets?

by Craig Goldwyn

Wine can be a great investment because it can increase in value rapidly, but the wine investor has several big problems, not the least of which is the fact that, as an investment, wine is not very liquid.

Except in a few isolated cases, it is illegal to sell alcoholic beverages without a license. So to whom do you sell your magnum of Château Haut Brion 1947, or your case of Heitz 1974 Martha's Vineyard Cabernet Sauvignon? A number of years ago a New Jersey wine collector advertised in a newspaper that he wanted to liquidate his $33,000 cellar. After a sting operation by the state, the entire cache was confiscated.

A few retail stores will buy wine "under the table," but most are not willing to risk their liquor licenses for a few rare bottles.

A few states permit you to sell your collection to licensed wholesalers, but wholesalers will pay only about one half to two thirds of its retail value so that they can take a markup when they resell it to the retailer and the retailer can also take a markup.

The buying and selling of wine between private individuals is illegal in most states, but it does indeed take place.

You could try to sell your wine at an auction. There are currently only a handful of wine auctions in the United States each year. The few wines that reach the block come mostly from the cellars of well-known collectors or merchants. They are usually case lots or large bottles. And there is, of course, no guarantee how much money they will bring. Whatever that amount, shipping costs and the auctioneer's commission must be subtracted.

The venerable English auction house Christie's holds auctions in Chicago several times per year. It charges the seller a 10% commission and buyers a 15% commission. For more information, contact Michael Davis, Christie's, 200 W. Superior, Chicago, IL 60610; telephone 312-951-1011.

Also in Chicago, the Chicago Wine Company holds several auctions where rare wines are sold to the highest mail bidder. It is actively seeking wine to sell. The Chicago Wine Company charges a 25% commission to the seller and no commission to the buyer. Contact John Hart or Phillip Tannenbaum, Chicago Wine Company, 5663 Howard St., Niles IL 60648; telephone 312-647-8789.

There are several other auctions that are primarily charity events and expect you to donate your cache.

Despite all the problems of liquidity, many individuals in this country have enhanced their portfolio of investments with a steadily appreciating collection of fine wines.

The buying and selling of wine between private individuals is illegal in most states but it does indeed take place. *International Wine Review* magazine (PO Box 285, Ithaca, NY 14851; telephone 607-273-6071) and the California newsletter *The Wine Trader* (881 Sneath Lane #114, San Bruno, CA 94066; telephone 415-588-9463) carry free classified-type advertisements from private individuals wishing to swap wines.

Then there is the question of the wine's condition. Wine must be stored at constant cool temperatures. Cellar-aged wines might not taste any better than closet-aged wines when they mature, but in cool cellars or vaults, wines age more slowly. Potential buyers will want to know the wine's pedigree: how long you have had the wine, who had it before you, and how it was stored.

The appearance of the label is important. Although the wine itself may be unaffected, a damaged label makes it less attractive and less sellable. A badly faded label is usually an indication that the bottle was not stored in the dark. Light is the bitter enemy of wine, and you should never leave your collector's items on a wine rack in the living room to impress the neighbors.

The ullage or air space in the bottle is also an important clue to the soundness of the wine, indicating if there has been excessive evaporation or leakage through the cork. The level of old wine should not be more than one inch below the cork.

Corks deteriorate with age, and very old wines should be recorked every 25-30 years. The corks of better wines usually have the winery name and vintage printed on them. If the bottle has been recorked, you should have the original cork and a certificate from the expert who recorked it.

Even if your wine passes muster on all these accounts, a prospective buyer may still want to taste a bottle to check its development and make sure it has been properly stored.

Despite all the problems of liquidity, many individuals in this country have enhanced their portfolio of investments with a steadily appreciating collection of fine wines.

For most consumers, the only investment worth making in wine is as a hedge against inflation. If you buy carefully today, the replacement cost of your purchase certainly will increase at least as fast as inflation, and when you drink an $80 wine that you bought 10 years ago for $8, it will surely taste better.

You should buy only the best vintages of the most famous estates. Most other wines are not collectable because they are not famous or scarce enough.

The most reliable investment wines are red Bordeaux from any of about 75 major chateaux. The best investments, by far, are the "first growths:" Château Lafite-Rothschild, Château Mouton Rothschild, Château Latour, Château Margaux, Château Haut Brion, Pétrus, Château Ausone, and Château Cheval Blanc. Most of these wines have been in highest demand for the past two centuries. For investment purposes you should buy only the best vintages: 1983, '82, '79, '78, '75, '70, '66, '61, '59, '55, '53, '49, '47, '45, '37, '29, '28, and a few older ones.

The best buys in futures come when the vintage is the first excellent vintage in several years.

The great sweet white Sauternes, Château d'Yquem, is bankable in better years ('75, '67, '59, '55, '53, '50, '47, '37, '29). Château d'Yquem is in a clear bottle, and its value is usually based on its color. Golden-to-amber is the color limit, although some necrophiliacs still buy them after they've turned brown.

Burgundy is a crapshoot because the best producers are very small, and even they are uneven in quality. The most bankable are the wines from the Domaine de la Romanée-Conti and Musigny from Comte Georges de Vogue.

The younger you can get any of these "investment wines," the better. Usually it is best to get in on the first offering of "futures," about 18 months after the harvest. This can be risky, however, because when the first offering of futures is made, the wines are still in the barrel, their quality is unknown, and the producers are given to hyperbole in describing them. The best buys in futures come when the vintage is the first excellent vintage in several years.

The 1982 vintage was an excellent investment. The first growths increased an average of 66% during the two years from first offering in spring 1983 to their arrival in the US in spring 1985. The second through fifth growths appreciated an average of about 37% during the same period.

Insiders are busily collecting the California Cabernet Sauvignons that have established a track record for both excellence and ageability. They are good candidates for investment because California Cabs are routinely consumed when too young, then become scarce. Those with the greatest growth potential are Beaulieu (BV) Private Reserve, Buehler, Buena Vista, Burgess, Caymus, Carneros Creek, Chappellet, Chateau Montelena, Clos du Val, Diamond Creek, Dry Creek, Duckhorn, Durney, Flora Springs, Freemark Abbey, Heitz, Inglenook Cask, Jekel, Jordan, Kenwood, Mayacamas, Mondavi, Mt. Eden, Mt. Veeder, Newton, Opus One, Phelps, Ridge, Sequoia Grove, Spring Mountain, Stag's Leap Wine Cellars, Sterling, and William Hill.

Usually the older the wine is, the more expensive it is, assuming it has been stored properly. But there is no way to accurately compute a wine's value. A wine's beauty is on the tongue of the beholder. There is no book listing values for rare wines, though Christie's does publish an index of prices paid at American and English auctions. In the end, if you cannot find someone willing to buy, legally or otherwise, your investment is worth only the pleasure found in drinking it. ❏

RED WINES

ABBREVIATIONS & SYMBOLS

RATINGS

★★★★—Like extremely or Platinum Medal
★★★1/2—Like very strongly or Gold Medal
★★★—Like strongly or Silver Medal
★★—Like slightly or Bronze Medal
★—Neither like nor dislike, a useful wine
(★)—Estimated peak score with aging
No Star—A wine with no star is a wine that won no medal in competition or a wine that the reviewer disliked.

WHO WROTE THE DESCRIPTIONS

AWC—American Wine Competition Judges
BC—Bordeaux Classic Judges
JB—John Binder
CC—Carole Collier
RF—Richard Figiel
CG—Craig Goldwyn
JDM—Jerry D. Mead
DM—Denman Moody Jr.
JPN—Judy Peterson-Nedry
CR—Christina Reynolds
S&PW—Sheldon & Pauline Wasserman

PRICES. Prices are typical of those in major metropolitan markets for standard, 750-ml bottles *at the time the review was written* (note the date following the descriptions). The prices of some wines are likely to rise as time passes. Prices may also vary *significantly* from state to state and store to store.

AVAILABILITY. Some wines may be hard to find because they are produced in small quantities, and distribution methods often make wines that are bestsellers in one city unavailable in another. Even large stores can't carry more than a fraction of the thousands of wines sold in the US and Canada, so many merchants are happy to order wines for you. If can't find wines you want in your area, try to shop when you're in other major cities.

BORDEAUX

Bordeaux is, by acclamation, the king of red wines. It comes from France's largest premium vineyard region, in the southwestern part of the country. Four districts within Bordeaux — Médoc, Graves, Pomerol, and St. Emilion — account for all of the area's great red wines, though many other very good and much less expensive wines are made in surrounding districts.

Red Bordeaux is made from one or more of five grape varieties: Cabernet Sauvignon, Merlot, Cabernet Franc, Verdot, and Malbec. Blends vary from district to district, vintage to vintage, and vineyard to vineyard, but the wines of Médoc and Graves generally highlight Cabernet while those of Pomerol and St. Emilion rely more on Merlot. As a result, Médocs tend to be harder, more austere wines in their youth, and more long-lived, but all of the best Bordeaux wines from good vintages require at least a few years of bottle age.

"Claret" is the British term for classic Bordeaux — wine which tastes harsh and awkward for its first five years or so, then flavors begin to harmonize, tannins soften, and the best wines gain amazing depth, complexity, and subtlety.

More than 130 years ago, the top wines of Médoc were officially classified into five quality levels, a classification that is still used today and has remained remarkably, though not perfectly, accurate. There are 61 châteaux included, collectively known as the "grands crus."

The best wines from Bordeaux are always labeled "Mis en Bouteilles au Château," meaning they were grown, made, and bottled by the estate named on the label. This doesn't guarantee top quality, but it makes it much more likely.

Ch. Cheval Blanc 1982 St. Emilion, 1st Grand Cru $60. Glorious nose of wood and intense, spicy fruit. A quilt of coffee, chocolate, tea, smoke, toast, mint, cedar flavors. Powerful, intense, but also shows real elegance and breed. Needs more than five years. (BC/Sept. '85) ★★★★

Ch. Cos d'Estournel 1982 St. Estèphe, 2nd Cru $30. Cassis, berries, coffee, spice. Complexity with harmony. Chewy. Long finish shows black cherries, licorice, and tannin. A keeper. (BC/Sept. '85) ★★★★

Ch. Duhart-Milon-Rothschild 1982 Pauillac, 4th Cru $18. Lush, concentrated, spicy fruit with hints of cedar, coffee, tobacco. Gracious balance and harmony. (BC/Sept. '85) ★★★★

Ch. Figeac 1983 St. Emilion, 1st Grand Cru $45. Intense, berry aromas with cedar, mint, vanilla, nutmeg, jasmine, and a vegetal note. Layers of flavor: currants, berries, and new oak. Soft. Should ascend for many years. (BC/July '86) ★★★★

Ch. Haut Brion 1982 Graves, 1st Cru $60. Huge fruit explodes with scents of wet stones, earth, and smoke. Dense, chewy, with tremendous length. Balanced from beginning to end. Needs more than five years. (BC/Sept. '85) ★★★★

Ch. La Lagune 1982 Haut-Médoc, 3rd Cru $25. Evolved nose: lots of new wood, spice, ripe fruit, cedar, vanilla, chocolate. Big, firm, well-structured. Great charm, breed. Soft tannins need five or more years. (BC/Sept. '85) ★★★★

Ch. Latour 1961 Pauillac, 1st Cru $300. A real powerhouse; the greatest of the huge-style '6ls. (DM/Mar. '86) ★★★★

Ch. Latour 1964 Pauillac, 1st Cru $200+. Great depth and character, drinking beautifully now. (DM/Mar. '86) ★★★★

Ch. Latour 1970 Pauillac, 1st Cru $200+. Very deep, attractive nose. Impressive fruit quality under a cloak of semi-tender tannin. (DM/Mar.'86) ★★★★

Ch. Margaux 1982 Margaux, 1st Cru $60. Lively, spicy, berry scents and aggressive new wood. Intense, ripe fruit. Well balanced with oak, acid, tannin. Long, elegant finish. Fleshy, exuberant. Long cellaring potential. (BC/Sept. '85) ★★★★

Ch. Margaux 1983 Margaux, 1st Cru $90. Remarkable nose with vanilla, new oak, plums, dill, cassis, mint, meat, violets. Intense fruit. Deep, well balanced. Good acidity and tannin. Power and elegance. Will improve for 20 years. (BC/July '86) ★★★★

Ch. Latour 1967 Pauillac, 1st Cru $75+ Surprisingly rich, floral bouquet, and full flavor. No acidity problem here, which plagues many of the '67s. Drink now. (DM/Mar. '86) ★★★1/2

Vieux Ch. Certan 1983 Pomerol $40. Cedar, lilacs, and apricots in the nose. Long, luscious, harmonious flavors of plum and bramble-berries. Great breed. Plenty of cellaring potential. (BC/July '86) ★★★1/2

Ch. Ausone 1983 St. Emilion, 1st Grand Cru $90. Fruit and cedar aromas. Understated and elegant. Perfect balance of fruit and wood. Needs at least five more years. (BC/July '86) ★★★1/2

Ch. Baret 1982 Graves $8.49. Rich, complex, deep fruit, suggesting raspberries, spice and earth. Big bodied and tannic. Classy. Needs more than five years. (BC/Sept. '85) ★★★1/2

Ch. Beauséjour 1983 St. Emilion, 1st Grand Cru $25. Mixture of fruity and vegetal aromas: cassis, cedar, bell pepper, black pepper. Excellent balance of fruit, tannin, alcohol, and acid. Well-structured. Long finish. (BC/July '86) ★★★1/2

Ch. Belair 1983 St. Emilion, 1st Grand Cru $25. Aroma of plums and cherries overlaid with tobacco, pepper, other spices. Tight structure. Tannins create a dusty impression. Should improve significantly with five-plus years of aging. (BC/July '86)

★★★1/2

Ch. Berliquet 1983 St. Emilion, Grand Cru $11.99. Fruit and cedar aromas. Lovely, mouth-filling, varietal Merlot character. Big, chewy, promising. Drink in three to seven years. (BC/July '86) ★★★1/2

Ch. Branaire 1982 St. Julien, 4th Cru $21.99. Balanced, intense, jammy fruit, lots of tannin, not too much oak. Elegant wine. Needs five or more years. (BC/Sept. '85) ★★★1/2

Ch. Branaire 1983 St. Julien, 4th Cru $15.95. Sweet, cherry-like nose has floral, vanilla, cedar, cinnamon tones. Concentrated, minty fruit. Lively acidity. Tannic finish. Needs five years. (BC/July '86) ★★★1/2

Ch. Brane-Cantenac 1982 Margaux, 2nd Cru $20. Big, powerful, with ripe fruit, still somewhat closed. Showing complexity, hints of smoke, earth, spice, coffee, chocolate. Needs five or more years. (BC/Sept. '85) ★★★1/2

Ch. Canon 1983 St. Emilion, 1st Grand Cru $25. Aromatic, jammy nose with cassis, cherries, chocolate, black pepper, some vegetal aromas. Complex layers of fruit flavors. Full-bodied and supple with a long finish. (BC/July '86) ★★★1/2

Ch. Cantemerle 1983 Haut-Médoc, 5th Cru $18. Rich, cassis, spicy berry-and-black-cherry nose. Rich, complex flavors still restrained. Dense, velvety texture. Needs five to ten years. (BC/July '86) ★★★1/2

Ch. Carbonnieux 1982 Graves, Cru Classé $12.49. Expansive, multi-layered, ripe fruit with solid acid backbone. Tight, conservative style. Should develop well for five years. (BC/Sept. '85) ★★★1/2

Ch. Cheval Blanc 1961 St. Emilion, 1st Grand Cru $200-300. Excellent bouquet. Lacks the balance or rich, lingering finish of the greatest 1961s, but still almost opulent compared to most other vintages. (DM/Jan. '86) ★★★1/2

Ch. Chicane 1983 Graves $8.49.
Rich aromas of black cherry, berries, chocolate, smoke. Complex, precocious, forward
flavors. Long, velvety, cedar-cassis finish.
Drink over next few years. (BC/July '86)
★★★1/2

**Ch. Clerc Milon 1982 Pauillac,
5th Cru $10.99.** Spicy oak, berry-like.
Generous balance of fruit and oak, full, firm
acidity, round tannins. Needs five years. (BC/
Sept. '85) ★★★1/2

**Ch. Corbin 1982 St. Emilion,
Grand Cru $18.** Full-bodied, with great
depth, structure and extract. Tremendous fruit
erupts from the glass. Needs five years or
more. (BC/Sept. '85) ★★★1/2

**Ch. Ducru Beaucaillou 1982 St. Ju-
lien, 2nd Cru $20.** Chocolate and coffee
nose with berry scents and cedary wood. Concentrated fruit, moderate tannin. Needs five
years. (BC/Sept. '85) ★★★1/2

**Ch. Figeac 1982 St. Emilion, 1st
Grand Cru $30.** Spicy, floral, with hints
of bell pepper, clove, and grass. Plenty of
tannin. Long, almost sweet finish. Needs five
years. (BC/Sept. '85) ★★★1/2

**Ch. Grand-Puy-Lacoste 1982 Pau-
illac, 5th Cru $12.** Dark, weighty,
brooding, within a tight, tannic structure.
Dense, ripe fruit. Needs more than five years.
★★★1/2

**Ch. Gruaud Larose 1982 St. Julien,
2nd Cru $25.** Bountiful, black cherry and
cassis aromas, still undeveloped. Plenty of
new wood, acidity, tannin. Great breed. Needs
five years plus. (BC/Sept. '85) ★★★1/2

**Ch. Gruaud Larose 1983 St. Julien,
2nd Cru $20.** Cassis and leathery, earthy
scents permeate rich, lush fruit. Deep, generous flavors. Intense, with lots of extract,
moderate oak, exquisite balance. Great, classic Bordeaux in 10 more years. (BC/July '86)
★★★1/2

**Ch. Haut Brion 1983 Graves, 1st
Cru $75.** Concentrated aromas of cassis,

spice, cedar, tobacco expand on the palate. Rich, distinguished, very well balanced, chocolate intensity. Aging potential: over 10 years. Marvelous claret. (BC/July '86) ★★★1/2

Ch. Haut-Bailly 1983 Graves, Cru Classé $19.99. Deep aromas of mint, cedar, wet earth. Firm, round, elegantly textured. Should peak within five years. (BC/July '86) ★★★1/2

Ch. L'Angélus 1983 St. Emilion, Grand Cru $18. Suggests leather, tobacco, coffee, ferns. Tightly knit. Concentrated, intense, soft-tannin, with terrific fruit and earthy flavors. Accessible now, but needs five years. (BC/July '86) ★★★1/2

Ch. L'Arrosée 1983 St. Emilion, Grand Cru $15. Complex nose of fruit, oak, and spice. Lush fruit flavors have earthy undertones. Needs at least three to five years aging. (BC/July '86) ★★★1/2

Ch. L'Evangile 1983 Pomerol $35. Concentrated nose of cedar, cigar box, berries. Deep, luscious, chewy flavors are packed right through the finish. A tannic backbone insures improvement well into the 1990s. A well-mannered monster. (BC/July '86) ★★★1/2

Ch. La Conseillante 1982 Pomerol $31.25. Luscious, complex nose and flavors, layered with cherry, raspberry, spice, cedar. Forward, with soft tannins, great balance and elegance. Long, chocolate finish. Needs at least five years. (BC/Sept. '85) ★★★1/2

Ch. La Dominique 1982 St. Emilion, Grand Cru $14.99. Fragrant, ripe nose with chocolate hints. Spicy. Well balanced. Big, concentrated, hard fruit and tannin. Needs more than five years. (BC/Sept. '85) ★★★1/2

Ch. La Mission Haut Brion 1982 Graves, Cru Classe $39. Complex nose of chocolate, cinnamon, clove. Nicely concentrated flavors. Long finish. Needs several years. (BC/Sept. '85) ★★★1/2

Ch. La Tour de Bessan 1983 Margaux $11.99. Sweet cassis and very concentrated, cherry-like fruit from start to finish. Multi-layered. Elegant texture. Moderate tannin should round out in five years. (BC/July '86) ★★★1/2

Ch. Lafite-Rothschild 1982 Pauillac, 1st Cru $70. Voluptuous flavors of various fruits, supported by acidity, spicy oak, hard tannins. Complexity, harmony will come in time. Needs over five years. (BC/Sept. '85) ★★★1/2

Ch. Lafleur 1982 Pomerol $45. Verges on overripeness. Complex, Port-like nose of tobacco, coffee, prunes. Very rich and tannic. Needs at least five years. (BC/Sept. '85) ★★★1/2

Ch. Langoa Barton 1982 St. Julien, 3rd Cru $15.95. Restrained nose, a hint of eucalyptus. Lush, forward fruit and vanilla-oak with good structure behind it. At peak in five years. (BC/Sept. '85) ★★★1/2

Ch. Lascombes 1982 Margaux, 2nd Cru $25. Intense, chewy powerhouse, but with balance and subtlety. Astringent. Big flavors of berries, cassis, and tobacco await release. Needs at least five years. (BC/Sept. '85) ★★★1/2

Ch. Lascombes 1983 Margaux, 2nd Cru $29. Vanilla and cedary-spicy scents of new barrels. Vibrant, expansive flavors of ripe, soft fruit; generous but delicate. Harmonious. Excellent acidity. (BC/July '86) ★★★1/2

Ch. Latour 1982 Pauillac, 1st Cru $65. Big fruit, with hints of bell pepper and coffee, dominated by bigger oak and tannin. Astringent, dense, solid. Needs more than five years. (BC/Sept. '85) ★★★1/2

Ch. Léoville Poyferré 1982 St. Julien, 2nd Cru $21.99. Dark, young, stuffed with concentrated, cassis fruit, lots of wood and a hint of earth. Fleshy. Needs five or more years. (BC/Sept. '85) ★★★1/2

Ch. Longueville au Baron de Pichon-Longueville 1982 Pauillac, 2nd Cru $16. Restrained hints of violets and oak. Lush flavors of ripe fruit, coffee, cassis and tobacco, well meshed with oak. Near-term potential, up to five years. (BC/Sept. '85) ★★★1/2

Ch. Longueville au Baron de Pichon-Longueville 1983 Pauillac, 2nd Cru $25. Powerful, fleshy, but still classically structured. Deep, very ripe flavors of blackberries, plums, cassis, coffee, dead leaves, earth. High tannin. Long. Needs five years. (BC/July '86) ★★★1/2

Ch. Lynch Bages 1983 Pauillac, 5th Cru $25. Youthful fruit, spice, herbs, and earthiness weave in and out of this subtle, elegant wine. Delicious streak of acidity. Soft tannins. (BC/July '86) ★★★1/2

Ch. Maucaillou 1983 Moulis $8.99. Hints of sweet cherries, berries, cinnamon in the nose. Very pleasant, youthful wine of modest proportions. Rich fruit, good balance and depth. Promises early maturity. (BC/July '86) ★★★1/2

Ch. Meyney 1982 St. Estèphe, Cru Grand Bourgeois Exceptionnel $10.95. Restrained melange of scents and flavors: wood, earth, tar, leather, flowers, berries, coffee, cassis. Good structure and elegance. Young and tannic, needs five plus years. ★★★1/2

Ch. Mouton Rothschild 1982 Pauillac, 1st Cru $70. Intense, aggressive, chocolate, raspberry, mint, smoke, and cassis nose. Dense, concentrated fruit leaps out, but is still undeveloped. Long, tannic finish. Needs at least five years. (BC/Sept. '85) ★★★1/2

Ch. Mouton Rothschild 1983 Pauillac, 1st Cru $80. Loads of oak, extract, dense fruit fill out this opulent, brawny wine. Complex nose and flavors show nuances of tar, chocolate, spice, smoke. Chewy texture. A keeper. (BC/July '86) ★★★1/2

Ch. Palmer 1982 Margaux, 3rd Cru $24.95. Spicy, cinnamon-cedar nose. Full flavored, with abundant, soft tannins. Approachable, harmonious. Long, elegant finish. (BC/Sept. '85) ★★★1/2

Ch. Palmer 1983 Margaux, 3rd Cru $30. Spicy new oak, plums, blackberries, cassis, chocolate, and mint mingle in a wine with good depth, medium weight. Velvety, supple, balanced. Long finish. Elegant. Needs another five years. (BC/July '86) ★★★1/2

Ch. Pavie 1983 St. Emilion, 1st Grand Cru $17. Berry and sweet, oaky-cedary aromas predominate. Fleshy, chewy flavors have terrific extract and a long finish. Very elegant. Needs at least five more years. (BC/July '86) ★★★1/2

Ch. Pichon-Longueville-Comtesse de Lalande 1983 Pauillac, 2nd Cru $50. Elegant; impeccable balance; well groomed. Black cherry and raspberry fruit has nuances of oak, vanilla, cassis, flowers. Dazzling finish. Needs another 5-10 years. (BC/July '86) ★★★1/2

Ch. Pichon-Longueville-Comtesse de Lalande 1982 Pauillac, 2nd Cru $19. Jammy ripe fruit nose, with notes of cinnamon-cardamom spice and newly cut wood. Soft, round, Merlot-type flavors. Peak in five years. (BC/Sept. '85) ★★★1/2

Ch. Rauzan-Gassies 1983 Margaux, 2nd Cru $14.99. Abundant, soft, ripe fruit suggests cassis, raspberries, blueberries, plums, cranberries. Very concentrated, tannic. Astringent finish. (BC/July '86) ★★★1/2

Ch. Taillefer 1982 Pomerol $15. Spicy, flowery, with notes of licorice and smoke. Soft, supple, medium-weight fruit, modest tannins. Needs up to five years. (BC/Sept. '85) ★★★1/2

Ch. Talbot 1983 St. Julien, 4th Cru $16. Gutsy wine. Leathery and barnyard scents mingle with expansive fruit and oak. Intense, concentrated fruit flavors laced with earthy, tarry, tobacco, bell pepper. Loads of extract, tannin, body. (BC/July '86) ★★★1/2

Ch. Tour Bicheau 1982 Graves $6.99. Fragrance of cassis, pepper, olives, vanilla, oak. Forward, attractive fruit. Light to medium bodied. Needs up to five years. (BC/Sept. '85) ★★★1/2

Domaine de Chevalier 1983 Graves, Cru Classé $28. Full aromas of spice, berries, new wood. Flavors of coffee, ripe cassis are lively, very long. Great breed. Needs more than five years aging. (BC/July '86) ★★★1/2

Pétrus 1982 Pomerol $200. Cassis, mint, berries, and coffee in the nose. Soft entry into big, round fruit. Rich, chewy texture. Lots of soft tannin. Long finish. Needs more than five years. (BC/Sept. '85) ★★★1/2

Pétrus 1983 Pomerol $125. Shy nose of vanilla, spice, cedar. Creamy, silky, with powerful flavors of blackcurrant and prunes. Hard and tannic; needs five-plus years cellar time. (BC/July '86) ★★★1/2

Ch. Batailley 1983 Pauillac, 5th Cru $15. Very attractive, forward, almost sweet, dried-fruit character. Round. Nice balance. Lovely finish. (BC/July '86) ★★★

Ch. Beychevelle 1982 St. Julien, 4th Cru $19.95. Big, round, with berryish fruit, lively tannin. Soft, chewy, California style. Peak within five years. (BC/Sept. '85) ★★★

Ch. Beychevelle 1983 St. Julien, 4th Cru $25. Violets, spice, and cassis on the nose. Sweet, black-cherryish fruit has lively acidity. Not big, but it has depth and elegance. (BC/July '86) ★★★

Ch. Bouscaut 1982 Graves, Cru Classé $12.99. Nose closed at first, opens to hints of cassis and plums. Soft, well-balanced, round fruit. Good drinking now, but can age for several years. (BC/Sept. '85) ★★★

Ch. Brane-Cantenac 1983 Margaux, 2nd Cru $19.99. Sweet, herbal, cedary nose. Smooth, elegant fruit. Understated.

Could use another five years of aging. (BC/
July '86) ★★★

**Ch. Cadet-Piola 1983 St. Emilion,
Grand Cru $13.50.** Spicy fruit, oak, and a
little alcoholic heat in the nose. Finesse and
style on the palate. (BC/July '86) ★★★

**Ch. Calon-Ségur 1983 St. Estèphe,
3rd Cru $22.** Medium-weight wine with
well-defined spiciness and cedary new wood in
the nose. Sweet cherry flavors are pleasant,
though not intense. (BC/July '86) ★★★

**Ch. Cantemerle 1982 Haut-Médoc,
5th Cru $13.** Generous, soft, big, forward
flavors with concentrated fruit, some depth.
Elegant, but low in acid. Peak in 5 years.
(BC/Sept. '85) ★★★

**Ch. Carbonnieux 1983 Graves, Cru
Classé $15.** Cassis, blackberries, wood,
herbs mingle in a round, supple wine. Good
depth, backbone. Medium weight. Long, tannic finish. Needs five more years to develop.
(BC/July '86) ★★★

**Ch. Cheval Blanc 1983 St. Emi-
lion, 1er Grand Cru $55.** Berry and vi-
nous aromas with some oak and cedar. Elegant, with a lingering finish. Modest tannins
call for three to five years more age. (BC/July
'86) ★★★

**Ch. Clerc Milon 1983 Pauillac,
5th Cru $15.** Toasty oak and very dry, rich
fruit, with a firm backbone of tannin and
acidity. Beautifully balanced. (BC/July '86)
★★★

**Ch. Cos d'Estournel 1983 St. Es-
tèphe, 2nd Cru $40.** An assertive nose
has cherry, toasty, smokey, vegetal, and coffee elements. More restrained, harmonious
flavor. Great structure. Fairly delicate except
strong tannins need more than five years to
resolve. (BC/July '86) ★★★

**Ch. d'Agassac 1983 Haut-Médoc
$11.99.** Spicy, sweet cherryish fruit. Sup-
ple, medium-light body. Solid structure. Moderate tannin should smooth out within a few
years. (BC/July '86) ★★★

Ch. de Sales 1982 Pomerol $12. Rounded berry nose. Full, jammy fruit extract. Should peak in five years. (BC/Sept. '85) ★★★

Ch. Deyrem-Valentin 1982 Margaux $10.99. Soft impressions of cassis and blackberries. Limited aging potential. (BC/Sept. '85) ★★★

Ch. du Beau Vallon 1982 St. Emilion $6.99. Chewy, rich, cherry-like extract. Considerable tannin. Excellent five year potential. (BC/Sept. '85) ★★★

Ch. Du Glana 1983 St. Julien, Cru Grand Bourgeois $10. Rich, sweet, raspberry nose. Deep, fat fruit leaps from the glass. Full and soft, but with astringent tannins. Needs more than five years aging. (BC/July '86) ★★★

Ch. du Tertre 1982 Margaux, 5th Cru $12.99. Pleasant, attractive fruit in good balance with moderate wood tannins. Medium-weight, with some delicacy. Five years may give elegance. (BC/Sept. '85) ★★★

Ch. Ducru-Beaucaillou 1983 St. Julien, 2nd Cru $45. An austere nose improves with airing. Closed but packed on the palate. Rich, firm, nicely structured. Rough tannins need plenty of time. (BC/July '86) ★★★

Ch. Duhart-Milon-Rothschild 1983 Pauillac, 4th Cru $22.95. Lush cassis and blackberry fruit mingles with oak in a classic manner. Big and powerful but still tightly locked up. Needs heavy-duty cellaring. (BC/July '86) ★★★

Ch. Fieuzal 1983 Graves, Cru Classé $12. Lush, fruity nose with smoke, cedar. Elegant. Soft. Short-term ageability. (BC/July '86) ★★★

Ch. Fonplegade 1982 St. Emilion, Grand Cru $15. Grapey fruit. Pronounced wood. Solid. Lots of tannin. Needs five years or more. (BC/Sept. '85) ★★★

Ch. Fonroque 1982 St. Emilion,

Grand Cru $10.99. Elegant nose of ripe fruit and new oak. Lean, with some tannin, modest finish. Needs up to five years. (BC/Sept. '85) ★★★

Ch. Fourcas-Hosten 1983 Listrac, Cru Grand Bourgeois $13. A hard, austere wine with the stuffing to come around. Plenty of extract. Restrained fruit has tarry or licorice undertones. Very dry finish. Needs lots of time. (BC/July '86) ★★★

Ch. Gazin 1983 Pomerol $20. Assertive nose delivers plums, spice, black cherry, and alcohol. Round, concentrated, expansive on the palate, with bitter tannins. Will reward long cellaring. (BC/July '86) ★★★

Ch. Giscours 1982 Margaux, 3rd Cru $24.99. Closed nose shows some cinnamon spice and berries. Ripe fruit flavors, not fully developed. Tannin enough for midterm aging. (BC/Sept. '85) ★★★

Ch. Gloria 1982 St. Julien $8.49. Very ripe, floral nose. Lean, elegant style. Good acidity. Needs up to five years aging. (BC/Sept. '85) ★★★

Ch. Grand-Puy Ducasse 1982 Pauillac, 5th Cru $13.79. Bready nose. Bright, forward fruit flavors. Prominent acidity. Will peak in five years, perhaps more. (BC/Sept. '85) ★★★

Ch. Grave-La-Cour 1983 St. Estèphe $9.99. Very ripe, sweet nose. Round, soft flavors with good acidity, velvety texture. Soft tannins. (BC/July '86) ★★★

Ch. Greysac 1982 Médoc, Cru Grand Bourgeois $6.99. Lush, ripe fruit in nose and flavor: berries, black cherries, licorice. Good structure. Stylish. Should keep, but not great potential. (BC/Sept. '85) ★★★

Ch. Kirwan 1982 Margaux, 3rd Cru $15.99. Surprisingly developed, mature. Easy-going, harmonious, with bright, simple strawberry and cassis fruit. Drink within a few years. (BC/Sept. '85) ★★★

Ch. L'Angélus 1982 St. Emilion,

Grand Cru $21.99. Briary nose of ripe fruit and chocolate. Medium-bodied, with chewy texture, hard finish. Needs five plus years. (BC/Sept. '85) ★★★

Ch. La Conseillante 1983 Pomerol $42. Prominent pine or mint quality in the nose. Lean, silky, graceful. Superb texture. Exotic character. (BC/July '86) ★★★

Ch. La Courolle 1983 Montagne-St. Emilion $8.99. Cedary wood combines with hints of berries in the nose. Well structured and balanced with fruit and tannin. Needs three to five years. (BC/July '86) ★★★

Ch. La Dominique 1983 St. Emilion, Grand Cru $14. Spicy fruit. Good depth of flavors and fruit intensity. Tannic finish. Age for five or more years. (BC/July '86) ★★★

Ch. La Lagune 1983 Haut-Médoc, 3rd Cru $13. A big, big wine. New oak dominates at this time. Intense, deep, California-Cabernet character. (BC/July '86) ★★★

Ch. La Mission Haut Brion 1983 Graves, Cru Classé $69.99. Deep scents of ripe fruit, cedar. Rich, supple flavors. Fine now, with the structure and round tannins to keep and build. (BC/July '86) ★★★

Ch. La Roque de By 1983 Médoc $7.99. Shy scents of cherries, leather, lilacs, raspberries. Good fruit and concentration. Minty flavors. Austere tannins dominate a long finish. Needs 5-10 years. (BC/July '86) ★★★

Ch. La Tour Carnet 1982 Haut-Médoc, 4th Cru $11.95. Rough, earthy, with plummy fruit well buried and undeveloped. Plenty of tannin, astringent finish. Good promise in 5-10 years. (BC/Sept. '85) ★★★

Ch. La Tour Haut Brion 1982 Graves, Cru Classé $49.99. Good concentration of ripe fruit, round and full, but somewhat hidden behind tannin. Best in five years. (BC/Sept. '85) ★★★

Ch. La Tour Martillac 1983 Graves, Cru Classe, $12. Herbaceous, earthy nose shows complexity. Ripe. Graceful. Pillow-soft texture. (BC/July '86) ★★★

Ch. Latour 1971 Pauillac, 1st Cru $75+. Bouquet falls short of elegant but is still attractive. Very enjoyable. Drink soon. (DM/Mar.'86) ★★★

Ch. Latour 1983 Pauillac, 1st Cru $60. Vivid nose of cedar, mint, spice, earth. Medium body. Good depth and concentration. Firm, tannic backbone. (BC/July '86) ★★★

Ch. Latour Figeac 1983 St. Emilion, Grand Cru $17.99. A rich, ripe nose shows lots of fruit and spice. Cassis and oak flavors have nicely rounded tannins. Well-structured. Almost ready. (BC/July '86) ★★★

Ch. LaTour Haut Brion 1983 Graves, Cru Classé $25. Almost yeasty, young scent with smokey nuances. Creamy. Tannic finish. (BC/July '86) ★★★

Ch. Le Gay 1982 Pomerol $11.50. Ripe, grapey, meaty, complex. Still tight with tannin. Needs more than five years. (BC/Sept. '85) ★★★

Ch. Léoville Barton 1982 St. Julien, 2nd Cru $16.95. Jammy, cedary nose. Ripe, concentrated fruit flavors and cedary-oak tones. Firm tannins, but a little short. Might improve in five years. (BC/Sept. '85) ★★★

Ch. Léoville Poyferré 1983 St. Julien, 2nd Cru $19. A tight, stately wine with lovely, tart fruit, cedary tones, nice acidity and balance. Good depth and complexity, but delicate. Soft tannins. (BC/July '86) ★★★

Ch. Léoville-Las-Cases 1983 St. Julien, 2nd Cru $23. Berryish fruit is closed up beneath cedary aromas and tannin. Big, rich, muscular, well-structured, with prominent acidity. (BC/July '86) ★★★

Ch. Meyney 1983 St. Estèphe, Cru

Bourgeois Exceptionnel $12. Rich, earthy, forceful. Plummy fruit. Plenty of potential needs plenty of time to develop. (BC/July '86) ★★★

Ch. Montrose 1982 St. Estèphe, 2nd Cru $20. Big, rich, intense. High alcohol, ripe fruit and oak flavors, rough tannins. Needs more than five years. (BC/Sept. '85) ★★★

Ch. Moulin des Carruades 1983 Pauillac $24.99. Bitter tannin masks ripe, dark, cassis-and-currant fruit, with cedary, vanilla, and cinnamon overtones. Should smooth out in 5-10 years. (BC/July '86) ★★★

Ch. Mouton-Baronne-Philippe 1982 Pauillac, 5th Cru $18.95. Classic, cedar-box nose. Fruit compacted by austere tannin. Restrained but powerful. Should open in five years. (BC/Sept. '85) ★★★

Ch. Perey 1983 Bordeaux $5.99. Beaujolais-type, cherry nose. Lively, well-balanced, supple, with light tannins. (BC/July '86) ★★★

Ch. Rausan-Ségla 1982 Margaux, 2nd Cru $17. Berry flavors heavily overlaid with sweet, spicy oak. Aggressive; somewhat out of balance. (BC/Sept. '85) ★★★

Ch. Rausan-Ségla 1983 Margaux, 2nd Cru $15.95. Cedar, cassis, and alcohol on the nose. Soft, fat, delicious fruit verges on overripeness. Powerful but smooth, until the hot, astringent finish. Needs serious cellaring. (BC/July '86) ★★★

Ch. Saint-Aubin 1983 Médoc $9.99. Bright, fresh fruit with minty and vegetal nuances. Well-balanced. Moderate weight and tannin. Good acidity. (BC/July '86) ★★★

Ch. Saint-Pierre 1983 St. Julien, 4th Cru $16.95. A contest between thick, ripe, chewy fruit and overwhelming tannin. Five to 10 years of aging required. (BC/July '86) ★★★

Ch. Smith-Haut-Lafite 1983

Graves, Cru Classé $15. Minty nose. Full bodied, generously fruity, with licorice hints and firm tannin. (BC/July '86) ★★★

Ch. St. Georges 1982 St. Georges-St. Emilion $11.99. Cinnamon, clove, mint, and wood scents. Full-bodied, ripe fruit. Harmonious. Will improve for several years. (BC/Sept. '85) ★★★

Ch. Trotanoy 1982 Pomerol $40. Big bodied. Ripe, concentrated fruit; pronounced vanilla-like oak. Excellent, long finish. Up to five years improvement. (BC/Sept. '85) ★★★

Ch. Trotanoy 1983 Pomerol $45. Hints of cherries, tea, pepper, and minty oak in a closed nose. Full bodied with densely packed flavors. Long, very tannic finish. Lots of promise, with lots of aging. (BC/July '86) ★★★

Clos des Jacobins 1982 St. Emilion, Grand Cru $14.95. Complex nose: chocolate, cedar, spice, pepper. Medium body. High acid balanced by high fruit. Needs time. (BC/Sept. '85) ★★★

Cos Labory 1982 St. Estèphe, 5th Cru $9.99. Earthy, dried-fruit nose with a hint of wood. Rich cedar, berries, and spice fill the glass. Fine balance. Going somewhere, in about five years. (BC/Sept. '85) ★★★

Domaine de L'Artigue 1982 Haut-Médoc $4.99. Bright fruit flavors with a stemmy note mid-palate, but not unpleasant. Soft, round, supported by moderate tannin. Peak within five years. (BC/Sept. '85) ★★★

Domaine La Grave 1982 Graves $7.50. Light to medium body. A bit closed, but complex nose: hints of cherry, chocolate, mint. Lean, tight, black-cherry fruit. Solid, tannic finish. Needs five years or more. (BC/Sept. '85) ★★★

La Cardonne 1982 Médoc, Cru Grand Bourgeois $5.99. Subdued nose. Fat fruit flavors; moderate-to-high tannin. Balanced, generous, though not complex.

Needs five years. (BC/Sept. '85) ★★★

Les Forts de Latour 1970 Pauillac $40. Beautifully developed bouquet showing a touch of mint. Concentrated, complex. (DM/Mar. '86) ★★★

Réserve de la Comtesse 1982 Bordeaux $10.25. Bouquet starting to develop. Unbelievably enticing and forward. Fruity and full. Already drinkable; good future. (DM/Jan. '86)) ★★★

Vieux Ch. Certan 1982 Pomerol $21.99. Multi-layered chocolate, cedar, flowers, and earth aromas. Lively fruit flavors well balanced by acid. Needs five years. (BC/Sept. '85) ★★★

Ch. Larrivaux 1982 Haut-Médoc, Cru Bourgeois $8. Ripe, mature, creamy aroma. Tobacco and cherry flavor. Fairly full body. (JPN/Mar. '86) ★★1/2

Ch. Latour à Pomerol 1983 Pomerol $35. Fruit aromas are laced with menthol, licorice, and cedar. Long in the mouth, with a nice splash of fruit mid-palate. (BC/July '86) ★★1/2

Font Villac 1983 St. Emilion, Grand Cru $12.50. Delicate, spicy fruit. Very appealing, fruity finish has moderate astringency. (BC/July '86) ★★1/2

Les Forts de Latour 1978 Pauillac $27.50. Some astringency, otherwise very well balanced. Full nose, lots of flavor. (DM/Mar.'86) ★★1/2

B&G 1983 St. Emilion $8.70. Clean nose with some cedar and spice. Well balanced. Medium body. Some tannin in the finish. (BC/July '86) ★★

Ch. Batailley 1982 Pauillac, 5th Cru $14.99. Robust fruit competes with bitter tannins. Flavors of black cherries and mint. Soft, short finish says drink in three to five years. (BC/Sept. '85) ★★

Ch. Beauséjour 1982 St. Estèphe $7.99. Rich, earthy aroma. Jammy fruit flavors have weight and charm but are simple. Surprisingly advanced. Drink in the next few years. (BC/Sept. '85) ★★

Ch. Belair 1982 St. Emilion, 1st Grand Cru $19. Round, bright, cherry fruit. Medium body. Soft tannins. Ready now. (BC/Sept. '85) ★★

Ch. Belgrave 1983 Haut-Médoc $7.99. Honest, harmonious, well-constructed wine. Bright, cherry and strawberry fruit has lively acidity. Medium weight. Enjoyable now. (BC/July '86) ★★

Ch. Bourgneuf-Vayron 1982 Pomerol $16.50. Full, ripe, losing its hard edges. Firm structure, medium-bodied. Will improve for five years. (BC/Sept. '85) ★★

Ch. Bouscaut 1983 Graves, Cru Classé $17. Jammy nose has elements of cedary cigar-box and barnyard. Big style but approachable now. Good balance, character. Finishes short. (BC/July '86) ★★

Ch. Canon 1982 St. Emilion, 1st Grand Cru $18. Smoky, with nice wood and fruit set in a jammy flavor. Good backbone, but finishes rough. Needs five-plus years. (BC/Sept. '85) ★★

Ch. Clos L'Oratoire 1983 St. Emilion, Grand Cru $17.99. Jammy nose with licorice notes. Subdued fruit flavors struggle against high alcohol. Medium body. Creamy texture. Ready in a few years. (BC/July '86) ★★

Ch. Coufran 1978 Haut-Médoc, Cru Grand Bourgeois $14/magnum. Characteristic but light, claret aroma. Fruit seems to have sweetness. Some tannin to shed, but can be enjoyed now. (S&PW/ Jan. '86) ★★

Ch. d'Angludet 1982 Margaux $12.99. Concentrated, not overly ripe fruit, still closed. Well-structured and balanced. Drink in about five years. (BC/Sept. '85) ★★

Ch. Dassault 1983 St. Emilion, Grand Cru $15. Cedary, leathery aromas with some barnyard propensities. Good fruit flavors; not intense, but with some depth. Medium-light body. (BC/July '86) ★★

Ch. de Ferrand 1982 St. Emilion,

Grand Cru $8.69. Heavy, almost sweet aroma. Spicy, soft. High alcohol. Tannic finish. Needs several years. (BC/Sept. '85) ★★

Ch. de La Dauphine 1982 Fronsac $9.50. Big, berry-like nose, a bit closed. Rich without a lot of complexity. High alcohol supports oak overtones. Tannin for short-term improvement. (BC/Sept. '85) ★★

Ch. de Lamarque 1982 Haut-Médoc, Cru Grand Bourgeois $6.99. Well integrated, balanced, solid wine of modest pedigree. Approachable now, but will develop. (BC/Sept. '85) ★★

Ch. de Marbuzet 1982 St. Estèphe, Cru Grand Bourgeois Exceptionnel $12.95. Closed nose hints at tar and wood. Rich fruit smothered in rough tannin now, but promising with five-plus years. (BC/Sept. '85) ★★

Ch. de Marbuzet 1983 St. Estèphe, Cru Grand Bourgeois Exceptionnel $12. Open, fresh, cherry-strawberry nose and flavors. Moderately light, balanced, harmonious. (BC/July '86) ★★

Ch. du Beau Vallon 1983 St. Emilion $8. Pleasant aromas of cherries, cedar, vanilla. Supple mouth feel. Medium body. Significant tannins require more than five years of aging. (BC/July '86) ★★

Ch. du Terte 1983 Margaux, 5th Cru $16.99. Sweet, ripe fruit with earthiness not far behind. Good extract. Moderate tannins. Promising. (BC/July '86) ★★

Ch. Fleur Pipeau 1983 St. Emilion $8.99. A slightly funky element in the nose ruffles elegant fruit scents. Medium-to-light body. Modest tannin level. Drink up. (BC/July '86) ★★

Ch. Gaudet-St. Julien 1983 St. Emilion, Grand Cru $15. Fruity, cherry nose with hints of prunes. Nice intensity on the palate. Medium body and finish. (BC/July '86) ★★

Ch. Gloria 1983 St. Julien $11.99. A complex wine in a controversial style.

(BC/July '86) ★★

Ch. Grand-Puy-Lacoste 1983 Pauillac, 5th Cru $29.99. Very closed, but with rich fruit and new oak in waiting. Good structure. Rough but promising; needs 5-10 years. (BC/July '86) ★★

Ch. L'Evangile 1982 Pomerol $25. Vibrant, big, plummy nose. Soft, fruity finish. A bit low in acid. Ready for drinking, but will hold awhile. (BC/Sept. '85) ★★

Ch. La Cardonne 1983 Médoc, Cru Grand Bourgeois $8.70. Fresh, ripe, sweet fruit. Well balanced. Attractive now, with some astringency to smooth out. (BC/July '86) ★★

Ch. La Croix 1982 Pomerol $12.99. Ripe, simple fruit with hints of violets and typical Merlot softness. Still opening up, but should peak soon. (BC/Sept. '85) ★★

Ch. La Pointe 1983 Pomerol $14.99. Cherry nose with mint. Well structured. On the light side. (BC/July '86) ★★

Ch. La Tour du Pin Figeac 1982 St. Emilion, Grand Cru $15. Ripe, dense, good extract. Tannic, bitter finish. Needs about five years. (BC/Sept. '85) ★★

Ch. Lafite-Rothschild 1983 Pauillac, 1st Cru $85. Elegant, spicy, vanilla-oak bouquet. Flavors are masked by hard tannins. Disjointed; needs serious cellaring. (BC/July '86) ★★

Ch. Lasseque 1982 St. Emilion, Grand Cru $10.99. Lively fruit flavors are a touch sweet. Considerable tannin. Hot finish. Needs five years. (BC/Sept. '85) ★★

Ch. Latour 1976 Pauillac, 1st Cru $60. Unexciting. A little light for Latour. Good flavor but lacks depth. (DN/Mar. '86) ★★

Ch. Lavignère 1983 St. Emilion $7.99. Light aromas of fruit, cedar, leather, mushrooms. Nice, fruity flavors with medium-to-light body and depth. Well-balanced, delicate, appealing. (BC/July '86) ★★

Ch. Léoville-Las-Cases 1982 St. Julien, 2nd Cru $25. Oak sticks out over scents and flavors of cherries, coffee, leather, cassis, plums, chocolate. High tannin. Needs at least five years. (BC/Sept. '85) ★★

Ch. Les Ormes de Pez 1983 St. Estèphe $16. Very ripe, berry-fruit, cassis, violets, and roses in the nose, but creamy fruit flavors are buried under bitter tannin. Needs cellaring. (BC/July '86) ★★

Ch. Les Vieux Maurins 1982 St. Emilion $5.99. Rich fruit aroma. A nice mouthful of flavor with light-to-moderate tannin. Ready now, with some room for improvement. (S&PW/Mar. '86) ★★

Ch. Lynch Bages 1982 Pauillac, 5th Cru $19.99. Intense, closed-in, Cabernet fruit lurks behind wood and soft tannins. Well endowed but not saying much yet. Give it five years, maybe more. (BC/Sept. '85) ★★

Ch. Marquis D'Alesme-Becker 1982 Margaux, 3rd Cru $14.95. Lean, pleasant fruit, relatively undeveloped. Rough tannin needs five to ten years. (BC/Sept. '85) ★★

Ch. Mouton-Baronne-Philippe 1983 Pauillac, 5th Cru $13. Ripe, varietal-Cabernet character with rich nuances, sharp tannin, firm acidity. Long finish. (BC/July '86) ★★

Ch. Pape Clément 1982 Graves, Cru Classé $21. Medium body, with light, attractive mint and fruit. Slightly stemmy. Drink within five years. (BC/Sept. '85) ★★

Ch. Pavie 1982 St. Emilion, 1st Grand Cru $15.99. Good fruit and peppery spice with a sweet hint. Soft acids. Quite tannic. Needs about five years. (BC/Sept. '85) ★★

Ch. Peyrabon 1982 Haut-Médoc, Cru Grand Bourgeois $6.99. Appealing, flowery bouquet. Straightforward, supple, attractive, cherry and cassis fruit. Not for long keeping. (BC/Sept. '85) ★★

Ch. Poujeaux 1983 Médoc, Grand Bourgeois Exceptionnel $13. Classy blend of new oak and concentrated, berryish fruit. Not big, but well structured, smooth. Finishes short. (BC/July '86) ★★

Ch. Prieuré-Lichine 1983 Margaux, 4th Cru $13. Cedary, spicy wood hovers over tight fruit. Moderate proportions are nicely filled out. (BC/July '86) ★★

Ch. Puyblanquet Carrille 1983 St. Emilion $9.99. Raspberries, licorice, tar, and a hint of prunes in the nose. Medium body. Good fruit flavors. A somewhat hot finish. Moderate ageability of one to five years. (BC/July '86) ★★

Ch. Rouget 1983 Pomerol $11. A complex interplay of qualities; controversial style. (BC/July '86) ★★

Ch. Saint-Pierre 1982 St. Julien, 4th Cru $12.99. Nose jumps from the glass: coffee, smoke, chocolate, raspberries, and plums. Matching complexity of flavors, very advanced. Bitter finish suggests aging five years. (BC/Sept. '85) ★★

Ch. St. André Corbin 1982 St. Georges-St. Emilion, Grand Cru $10.99. Light, lean, but well balanced, with good acidity and some complexity. Tannic finish. Needs five years or more. (BC/Sept. '85) ★★

Ch. St. André Corbin 1983 St. Georges-St. Emilion, Grand Cru $5.95. Delicate, fruity, spicy nose. Light but well-balanced flavor and body. (BC/July '86) ★★

Ch. Taillefer 1983 Pomerol $10. Fruit aromas with notes of mushrooms or wet soil. Big and full bodied but unyielding, with rough tannins in the finish. Needs more than five years cellaring. (BC/July '86) ★★

Domaine de Chevalier 1982 Graves, Cru Classé $18.99. Spice and pine in the nose. Dusty, Rioja-like fruit in the mouth with plenty of vanilla oak. (BC/Sept. '85) ★★

Les Forts de Latour 1975 Pauillac $32. Lack of fruit in the nose. Lots of tannin. High acidity. Fruit just peeking through. (DM/Mar.'86) ★★

Maître d'Estournel 1983 Bordeaux $5.99. Pale garnet color with brownish edges. Light aroma of cherries, chocolate. Simple, soft, pleasant. (BC/July '86) ★★

Ch. Latour 1973 Pauillac, lst Cru $45. Appealing bouquet. Soft on the palate. Immediate drinkability. (DM/Mar. '86) ★1/2

B&G 1983 Margaux $10.79. Medium weight and richness. Some potential. (BC/July '86)

B&G 1983 Médoc $6.99. Light, tart fruit. (BC/July '86)

B&G 1983 St. Julien $11.99. An odd quality in the nose detracts from generous flavors with some depth. Very astringent. (BC/July '86)

Beau-Rivage 1982 Bordeaux $5.49. Mild aroma with hints of cherry and coffee. Drink now. (BC/Sept. '85)

Beau-Rivage 1983 Bordeaux $5.99. Light color, aroma, body, but high alcohol, significant tannins. (BC/July '86)

Ch. Ausone 1982 St. Emilion, 1st Grand Cru $175. Flowery, cherry-like fruit. Straightforward flavors. Modest tannin. Ready now, but may improve. (BC/Sept. '85)

Ch. Barthez de Luze 1982 Haut-Médoc $5.99. Curious bouquet of cinnamon, eucalyptus, earth, tar, and tea. For near-term drinking. (BC/Sept. '85)

Ch. Beauregard 1983 Pomerol $20. A musty, stale aroma precedes long, appealing flavors with good concentration. (BC/July '86)

Ch. Beauséjour 1983 Côtes de Castillon, Bordeaux $5.99. Light fruit aroma. Medium body with some tannin. (BC/July '86)

Ch. Beauséjour 1983 St. Estèphe $8. Sweet, ripe-to-overripe fruit; soft and seductive. Light-to-medium bodied. (BC/July

'86)

Ch. Bel Air 1982 Haut-Médoc $6.49. Stinky nose cleans up with air. Balanced, ripe, black cherry flavors. Supple, lean, soft; on the light side. Ready now. (BC/Sept. '85)

Ch. Bellegrave 1983 Pauillac, Cru Bourgeois $16. Gobs of bitter tannin overwhelm anything else present. (BC/July '86)

Ch. Boyd-Cantenac 1983 Margaux, 3rd Cru $14. Vegetal, musty nose. Supple, sweet fruit flavors. Very astringent. (BC/July '86)

Ch. Cantenac Brown 1982 Margaux, 3rd Cru $14. Pleasant, mixed berries, oak, and cassis smells and flavors. Light-medium weight. Well made and balanced. Near its peak. (BC/Sept. '85)

Ch. Cantenac Brown 1983 Margaux, 3rd Cru $14.95. An odd nose and excessive tannin detract from intense, ripe fruit flavors. (BC/July '86)

Ch. Cap de Haut 1982 Haut-Médoc $8.99. Light bodied with flavors of black cherries. Somewhat dumb. Not distinguished. (BC/Sept. '85)

Ch. Caze Montfort 1983 Bordeaux $3.99. Raspberry, cherry aromas; hint of oak. Pleasant, simple. (BC/July '86)

Ch. Cissac 1983 Haut-Médoc, Cru Grand Bourgeois Exceptionelle $10.99. Light weight, shallow flavors, astringent tannin. (BC/July '86)

Ch. Clarke 1982 Listrac $11.50. Black cherry and spice nose. Forward, elegant fruit. Harmonious, rather light. (BC/Sept. '85)

Ch. Clinet 1982 Pomerol $11. Well-structured, modest fruit. (BC/Sept. '85) .

Ch. Clinet 1983 Pomerol $18. Spicy, peppery nose. Good, straightforward flavors lack depth and concentration. (BC/July '86)

Ch. Cos Labory 1983 St. Estèphe, 5th Cru $16. Leathery, oddly mature aroma. Light weight and brief. (BC/July '86)

Ch. Coufran 1982 Haut-Médoc, Cru Grand Bourgeois $8.99. Full, chewy, high extract underneath hard, astringent tannin. Flavors still undeveloped, but low acidity suggests limited ageability. (BC/Sept. '85)

Ch. Croizet-Bages 1983 Pauillac, 5th Cru $12. Ample, seductive fruit. Overripe. (BC/July '86)

Ch. Croque Michotte 1983 St. Emilion, Grand Cru $16.99. Aromas of spice, cedar, cigar box, and a hint of barnyard and weeds. Medium-full body. Soft and supple. Modest finish. (BC/July '86)

Ch. de Bel-Air 1983 Lalande de Pomerol $15. Overripe prunes in the nose. Round and soft on the palate. Low acidity. Tannins overpower the finish. (BC/July '86)

Ch. de La Dauphine 1983 Fronsac $6.99. Subdued nose, hints of berry fruit. Good body, structure. Tannic; needs a few years. (BC/July '86)

Ch. de Malleret 1982 Haut-Médoc, Cru Grand Bourgeois $6.99. Medium bodied, up-front flavors are soft, supple, diffused. Already approaching peak. (BC/Sept. '85)

Ch. de Montdespic 1983 Bordeaux Supérieur-Côtes de Castillon $7.50. Light, pleasant fruit aromas, flavors. Clean, simple. (BC/July '86)

Ch. de Pez 1982 St. Estèphe $13.50. Overripe fruit character that shades to coffee and tobacco with aeration. Flavors are soft and fat, with berry fruit through to the finish. High alcohol. (BC/Sept. '85)

Ch. de Ricaud 1983 1er Côtes de Bordeaux $5.75. Cooked vegetable aroma. Moderate fruit, body. Slightly sweet finish. (BC/July '86)

Ch. de Sales 1983 Pomerol $10. Forward, jammy aromas have a whiff of cedar. Roughly tannic. (BC/July '86)

Ch. Ducla 1982 Bordeaux $3.99. Light bodied, but tannic. Hints of olive and light fruit. Drink soon. (BC/Sept. '85)

Ch. Ducla 1983 Bordeaux $3.99.
Scents of black cherries, tobacco, black pepper, tar. Medium-light body. Has character. Moderate tannins. (BC/July '86)

Ch. Fontaine Royale 1983 Listrac $5.99. Thin, with elusive, overripe fruit. (BC/July '86)

Ch. Fourney 1982 St. Emilion, Grand Cru $7.99. An off, barnyard nose disrupts lilac and cherry fruit. (BC/Sept. '85)

Ch. Franc Lartigue 1983 St. Emilion, Grand Cru $9.99. Modestly spicy, ripe-fruit nose. Medium body and flavor with good structure. (BC/July '86)

Ch. Gaillard de La Gorce 1982 St. Emilion, Grand Cru $11.29. Tannic and hard, with good acid. Closed up. Uncertain future. (BC/Sept. '85)

Ch. Gazin 1982 Pomerol $14.99. Some spiciness but short on fruit. Tannic, but not enough body or fruit to build on. (BC/Sept. '85)

Ch. Grandes Murailles 1983 St. Emilion $9.99. Unpleasant aromas lurk in an herbaceous, spicy wine. (BC/July '86)

Ch. Haut-Batailley 1983 Pauillac, 5th Cru $17. Cassis, strawberry in the nose. Soft fruit and tannin. Simple. (BC/July '86)

Ch. Haut-Brignon 1983 1er Côtes de Bordeaux $7.99. Vegetal, overripe character in nose and taste; suggestions of prunes, cloves, oak. Controversial style. (BC/July '86)

Ch. Huissant 1983 St. Estèphe, Cru Bourgeois Exceptionnel $9.99. Floral nose. Fresh fruit flavors with lively acidity, light weight. Good but atypical Bordeaux. (BC/July '86)

Ch. L'Eglise-Clinet 1982 Pomerol $18.95. Tannic, hard, with only modest fruit. Five years age may bring improvement. (BC/Sept. '85)

Ch. La Louvière 1983 Graves

$10.99. Rubbery nose mars a soft, balanced, medium-bodied, elegant wine. (BC/July '86)

Ch. La Tour Carnet 1983 Haut-Médoc, 4th Cru $15. Musty, earthy aromas and flavor. Light. (BC/July '86)

Ch. Lafitte-Carcasset 1983 St. Estèphe $9.99. Light, soft, simple, diffuse. (BC/July '86)

Ch. Lafleur 1983 Pomerol $45. A prominent, herbal, grassy quality permeates lovely, almost overripe fruit. Viscous texture. (BC/July '86)

Ch. Lafon Rochet 1983 St. Estèphe, 4th Cru $7.99. Not enough to back up austere, coarse tannins. (BC/July '86)

Ch. Laroque 1982 St. Emilion, Grand Cru $10. Lean, compact, with jammy flavors. Structured for aging, but high alcohol throws it off balance. (BC/Sept. '85)

Ch. Larose-Trintaudon 1982 Haut-Médoc, Cru Grand Bourgeois $6.49. Medium weight. Prominent tannins need five years to soften. (BC/Sept. '85)

Ch. Le Gay 1983 Pomerol $20. Ripe nose. Very full and tannic; will improve significantly with five years in the cellar. (BC/July '86)

Ch. Léon 1983 1er Côtes de Bordeaux $5.99. Musty nose. Lacks character. (BC/July '86)

Ch. Les Hauts de Pontet 1983 Pauillac $11.99. Candied fruit aroma. Light. Nicely structured. (BC/July '86)

Ch. Liouner 1982 Listrac $8.99. Strawberries, cherries and prunes in the nose and mouth, with a cedary overlay. Light, tart, simple. Drink now. (BC/Sept. '85)

Ch. Lynch-Moussas 1983 Pauillac, 5th Cru $15. Soft, juicy fruit. Light body. Supple and attractive. (BC/July '86)

Ch. Magnol 1983 Haut-Médoc, Cru Bourgeois $7.99. Sweet cherry aroma. A little fat, with a very dry, bitter finish. (BC/July '86)

Ch. Malescot St. Exupéry 1982 Margaux, 3rd Cru $18.98. Developed aromas of cherries, dried herbs, blackcurrants, and cedar. Fruit flavors are round but somewhat shallow. One-to-five-year potential. (BC/Sept. '85)

Ch. Mauvinon 1983 St. Emilion, Grand Cru $9.99. Standard quality. (BC/July '86)

Ch. Montrose 1983 St. Estèphe, 2nd Cru $20. Round, forward fruit is a little jammy. Smooth and pleasant. (BC/July '86)

Ch. Nenin 1982 Pomerol $12.95. Modest, slightly underripe fruit. Medium bodied. Could use a few years aging. (BC/Sept. '85)

Ch. Panigon 1982 Médoc, Cru Bourgeois $5. Simple, light fruit flavors and a slightly sweet impression. A little thin, but enough tannins to need a few more years. (BC/Sept. '85)

Ch. Pape Clément 1983 Graves, Cru Classé $24.99. Musty smells and flavors. (BC/July '86)

Ch. Petit Village 1982 Pomerol $20. Oaky, toasty, with moderate fruit. (BC/Sept. '85)

Ch. Petit Village 1983 Pomerol $19. A low-key wine with some elegance and harmony. (BC/July '86)

Ch. Phélan Ségur 1983 St. Estèphe, Cru Bourgeois Exceptionnel $8.99. A stinky, dirty nose is hard to get past. (BC/July '86)

Ch. Pichon 1983 Haut-Médoc $7.50. Lovely, fat fruit has cinnamon, clove, and vegetal undertones. (BC/July '86)

Ch. Pilot Caillou 1983 Lussac-St. Emilion $5.49. Weedy, vegetal, bell pepper character. (BC/July '86)

Ch. Plantey 1983 Pauillac $10.99. Full, forward flavors have a streak of astringent tannin. (BC/July '86)

Ch. Pontet-Canet 1983 Pauillac,

5th Cru $10. Very ripe, berryish flavors. Good acidity. Some oaky tones. (BC/July '86)

Ch. Prieuré-Lichine 1982 Margaux, 4th Cru $12. Light, easy going, simple, cherry flavors. Light tannins don't preclude enjoyment now. (BC/Sept. '85)

Ch. Senejac 1982 Médoc $7.99. Light, short, simple, pleasant. Ready to drink. (BC/Sept. '85)

Ch. Sigognac 1982 Médoc, Cru Grand Bourgeois $5.99. Dried herbs, flowers in the nose. Some oxidation and overripe, medicinal flavors (BC/Sept. '85)

Ch. Sociando Mallet 1982 Haut-Médoc, Cru Grand Bourgeois $10.99. Bouquet of cinnamon, berries, flowers and oak, as well as bothersome wet leaves. (BC/Sept. '85)

Ch. Soudars 1983 Haut-Médoc, Cru Bourgeois $8.99. Funky, vegetal nose. Soft, well-developed flavors of fruit, earth, and oak. (BC/July '86)

Ch. Talbot 1982 St. Julien, 4th Cru $12.99. Complex nose of prunes, tar, olives, mint. Forceful, chewy, earthy, like a barrel sample. Very ripe. Low acid, high tannin. Needs five-plus years. (BC/Sept. '85)

Ch. Tour du Haut Moulin 1982 Haut-Médoc, Cru Grand Bourgeois $9.49. Slightly burnt, overripe quality is not unpleasant. Fruit is quiet but there. Straightforward, well made. Ageability: about five years. (BC/Sept. '85)

Ch. Tour Pomys 1982 St. Estèphe $5.99. Light-to-medium body. Clean, simple fruit. Short but pleasant. Drink within the next few years. (BC/Sept. '85)

Ch. Troplong Mondot 1982 St. Emilion, Grand Cru $12.99. Ripe, cherry fruit. Moderate tannins. Will improve with five years. (BC/Sept. '85)

Ch. Valoux 1983 Graves $7.99. Cherry-like aromas. Standard quality Graves. (BC/July '86)

Chapelle de la Trinité 1982 St.

Emilion $6.49. Curious, spicy, skunky smells. (BC/Sept. '85)

Clos des Jacobins 1983 St. Emilion, Grand Cru $15. Strongly vegetal character. (BC/July '86)

Clos L'Eglise 1982 Pomerol $15.95. Prune-like nose shows signs of oxidation. Flabby. (BC/Sept. '85)

Clos L'Eglise 1983 Pomerol $15.99. Good, fruity, Merlot aroma. Pleasant, supple. (BC/July '86)

Jean Pierre Mouiex 1982 St. Emilion $7.49. Smoky, lean style. Good fruit with sweet overtones. Well structured with acid for aging. (BC/Sept. '85)

Jean Pierre Mouiex 1983 Fronsac $5.95. Hints of fruit, mint, wood, but lacks concentration and interest. (BC/July '86)

Jean Pierre Mouiex 1983 Pomerol $8.50. All starts and finishes with no middle. (BC/July '86)

La Rose Blanche 1982 St. Emilion $8.99. Closed, vegetal nose. Quite hard. May improve with three or more years age. (BC/Sept. '85)

Les Douelles 1982 Bordeaux $2.99. Pleasant, light fruit, with a hint of strawberry. Serviceable. (BC/Sept. '85)

Maître d'Estournel 1982 Bordeaux $5.49. Medium bodied with considerable tannin. Simple, jammy, pleasant. Drink over the next two years. (BC/Sept. '85)

Mouton-Cadet 1982 Bordeaux $5.99. Balanced, ripe, simple fruit. (BC/Sept. '85)

Mouton-Cadet 1983 Bordeaux $5. Slight licorice or tarry aroma. Soft, simple. (BC/July '86)

Verdillac 1983 Bordeaux Supérieur $5. Moderately intense aromas of black cherries, menthol, cloves. Simple fruit flavors. Medium body. Some ageability. (BC/July '86)

Vicomte Médoc 1982 Médoc $4.89. Light, strawberry, cherry fruit smells and flavors. Simple, precocious, almost sweet. Beaujolais style. (BC/Sept. '85)

Vicomte St. Estèphe 1982 St. Estèphe $6.49. Extremely ripe, pruney, and cumbersome with oxidation showing. (BC/Sept. '85)

BURGUNDY

The name Burgundy has become synonymous with red wine, but true red Burgundy comes only from vineyards in the Saône River area, 150 miles southeast of Paris, accounting for a mere 5% of France's appellation contrôlée (high quality wine) acreage. The wine's scarcity, coupled with a reputation for excellence that dates back to the days of Charlemagne, has led to generally high prices. As with the top wines of Bordeaux, the market has stayed strong for Burgundy even as prices have continued to climb. Unlike Bordeaux, many winemakers in Burgundy have become complacent about quality standards. As a result, good, reasonable Burgundy is rare indeed, and even among expensive Burgundies, finding superior wines requires very careful selection.

The Côte d'Or ("slope of gold") is the heart of Burgundy, the source of its greatest wines, and the home of the Pinot Noir grape. It is divided into the Côte de Nuits and Côte de Beaune — names that appear on the labels of their regional wines. The more expensive wines (they are not always better) carry village, commune, and/or specific vineyard names. Even specific vineyards are often divided up between several independent growers, whose names may also appear on labels. Hence Burgundy labels offer a challenge even to knowledgeable wine drinkers.

One solution is to look for the names of reliable proprietors, shippers, or négociants. Négociants offer wines from many different vineyards and areas, often also making up their own blends. The name of a reliable négociant on a label is a good clue to quality and style. When you find one you like, you'll have a foot in the door to one of the wine world's most rewarding experiences.

When you are spending as much as you do for French Burgundy, tasting notes are a vital guide. The reviews below focus on the best wines and the best values from the Côte d'Or and from the Côte Chalonnaise, a district immediately to the south that offers some of Burgundy's more affordable wines. Wines from all these areas are made entirely from Pinot Noir grapes. They are generally lighter, more supple wines than Bordeaux, and rarely have aromas or flavors associated with fresh fruits. Words like "earthy," "stinky," even "barnyard" often turn up in Burgundy tasting notes. In this case they are generally not pejorative; rather they are reaching to describe the complex qualities of these wines.

Joseph Faiveley 1981 Chambolle-Musigny $22. Earthy, vegetal; smacks of stems. Rich, smooth, smoky in the mouth. Abundant fruit. (JPN/Mar. '86) ★★★ (★★★1/2)

Latour-Giraud 1982 Côte de Beaune-Villages $9.99. Loads of penetrating fruit with excellent, varietal definition. Mouthfilling and complex. (CC/Mar. '86) ★★★ (★★★1/2)

Les Caves des Hauts-Côtes 1983 Nuits-St.-Georges $13. Concentrated, cherry-cranberry aromas and flavors; hints of tobacco, chocolate. Adequate structure, full bodied, fleshy. Delicious already, but astringent tannins need brief cellaring. Very good value. (CC/May '86) ★★★

Simon Bize & Fils 1982 Bourgogne, Aux Perrières $9.99. Violet scent. Nicely maturing Pinot Noir fruit. Good acidity. Medium body. (CC/Mar. '86) ★★3/4

Joseph Drouhin 1983 Morey-St.-Denis, Clos de la Roche $31. Plummy, somewhat closed nose. Ripe fruit evident in slightly smoky flavors. Hint of goût de terroir in finish; sharp, dry note. Excellent structure and depth. Nicely balanced. (CC/May '86) ★★1/2 (★★★)

Joseph Faiveley 1980 Mazis-Chambertin, Sélection Chevaliers du

Tastevinage $28.19. Lovely, open bouquet has woodsy nuances. Some tannin and lots of flavor. Enjoyable now, and will improve. (S&PW/Jan. '86) ★★1/2 (★★★)

Joseph Faiveley 1981 Gevrey-Chambertin, Les Cazetier $25. Stinky, almost sour-cream aromas with oak, other nice scents. Moderate, oak and cherry flavors. Medium body. (JPN/Mar. '86) ★★1/2 (★★★)

Joseph Faiveley 1981 Morey-St.-Denis $19. Closed nose, hints of cedar. Good body and balance. Fruit intensifies in the glass. (JPN/Mar. '86) ★★1/2 (★★★)

Joseph Faiveley 1982 Nuits-St.-Georges, Clos de la Maréchale $21. Spicy rather than fruity. Very tight and closed. Hints of violet as it opens. (JPN/Mar. '86) ★★1/2 (★★★)

Joseph Faiveley 1983 Nuits-St.-Georges, Clos de la Maréchale $40. Bouquet exudes elegant goût de terroir and a scent of weeds and wildflowers. Restrained flavors; long finish. Moderately astringent. (CC/May '86) ★★1/2 (★★★)

Moillard 1983 Clos de Vougeot $36. Delicate, plum and cream aromas. Ripe fruit taste with pleasant oak flavor in the finish. (JPN/Jan. '87) ★★1/2 (★★★)

Joseph Faiveley 1981 Mercurey, Clos des Myglands $12. Chocolate-and-toast aroma. Good balance of fruit and oak. Medium body. Plenty of acid. (JPN/Mar. '86) ★★ (★★★)

Lupé-Cholet 1983 Nuits-St.-Georges, 1er Cru, Château Gris $24. Ripe fruit and vanilla-oak aromas. Berry and chocolate flavors. Engaging, forward style, full bodied, with substantial tannins. Needs five years. (CC/May '86) ★★ (★★3/4)

Caves des Vignerons de Buxy 1983 Bourgogne $5.59. Almost metallic hardness in the nose; unyielding. Firm fruit in the mouth; mushrooms and earth. Medium body. (RF/Mar. '86) ★★ (★★1/2)

Joseph Drouhin 1983 Beaune, Clos

des Mouches Rouge $19.89. Youthful, berry-like aroma with a touch of spice. Moderate tannin. Flavorful. Moderately long finish. Needs a few years to develop. (S&PW/Mar. '86) ★★ (★★1/2)

Joseph Faiveley 1983 Nuits-St.-Georges $35. Berryish bouquet with chocolate and mocha nuances. Moderately astringent tannins. Should open in about five to seven years. (CC/May '86) ★★ (★★1/2)

Moillard 1983 Fixin, Clos d'Entre Deux Velles $15. Closed, black pepper aroma carries into flavor. Tightly structured; holding back. (JPN/Jan. '87) ★★ (★★1/2)

Daniel Rion 1981 Côte de Nuits-Villages $10.49. Berryish fruit aroma and flavor, laced with minty, menthol-like overtones. (CC/Mar. '86) ★★

Domaine de Lambray 1983 Clos des Lambrays, Grand Cru $43. Bright, cherryish fruit. Leather, vanilla, bitter-licorice flavors. Lean and tannic; symptomatic of vintage at this point. (CC/May '86) ★★

Joseph Drouhin 1983 Chambertin $35. Pungent aroma laced with cranberries, tobacco, vanilla. Tannic, austere, tart. Flavors and finish closed. (CC/May '86) ★★

Joseph Drouhin 1983 Echézeaux $33. Sharp, oaky aromas. Unyielding flavors with complex smokiness. Sharp acidity; restrained, astringent finish. Needs time. (CC/May '86) ★★

Joseph Faiveley 1982 Fixin, Tastevin Selection $13. Delicate fruit flavor with some toastiness. Somewhat closed, fairly light body. (JPN/Mar. '86) ★★

Joseph Roty 1983 Gevrey-Chambertin $20. Somewhat closed nose hints of vanilla, coconut. Lean and tannic. Somewhat hot finish. Promising. (CC/May '86) ★★

Moillard 1982 Chambolle-Musigny $15. Spice and black cherry aromas and flavors. Some vanilla in the finish. Pleasant now. (JPN/Jan. '87) ★★

Moillard 1983 Nuits-St.-Georges, Clos de Thorey $25. Caramel and plums in the aroma and taste. Medium bodied. Some harsh tannin in the finish. (JPN/Jan. '87) ★1/2 (★★1/2)

Vadey-Castagnier 1983 Chambolle-Musigny $17. Rich, ripe-fruit aromas. Tart, spicy flavors. Aggressive tannins will mature a bit sooner than others of this vintage. (CC/May '86) ★1/2 (★★)

Chanson Père et Fils 1982 Beaune, Clos des Fèvres $15. Smoky, oaky, and coffee qualities. Tight, fairly well balanced. Not enough fruit. (JPN/Jan. '87) ★1/2

Chanson Père et Fils 1983 Côte de Beaune-Villages $11. Ripe raspberry, slightly perfumy aroma. Moderate cherry taste. Somewhat watery middle. Drink now. (JPN/Jan. '87) ★1/2

Joseph Faiveley 1981 Côte de Nuits-Villages, Tastevin Selection $13. Slightly stinky. Pleasant, cherry-and-spice flavor. A bit watery. (JPN/Mar. '86) ★1/2

Daniel Rion 1982 Côte de Nuits-Villages $10.49. Aromatic, fruity, earthy. Youthfully simple and short. (CC/Mar. '86) ★

Lupé-Cholet 1983 Chambolle-Musigny $17. Vinous, fruited aroma. Delicate, flowery undertones in flavors. Substantial tannins. Clean, simple, short. (CC/May '86) ★

B. de Monthélie 1982 Bourgogne, Pinot $6. Candyish, jammy, mouthwash-like aroma with obtrusive, earthy and woody accents. (CC/Mar. '86)

B. de Monthélie 1982 Gevrey-Chambertin, 1er Cru, Les Cazetiers $14. Putrid, brackish, and bitter. (CC/Mar. '86)

B. de Monthélie 1982 Nuits-St.-Georges, 1er Cru, Les Damodes $13. Swampy, vegetal stink. Very bitter. (CC/Mar. '86)

B. de Monthélie 1982 Savigny-

Les-Beaune, Domaine Chénu $11.50. Smells artificially sweet with sweaty undertones. Weak, dirty flavors. (CC/Mar. '86)

Bernard Mugneret-Gouachon 1983 Nuits-St.-Georges, Les Perdrix $17. Sweet, concentrated perfume, but with subtle, dirty undertones in the finish. (CC/May '86)

Daniel Rion 1980 Côte de Nuits-Villages $10.49. Complex, oak-induced aromas and flavors. (CC/Mar. '86)

Henri Magnien 1983 Gevrey-Chambertin $17. Smoky aroma and flavor; very astringent. Painfully dry. Age for a minimum of 10 years. (CC/May '86)

Mommessin 1983 Clos de Tart $50. Aroma suggests vanilla pudding. Simple, cherryish flavors with hint of earthiness. Austere structure, unbearably astringent. (CC/May '86)

CABERNET SAUVIGNON

In 1985 approximately 12 million gallons of Cabernet Sauvignon were fermented in California, making this variety the most important premium red wine in the United States. The major grape variety of French Bordeaux, Cabernet has clearly established another home in California, and particularly in the Napa Valley. More than any other varietal, it has made the Napa Valley America's premier wine district.

The Cabernet vine requires a relatively long growing season. Outside of California, it has begun to show potential in the warm, eastern part of Washington State, and in a Middle-Atlantic crescent from Virginia through Maryland and Pennsylvania to Long Island. Further afield, very fine Cabernet Sauvignon is produced in Australia, and in Chile.

The flavors encountered in a bottle of Cabernet range from a berry or jammy fruitiness to a complex melange of spices, cedar, eucalyptus, and mint, with an herbaceous underlay. It is always dry, though perhaps not quite so dry as Bordeaux. In the last several years, many American winemakers have begun blending Cabernet Sauvignon with Merlot and sometimes with Cabernet Franc, the varieties most prominent in the blending of Bordeaux. The addition of Merlot, in particular, tends to mitigate some of the roughness of Cabernet, at least in its youth. Winemakers are generally striving to make more subtle, complex, supple wines. If the wine is at least 75% Cabernet, other varieties need not be mentioned on the label. But in recent years, more wines are being made with higher percentages of Merlot and Cabernet Franc and labeled with proprietary names rather than as Cabernet, such as the Mondavi-Rothschild Opus One and Joseph Phelps' Insignia.

AMERICAN

Charles Krug 1974 Cabernet Sauvignon, Vintage Selection, Lot F-1, Napa Valley, CA $35. Beautifully developed, cedary bouquet. Earthy flavors with subtle, Cabernet herbaceousness, hints of mint, green olive, spice, ripe cherry. Very complex. Should be decanted. Mature but should cellar well for at least another decade. Be sure the label says Lot F-1. (JDM/Mar. '86) ★★★★

Crystal Valley 1983 Cabernet Sauvignon, Reserve Edition, North Coast, CA $12. Scents of plums, berries, chocolate, cedar, leather. Rich, multi-layered flavors still tightly wound up with intense tannins. Loads of extract. Very well structured. Needs 5-10 years. (AWC/Nov. '86) ★★★★

Inglenook 1981 Cabernet Sauvignon, Limited Cask Reserve Selection, Napa Valley, CA $15.50. Fruity nose has overtones of minerals and tobacco. Impeccably balanced. Strong tannin, firm acidity, intense fruit. Long finish. Will gain with five years. (AWC/Nov '86) ★★★★

Newton 1981 Cabernet Sauvignon, Napa Valley, CA $12.50. Big, rich, weighty; with elegance. Jasmine, mint, black cherry nose. Generous but not ponderous. Plummy fruit. Peppery, spicy finish. Firm tannin and acid. Needs five years. (AWC/Nov. '85) ★★★★

Susine 1982 Cabernet Sauvignon, Suisin Valley, CA $8. Very intense but not overly extracted or overripe. Plum and black cherry flavors show French oak and a complex, cedary quality. A great bargain. (JDM/Mar. '86) ★★★★

Ch. Montelena 1980 Cabernet Sauvignon, Estate Bottled, Napa Valley, CA $24. Undeveloped, delicate aromas of violets and berries. Fruit taste is rich but understated. Firm structure. No harsh tannins or overripeness. Wonderful now, should age gracefully. (JPN/Jan. '87) ★★★1/2 (★★★★)

Davis Bynum 1981 Cabernet Sauvignon, Artist's Label Reserve, Sonoma County, CA $25. Charming, cedary bouquet followed by complex flavors of green olive, cherry, and cassis. Very enjoyable now, but further development is assured. (JDM/Mar. '86) ★★★1/2 (★★★★)

Laurel Glen 1982 Cabernet Sauvignon, Sonoma Valley, CA $12.50. Beginning to develop a lovely, Bordeaux-like, cedary bouquet. Complex flavors are big, bold, intense, but also have finesse. Time should bring the polish of greatness. Good value. (JDM/Mar. '86) ★★★1/2 (★★★★)

Lyeth 1982 Estate Bottled, Alexander Valley, CA $16. A Bordeaux-style blend of Cabernet Sauvignon, Cabernet Franc, Merlot, and Malbec. Many layers of complexity enhanced by judicious oak aging. Enjoyable in youth but balanced for aging. (JDM/Mar. '86) ★★★1/2 (★★★★)

Acacia 1983 Cabernet Sauvignon, Napa Valley, CA $18.49. Still closed up, but starting to reveal good depth, lots of extract and intensity, fine balance. Long, astringent finish. Lay it down. (AWC/Nov. '86) ★★★1/2

Adelaida 1982 Cabernet Sauvignon, Paso Robles, CA $9.75. Ripe cassis nose. Beautiful balance of luscious fruit, soft tannin, with a smooth texture, good length. Elegant. (AWC/Nov. '86) ★★★1/2

Beaulieu (BV) 1980 Cabernet Sauvignon, Private Reserve de Georges de Latour, Napa Valley, CA $21. Oak and mint with big, rich, berry flavors bordering on overripe. Toasty-smoky nuances. Complex. Very well balanced. Mature but still going up. (AWC/Nov. '86) ★★★1/2

Buena Vista 1982 Cabernet Sauvignon, Carneros—Sonoma Valley, CA $11. Big, Cabernet nose has peppery spice and cassis highlights. Full fruit flavors with strong acidity. Medium weight. Well balanced. (AWC/Nov. '86) ★★★1/2

Burgess 1982 Cabernet Sauvignon, Vintage Selection, Napa Valley, CA $15.95. Cedary wood tones in a berry-fruit nose. Chewy, deep, very ripe, spicy fruit flavors. Elegant structure. (AWC/Nov. '86) ★★★1/2

Byrd 1982 Cabernet Sauvignon, Estate Bottled, Catoctin, MD $10. Hints of vanilla, cedar and cinnamon. Luscious fruit, slightly dusty, with high tannin and acidity. Vigorous; needs time. (AWC/Nov. '85) ★★★1/2

Cain 1982 Cabernet Sauvignon, Napa Valley, CA $11. Restrained nose of cedar and spice. Full, intense fruit hiding behind hard tannins. Demands five or more years cellaring. (AWC/Nov. '86) ★★★1/2

Columbia 1982 Cabernet Sauvignon, Red Willow Vineyard, Yakima Valley, WA $12. Tea, spices, cedar, cherry, blueberry nose. Lean flavors suggest black currant. Good acidity and tannin for aging. Long, elegant finish. Médoc-style. (AWC/Nov. '86) ★★★1/2

Concannon 1983 Cabernet Sauvignon, Estate Bottled, Livermore Valley, CA $11.50. Currants and cassis highlight rich, sweet fruit flavors. Complex, opulent style. Lowish acidity. Classic, plush, ultra-ripe California Cab. (AWC/Nov. '86) ★★★1/2

De Loach Vineyards 1983 Cabernet Sauvignon, Dry Creek Valley, CA $11. Superb, spicy, berry-fruit nose of flowers, peaches, cassis. Cedary wood complements firm, ripe fruit flavors. Weighty but well structured. Soft tannin calls for a few years cellaring. (AWC/Nov. '86) ★★★1/2

Duckhorn 1983 Cabernet Sauvignon, Napa Valley, CA $18. Hints of tar and leather in a berry-mint nose. Rich, Cabernet fruit, high extract, but austere tannins dominate. In an awkward stage; needs at least 5-10 years. (AWC/Nov. '86) ★★★1/2

Eberle 1982 Cabernet Sauvignon, Paso Robles, CA $10. Well-defined, jammy, Cabernet aromas show classic cassis and mint. Rich fruit; good extract. Medium weight. Velvety texture. Bitter tannin calls for two to five years aging. (AWC/Nov. '86) ★★★1/2

Estrella River 1982 Cabernet Sauvignon, Estate Bottled, Paso Robles, CA $10. Minty Cabernet nose has earthy-woody tones. Generous, raspberryish flavors show lively acidity. Austere, tannic backbone and finish needs five years to smooth out. (AWC/Nov. '86) ★★★1/2

Grgich Hills 1980 Cabernet Sauvignon, 34% Napa County/66% Sonoma County, CA $16. Roundness, harmony, complexity. Fruit is dry but not lean; suggests cranberries, strawberries. Lingering, tart finish. (AWC/Nov. '85) ★★★1/2

Groth 1983 Cabernet Sauvignon, Napa Valley, CA $13. Cranberry, mint, and herb scents. Oak and supple Cabernet fruit flavors are in good balance with soft tannins. Very elegant. Drink now. (AWC/ Nov. '86) ★★★1/2

Jekel 1982 Cabernet Sauvignon, Monterey, CA $11. Complex nose of cigar box, oak, figs, eucalyptus, black pepper, vanilla, mint. Mellow, sweet fruit flavors have vanilla-oak highlights. Soft texture. Nice balance. Ready to drink. (AWC/Nov. '86) ★★★1/2

Joseph Phelps 1981 Cabernet Sauvignon, Eisele Vineyard, Napa Valley, CA $30. Gentle, strawberry nose. Mellow fruit flavors show slight sweetness, peppery spice. Strong tannins for five years or more aging. (AWC/Nov. '85) ★★★1/2

Lambert Bridge 1981 Cabernet Sauvignon, Estate Bottled, Sonoma County, CA $10. Luscious, round fruit with hints of pepper and dill. Rich, full bodied; viscous texture. Drink in the next few years. (AWC/Nov. '85) ★★★1/2

Markham 1980 Cabernet Sauvignon, Yountville, Napa Valley, CA $13. Rich, jammy fruit laced with black currants, molasses, toffee, figs, chocolate, coffee. Full body and extract. Lots of tannin in a long finish. Needs more than five years. (AWC/Nov. '85) ★★★1/2

Markham 1981 Cabernet Sauvignon, Markham Vineyard—Yountville, Napa Valley, CA $13. Cedar and spice highlight rich, grape aromas. Intense, ripe, cherry-cassis flavors. Full bodied. Wonderful finish. Requires at least five more years. (AWC/Nov. '86) ★★★1/2

Robert Young Vineyard (Belvedere Winery) 1982 Cabernet Sauvignon, Alexander Valley, CA $12. Licorice and pepper nose. Big, round, plum-like fruit with elegant overtones of smoke and roasted meat. Full body. Strong tannins. Needs more than five years. (AWC/Nov. '85) ★★★1/2

Round Hill 1982 Cabernet Sauvignon, Napa Valley, CA $9. Packed with aromas and flavors of deep, berry-fruit, cedar, mint. Excellent balance. Still youthful; needs more than five years. (AWC/Nov. '86) ★★★1/2

Rutherford Ranch Brand 1982 Cabernet Sauvignon, Napa Valley, CA $12. A big, earthy powerhouse. Spicy, cassis, and mint nose. Loads of plummy fruit and tannin. Needs more than five years. (AWC/Nov. '86) ★★★1/2

Sequoia Grove 1983 Cabernet Sauvignon, Napa Valley/Alexander Valley, CA $12. Big, sweet fruit of raspberries, cherries, blueberries, with nuances of chocolate, leather. Fleshy texture, good balance and structure, loads of tannin. A keeper. (AWC/Nov. '86) ★★★1/2

Simi 1981 Cabernet Sauvignon, Alexander Valley, CA $11. Cassis fruit up front, joined by raspberry, chocolate, and mint. Gentle fruit edged with assertive acidity and hard tannins. Needs three to five years. (AWC/Nov. '85) ★★★1/2

V. Sattui 1982 Cabernet Sauvignon, Reserve Stock, Preston Vineyard, Napa Valley, CA $17.50. Complex nose. Rich, round flavors with well-integrated oak. Long finish. Mature Cabernet still ascending. (AWC/Nov. '86) ★★★1/2

Clos du Bois 1980 Cabernet Sauvignon, Dry Creek Reserve, Sonoma County, CA $15. Classy Cabernet in the Bordeaux mold: lean, tight, firm structure. Earthy flavors have hints of black cherry. Long, complex aftertaste. Excellent ageability. (JDM/Mar. '86) ★★★ (★★★1/2)

Smith-Madrone 1982 Cabernet Sauvignon, Napa Valley, CA $12. Very Bordeaux-like in its lean, firm structure and pleasant, tart acidity. Firm but not unruly tannin. Green olive flavors up front progress to more earthy, black olive, with hints of black cherry. (JDM/Mar. '86) ★★★ (★★★1/2)

Bargetto 1983 Cabernet Sauvignon, Napa Valley, CA $11. Soft, elegant fruit throughout. Very harmonious, well-balanced. Smooth texture. (AWC/Nov. '86) ★★★

Beringer 1981 Cabernet Sauvignon, Reserve, Napa Valley, CA $18. Assertive nose. Soft, deep, jammy fruit flavors, well balanced with round tannins. Excellent finish. (AWC/Nov. '86) ★★★

Buena Vista 1981 Cabernet Sauvignon, Private Reserve, Carneros, Sonoma Valley, CA $18. Dense, burly, high extract, with round, concentrated, berry-fruit flavors. Soft tannins. (AWC/Nov. '85) ★★★

Burgess 1981 Cabernet Sauvignon, Vintage Selection, Napa Valley, CA $15.95. Straightforward, full, plummy, with spicy mint and pepper. (AWC/Nov. '85) ★★★

Byrd 1983 Cabernet Sauvignon, Estate Bottled, Catoctin, MD

$16.50. Jammy, cedary nose. Youthful, berryish, rich, with wood tones. Developing complexity. Needs more time. (AWC/Nov. '86) ★★★

Ch. Boswell 1982 Cabernet Sauvignon, Private Reserve, Napa Valley, CA $15. Shy, sweet-berry nose has cedary overtones. Big, chewy, intense fruit. (AWC/Nov. '86) ★★★

Ch. Diana 1983 Cabernet Sauvignon, Napa Valley, CA. Aromatic nose mingles cherries, blackberries, cranberries. Easy-drinking wine with balance, spry acidity, long finish. (AWC/Nov. '86) ★★★

Ch. Montelena 1982 Cabernet Sauvignon, Estate Bottled, Napa Valley, CA $16. Cedar and currant nose. Rich fruit extract with woody, earthy highlights. Sharp tannins. (AWC/Nov. '86) ★★★

Ch. Ste. Michelle 1980 Cabernet Sauvignon, Chateau Reserve, Cold Creek Vineyards, Benton County, WA $19.50. Strong wood tones of cedar and oak, with plenty of fruit and soft tannins. Some elegance. Good length. (AWC/Nov. '86) ★★★

Christian Brothers 1980 Cabernet Sauvignon, Napa Valley, CA $8. Mature, tarry aroma. Good weight in the mouth. Broad, supple, ready to drink. Nice, tar-and-tobacco flavors. Good value. (JPN/Mar. '86) ★★★

Clos du Bois 1980 Cabernet Sauvignon, Briarcrest, Alexander Valley, CA $12.75. Forward, fragrant fruit and cedary nose. Opens in the glass to tart, berry and vanilla flavors. Tight, well-woven. (AWC/Nov. '85) ★★★

Clos du Bois 1981 Cabernet Sauvignon, Alexander Valley, CA $9. Oaky, coffee nose; also cherries, vanilla, smoke. Berry fruit and mocha. High alcohol, firm tannins. (AWC/Nov. '85) ★★★

Clos du Val 1978 Cabernet Sauvignon, Reserve, Napa Valley, CA $35.

Big, robust. Chocolate, raspberry, anise, coffee, cassis, wood are all there. Remarkable balance. (AWC/Nov. '85) ★★★

Clos du Val 1982 Cabernet Sauvignon, Napa Valley, CA $13.25. Varietal Cabernet aromas and a scent of dill. Round, soft, earthy-berryish flavors show complexity from bottle age. Fine balance. Good length. (AWC/Nov. '86) ★★★

Crystal Valley 1983 Cabernet Sauvignon, North Coast, CA $8.50. Toast and cassis in good Cabernet aromas. Abundant fruit and soft, peppery tannins. Good structure for short-term aging. (AWC/Nov. '86) ★★★

Davis Bynum 1981 Cabernet Sauvignon, Sonoma County, CA $9. Spicy, rich, direct, fruit flavors. (AWC/Nov. '85) ★★★

Fairmont Cellars 1982 Cabernet Sauvignon, Private Selection, Napa Valley, CA $10.50. Assertive cherry fruit and wood, and a grassy scent. Full, smooth fruit competes with bitter tannins. Needs a few years. (AWC/Nov. '85) ★★★

Firestone 1978 Cabernet Sauvignon, Vintage Reserve, Santa Ynez Valley, CA $18. Big, rich-fruit, varietal aroma. Firm and flavorful. Still has a tannic spine. (S&PW/Mar. '86) ★★★

Freemark Abbey 1982 Cabernet Sauvignon, Cabernet Bosche, Napa Valley, CA $15. Youthful nose shows loads of sweet, ultra-ripe fruit. Very rich, ripe flavors are still a bit raw. Needs a few more years. (AWC/Nov. '86) ★★★

Glen Ellen 1983 Cabernet Sauvignon, Glen Ellen Estate, Sonoma Valley, CA $9.75. Mint and eucalyptus character is quite pronounced. High fruit extract with strong tannin. Well structured. (AWC/Nov. '86) ★★★

Haywood 1982 Cabernet Sauvignon, Sonoma Valley, CA $11. Dense, powerful fruit; rich and round. Alcohol, wood, and tannin also prominent. Depth without complexity. Needs up to five years. (AWC/Nov. '85) ★★★

Hogue 1983 Cabernet Sauvignon, Reserve, WA $14. Big, deep. A complex nose of smoke, coffee, shoe leather, jasmine. Intense, rich fruit, excellent balance. (AWC/ Nov. '85) ★★★

Hogue 1984 Cabernet Sauvignon, Reserve, WA $17.95. Straightforward, berryish fruit resembles a young Rhône. Well-balanced, lighter style Cabernet. (AWC/ Nov. '86) ★★★

Husch 1982 Cabernet Sauvignon, Estate Bottled, La Ribera Ranch, Mendocino County, CA $10. Scents of peppermint, eucalyptus. Very ripe, mouthfilling fruit. Soft; low acidity. (AWC/Nov. '85) ★★★

J. Lohr 1983 Cabernet Sauvignon, CA $5. Minty, fresh cherry nose. Forward, lively, berry flavors with peppery accents. (AWC/Nov. '85) ★★★

Jordan 1982 Cabernet Sauvignon, Estate Bottled, Alexander Valley, CA $16.99. Big wine with bell-peppery fruit and oak in balance. Fleshy. High alcohol and peppery tannin need mellowing out. (AWC/ Nov. '86) ★★★

Kendall-Jackson 1983 Cabernet Sauvignon, Cardinale, CA $9. Powerful. Still relatively closed up with tannin. (AWC/Nov. '85) ★★★

Lakespring 1981 Cabernet Sauvignon, Napa Valley, CA $11. Aromatic, cedary nose with hints of licorice. Plummy, Merlot-Cabernet fruit. (AWC/Nov. '85) ★★★

Monticello Cellars 1982 Cabernet Sauvignon, Corley Reserve, Napa Valley, CA $14.50. Expansive nose of currants, flowers, plums. Big body, chewy tannins, good acidity, high alcohol. Needs at least five years. (AWC/Nov. '85) ★★★

Monticello Cellars 1983 Cabernet Sauvignon, Jefferson Cuvee, Napa

Valley, CA $10. Aromatic nose of cigar-box cedar and peaches. Concentrated, port-like flavors. Firm structure. Plenty of tannin. (AWC/Nov. '86) ★★★

Newton 1982 Cabernet Sauvignon, Napa Valley, CA $12.50. Cedar, spice, and plummy fruit. Bright acidity. Peppery tannin. Well crafted; almost delicate. (AWC/Nov. '86) ★★★

Quail Run 1983 Cabernet Sauvignon, Yakima Valley, WA $9.49. Big, powerful, concentrated wine. High alcohol. Intense layers of aroma and flavor. (AWC/Nov. '86) ★★★

Raymond 1981 Cabernet Sauvignon, Private Reserve, Napa Valley, CA $16. Jammy cassis on the nose. Oak is nicely woven through soft fruit. Medium-light body. Classic structure with strong tannin, good aging potential. (AWC/Nov. '86) ★★★

Robert Mondavi 1980 Cabernet Sauvignon, Reserve, Napa Valley, CA $31.25. Minty, smoky nose with woody notes. Lean, well-structured, oak, pepper, leather, and cherry flavors. (AWC/Nov. '85) ★★★

Robert Mondavi 1981 Cabernet Sauvignon, Reserve, Napa Valley, CA $27.50. Floral, high-toned, berry nose has minty, lemony nuances. Complex fruit, wood, and leathery flavors are nicely balanced. Subtle wine with good potential. (AWC/Nov. '86) ★★★

Round Hill 1981 Cabernet Sauvignon, Napa Valley, CA $9. Ripe nose of plums, cassis, and raisins. Concentrated, rich, currant fruit with mint and tobacco flavors, pepper, and high alcohol. Needs more than five years. (AWC/Nov. '85) ★★★

Sierra Vista 1982 Cabernet Sauvignon, Estate Bottled, El Dorado, CA $8.50. Forward, cherry-raspberry nose and flavor. Good balance of acid and tannin with high alcohol. (AWC/Nov. '85) ★★★

Smith & Hook 1982 Cabernet Sau-

vignon, Estate Bottled, Monterey, CA $13. Round, aggressive, ready now, with some tannin for keeping. (AWC/Nov. '85) ★★★

Steltzner 1983 Cabernet Sauvignon, Napa Valley, CA $15. Austere tannins matched by very ripe, slightly pruney fruit with cedary, spicy overtones. Needs five years or more. (AWC/Nov. '86) ★★★

Stratford 1982 Cabernet Sauvignon, CA $7.50. Aromatic, spearmint bouquet. Plenty of fruit, and a warm, peppery quality. Well put together. (AWC/Nov. '85) ★★★

V. Sattui 1983 Cabernet Sauvignon, Napa Valley, CA $9.75. Lightly aromatic wine of medium body, with fleshy texture, supple berry and cassis flavors, high tannin. Needs a few more years. (AWC/Nov. '86) ★★★

Whitehall Lane 1982 Cabernet Sauvignon, Napa Valley, CA $12. Open, youthful nose of berries and spice. Simple, mellow flavors of plums, mint, vanilla. Alcohol slightly high, and plenty of tannin for aging. Needs more than five years. (AWC/ Nov. '85) ★★★

Ch. Montelena 1981 Cabernet Sauvignon, Estate Bottled, Napa Valley, CA $24. Closed aroma of cassis. Lots of ripe fruit. Chocolate, tannic finish. Needs more bottle age. (JPN/Jan. '87) ★★1/2 (★★★1/2)

Eberle 1981 Cabernet Sauvignon, Paso Robles, CA $12. Complex, herbs and berry aroma. Rich, enjoyable, somewhat tarry, briary-berry flavors. Should age well for a few more years. (JPN/Jan. '87) ★★1/2 (★★★)

Mont St. John 1981 Cabernet Sauvignon, Private Reserve, Napa Valley, CA $11. Earthy and chocolaty. Substantial tannins are not offensive and promise long life. (JDM/Mar. '86) ★★1/2 (★★★)

Stag's Leap Wine Cellars 1982 Ca-

bernet Sauvignon, Stag's Leap Vineyard, Napa Valley, CA $16.50. Rich fruit and herbal nose. Flavors are rich with tar, cherries, slight mint. Good potential. (JPN/Jan. '87) ★★1/2 (★★★)

Ultravino 1982 Cabernet Sauvignon, Napa Valley, CA $9. Firm, almost hard, Bordeaux-like structure with pleasant, green-olive and berry qualities. (JDM/May '86) ★★1/2 (★★★)

Cecchetti-Sebastiani 1983 Cabernet Sauvignon, Sonoma, CA $14. Youthful but precocious, with rich, chocolate overtones. Ready. Pricey. (JDM/Mar. '86) ★★1/2

Devlin 1982 Cabernet Sauvignon, Sonoma County, CA $7. Voluptuous, forward, ripe, very intense, with underlying notes of black cherry and cassis. (JDM/May '86) ★★1/2

River Oaks 1983 Cabernet Sauvignon, Sonoma, CA $6. Soft fruit and tannin. Straightforward, slightly herbaceous flavors with a hint of mint. (JDM/Mar. '86) ★★1/2

Stag's Leap Wine Cellars 1983 Cabernet Sauvignon, Napa Valley, CA $11. Rich cherry, mushroom, and earth aromas. Flavor is more herbal than fruity. Nice balance on the light side. (JPN/Jan. '87) ★★1/2

Rodney Strong 1980 Cabernet Sauvignon, Alexander's Crown, CA $12. Big, rich, intense aroma. Enormous richness and concentration with the sweetness of ripe fruit. Well structured, with real character. Needs another three to four years. (S&PW/May '86) ★★ (★★★)

Woodward Canyon 1983 Cabernet Sauvignon, WA $16.50. Brambly, fruity nose. Firm, youthful texture. Lots of fruit. Nice, acidic liveliness; pleasant oak flavors. A bit alcoholic. (JPN/May '86) ★★ (★★★)

Bellerose 1983 Cabernet Sauvignon, Cuvee Bellerose, Dry Creek

Valley, CA $12. Reticent nose hints of green olives and tobacco. Soft tannin, some firmness, fruity, soft-centered. Moderate length. Approachable now but needs three more years. (S&PW/May '86) ★★ (★★1/2)

Flora Springs 1981 Cabernet Sauvignon, Napa Valley, CA $14.99. Light, refined, varietal aroma. Lean, austere style. Quite flavorful. Still somewhat closed, but quality is very evident. (S&PW/Mar. '86) ★★ (★★1/2)

Almaden 1982 Cabernet Sauvignon, Monterey County, CA $4.99. Suggestions of flowers and soft, berryish fruit in a light, balanced, easy-drinking wine. (AWC/ Nov. '86) ★★

Buena Vista 1980 Cabernet Sauvignon, Special Selection, Sonoma Valley, CA $18. Very ripe, Port-like aromas of caramel and coffee. Flavors are rich, deep, but unusual. (AWC/Nov. '85) ★★

Chalk Hill 1982 Cabernet Sauvignon, Sonoma County, CA $9. Chocolaty, leathery nose. Rich, ripe fruit flavors. Tannic, with a brief, hot finish. (AWC/Nov. '86) ★★

Christophe 1982 Cabernet Sauvignon, CA $4.49. Minty fruit. Soft, light body, well balanced. (AWC/Nov. '85) ★★

Clos du Bois 1981 Cabernet Sauvignon, Briarcrest Vineyard, Alexander Valley, CA $15. Rich, soft, almost sweet fruit shows overripeness and complexity. (AWC/Nov. '86) ★★

Colony 1982 Cabernet Sauvignon, Sonoma County, CA $6.99. Jammy character is generous and long, verging on overripe. (AWC/Nov. '86) ★★

Delicato 1983 Cabernet Sauvignon, Golden Anniversary, Napa Valley—Carneros, CA $12. (AWC/Nov. '86) ★★

Flora Springs 1982 Cabernet Sauvignon, Napa Valley, CA $10.99. Lovely aroma of oak and fruit. Well balanced, firm, with moderate tannin. A well-made though somewhat lean wine. (S&PW/Mar. '86) ★★

Gainey 1981 Cabernet Sauvignon, Limited Selection, Santa Ynez Valley, CA $11. Forward, coffee and berry nose. Flavors of supple fruit with chocolate and coffee. Low tannin and acidity. (AWC/ Nov. '85) ★★

Glen Ellen 1983 Cabernet Sauvignon, Proprietor's Reserve, CA $5. A bargain in the light, easy-to-quaff style. Berry flavors are fairly one-dimensional. Fine, everyday wine. (JDM/Mar. '86) ★★

Guenoc 1983 Cabernet Sauvignon, Lake County, CA $8.75. A sweet, mint-and-berry nose has a slightly burnt quality. Light but elegant. (AWC/Nov. '86) ★★

Joseph Phelps 1982 Cabernet Sauvignon, Napa Valley, CA $12. Aromatic, minty-spicy nose. Elegant fruit flavors are buried in tannin. (AWC/Nov. '86) ★★

Kenwood 1982 Cabernet Sauvignon, Artist Series, Sonoma Valley, CA $25. Rich peppery, earthy, vanilla, coffee, mint flavors woven together nicely; but fruit is short. Should hold up well. (AWC/ Nov. '85) ★★

Laurel Glen 1982 Cabernet Sauvignon, Sonoma Mountain, CA $12.50. Aromatic, minty-eucalyptus nose. Flavors are youthful, with sweet fruit, wood, tart acidity. (AWC/Nov. '85) ★★

Louis J. Foppiano 1981 Cabernet Sauvignon, Russian River Valley, CA $5.50. Spicy, cedary, earthy nose. Rich fruit extract. Bitter, tannic finish needs time. (AWC/Nov. '86) ★★

M. Marion 1983 Cabernet Sauvignon, CA $4.50. Abundant fruit. Soft, round, herbaceous. Good balance and structure. (AWC/Nov. '86) ★★

Mirassou 1982 Cabernet Sauvignon, Harvest Reserve, Napa Valley, CA $12. Lean, smooth, elegant flavors. Well balanced. Toasty finish. (AWC/Nov.

'86) ★★

Pine Ridge 1982 Cabernet Sauvignon, Pine Ridge Stag's Leap Vineyard, Napa Valley, CA $20. Mineralfruit nose. Ripe blackberry flavors. Good balance. Soft tannins. Short finish. (AWC/Nov. '86) ★★

Ridgemont 1983 Cabernet Sauvignon, American, winery in WA $8.50. Shy, berryish nose. Soft, round fruit nicely balanced with acidity and light tannin. (AWC/Nov. '86) ★★

Robert Stemmler 1982 Cabernet Sauvignon, Sonoma County, CA $15. Complex nose and flavors: very ripe grapes, old oak, coffee, mint, sage, and a slightly musty, barnyardy note. Ready now. (AWC/Nov. '85) ★★

Shafer Vineyards 1983 Cabernet Sauvignon, Napa Valley, CA $13. Good balance of acidity and raspberryish fruit, with nuances of green pepper and tobacco. Firm structure. (AWC/Nov. '86) ★★

Sterling 1980 Cabernet Sauvignon, Estate Bottled, Reserve, Napa Valley, CA $22.50. Solid but gentle scents of vanilla, alcohol, currants, fresh fruit. Balanced. Straightforward. (AWC/Nov. '85) ★★

Sterling 1982 Cabernet Sauvignon, Diamond Mountain Ranch, Napa Valley, CA $15. Layered fruit overshadowed by high tannin and sturdy acidity. Needs three to five years. (AWC/Nov. '85) ★★

Taylor California Cellars (nonvintage) Cabernet Sauvignon, CA $3.99. Fresh, berry nose. Sweet, raspberry fruit. (AWC/Nov. '85) ★★

Valley View Vineyard 1979 Cabernet Sauvignon, OR $17. A huge, fat, viscous Cabernet with a lot going on — tarry, minty, weedy, mushroomy, plus abrasive tannins. (AWC/Nov. '86) ★★

Vichon 1982 Cabernet Sauvignon, Fay Vineyard, Napa Valley, CA $15. Full, forward, berryish fruit has leathery nuances. Good balance. Hard tannins. (AWC/ Nov. '86) ★★

William Hill 1981 Cabernet Sauvignon, Napa Valley—Mt. Veeder, CA $14.50. Round, very ripe flavors have sweaty, leathery, tobacco qualities and an austere, tannic grip. Needs more than five years aging. (AWC/Nov. '86) ★★

Zaca Mesa 1983 Cabernet Sauvignon, Central Coast, CA $8.50. Good balance and structure. Forward flavors of ripe berries and green pepper. Short finish. (AWC/ Nov. '86) ★★

Tepusquet 1984 Cabernet Sauvignon, Santa Maria Valley, CA $6. Mint, herbs, and some vegetal character in the nose. Fairly tannic and not very fruity. Ponderous. (JPN/Jan. '87) ★

Allegro 1984 Cabernet Sauvignon, York County, PA, $10.90. (AWC/Nov. '86)

Almaden (nonvintage) Cabernet Sauvignon, CA $6.99/liter. Berry aromas, uneven flavors. (AWC/Nov. '85)

Angelo Papagni 1981 Cabernet Sauvignon, CA $7. (AWC/Nov. '86)

Arbor Crest 1982 Cabernet Sauvignon, Bacchus Vineyard, WA $17.50. (AWC/Nov. '85)

Arbor Crest 1983 Cabernet Sauvignon, Bacchus Vineyard, Columbia Valley, WA $17.50. (AWC/Nov. '86)

August Sebastiani (nonvintage) Cabernet Sauvignon, Country, CA $7/ 1.5 liters. Beaujolais style; cherry-raspberry flavors. (AWC/Nov. '85)

Bandiera 1983 Cabernet Sauvignon, North Coast, CA $4.50. (AWC/ Nov. '86)

Belvedere 1982 Cabernet Sauvignon, York Creek, Napa Valley, CA $12. (AWC/Nov. '86)

Beringer 1981 Cabernet Sauvignon, Knight's Valley, CA $9. (AWC/ Nov. '85)

Beringer 1982 Cabernet Sauvignon, Napa Valley, CA $9. (AWC/Nov. '85)

Beringer 1982 Cabernet Sauvignon, Proprietor Grown, Knights Valley, CA $9. (AWC/Nov. '86)

Buena Vista 1982 Cabernet Sauvignon, Private Reserve, Sonoma Valley—Carneros, CA $18. (AWC/Nov. '86)

Calafia 1982 Cabernet Sauvignon, Kitty Hawk Vineyard, Napa Valley, CA $11. (AWC/Nov. '85)

Catoctin Vineyards 1983 Cabernet Sauvignon, MD $10.95. (AWC/Nov. '86)

Ch. Biltmore 1983 Cabernet Sauvignon, Inaugural Release, NC $14.95. (AWC/Nov. '86)

Ch. Georges 1984 Cabernet Sauvignon, American, NY $6. (AWC/Nov. '86)

Ch. Potelle 1983 Cabernet Sauvignon, Alexander Valley, CA $12. (AWC/Nov. '86)

Ch. Rutherford 1979 Cabernet Sauvignon, Special Reserve, Napa Valley, CA .$13.50. (AWC/Nov. '85)

Ch. Ste. Michelle 1977 Cabernet Sauvignon, WA $13.40. (AWC/Nov. '85)

Ch. Ste. Michelle 1980 Cabernet Sauvignon, WA $8.65. (AWC/Nov. '85)

Ch. Ste. Michelle 1982 Cabernet Sauvignon, WA $9.85. (AWC/Nov. '86)

Chappellet 1980 Cabernet Sauvignon, Napa Valley, CA $18. (AWC/Nov. '85)

Chappellet 1981 Cabernet Sauvignon, Napa Valley, CA $9.99. (AWC/Nov. '86)

Charles Krug 1980 Cabernet Sauvignon, Napa Valley, CA $6.50. (AWC/Nov. '85)

Charles Lefranc 1981 Cabernet

Sauvignon, Monterey County, CA
$10.59. (AWC/Nov. '86)

Cilurzo 1982 Cabernet Sauvignon,
Temecula, CA $9.50. (AWC/Nov. '86)

Clos du Bois 1980 Cabernet Sauvignon, Proprietor's Reserve, Dry
Creek Valley, CA $15. (AWC/Nov. '86)

Clos du Bois 1982 Cabernet Sauvignon, Alexander Valley, CA $9.
(AWC/Nov. '86)

Columbia 1981 Cabernet Sauvignon, Sagemoor Vineyards, WA $12.
(AWC/Nov. '85)

Columbia 1982 Cabernet Sauvignon, Otis Vineyards, Yakima Valley, WA $13.50. Cedar, spice, plummy
fruit, but hard. High acid. (AWC/Nov. '85)

Columbia 1982 Cabernet Sauvignon, Yakima Valley, WA $9. (AWC/
Nov. '85)

Columbia 1983 Cabernet Sauvignon, WA $9. (AWC/Nov. '86)

Concannon 1982 Cabernet Sauvignon, Estate Bottled, Livermore Valley, CA $10.25. (AWC/Nov. '85)

Conn Creek 1982 Cabernet Sauvignon, Napa Valley, CA $17. (AWC/
Nov. '86)

Corbett Canyon 1983 Cabernet
Sauvignon, Coastal Classic, Central
Coast, CA $7.99/liter. (AWC/Nov. '85)

Corbett Canyon Vineyards 1983
Cabernet Sauvignon, Central Coast,
CA $7. (AWC/Nov. '86)

Corbett Canyon Vineyards 1984
Cabernet Sauvignon, Coastal Classic, Central Coast, CA $8. (AWC/Nov.
'86)

Creston Manor 1983 Cabernet Sauvignon, Edna Valley, CA $12. (AWC/
Nov. '86)

Cuvaison 1981 Cabernet Sauvignon, Napa Valley, CA $11.95.
(AWC/Nov. '86)

David Bruce 1983 Cabernet Sauvignon, Vintner's Select, CA $9.50. (AWC/Nov. '86)

Davis Bynum 1983 Cabernet Sauvignon, Alexander Valley, CA $10. (AWC/Nov. '86)

De Moor 1982 Cabernet Sauvignon, Napa Valley, CA $11.25. (AWC/Nov. '86)

Domain San Martin 1982 Cabernet Sauvignon, Central Coast, CA $7.75. (AWC/Nov. '86)

Domaine Laurier 1982 Cabernet Sauvignon, Estate Bottled, Green Valley, Sonoma County, CA $12. (AWC/Nov. '85)

Domaine St. George 1983 Cabernet Sauvignon, Mendocino County, CA $5.99. (AWC/Nov. '86)

Dry Creek 1980 Cabernet Sauvignon, Sonoma County, CA $13. (AWC/Nov. '86)

Dry Creek 1982 Cabernet Sauvignon, Sonoma County, CA $9.50. (AWC/Nov. '85)

Durney 1982 Cabernet Sauvignon, Estate Bottled, Carmel Valley, CA $11.99. (AWC/Nov. '86)

Edmeades 1982 Cabernet Sauvignon, Anderson Valley, CA $9. Hard to find distinguishing character. (AWC/Nov. '85)

Ernest & Julio Gallo 1978 Cabernet Sauvignon, Limited Release, CA $8. Dusty, port-like nose and flavors. (AWC/Nov. '85)

Ernest & Julio Gallo 1980 Cabernet Sauvignon, Oak Cask Vintage, CA $8. (AWC/Nov. '86)

Estancia 1980 Cabernet Sauvignon, Alexander Valley, CA $6. (AWC/Nov. '86)

Estrella River 1980 Cabernet Sauvignon, Estate Bottled, San Luis Obispo County, CA $10. (AWC/Nov. '85)

Fetzer 1982 Cabernet Sauvignon, Barrel Select, Mendocino, CA $8.50. (AWC/Nov. '86)

Firelands 1983 Cabernet Sauvignon, Lake Erie, OH $5.95. (AWC/Nov. '86)

Firestone 1979 Cabernet Sauvignon, Vintage Reserve, Santa Ynez Valley, CA $15. (AWC/Nov. '86)

Flora Springs 1983 Cabernet Sauvignon, Napa Valley, CA $12.50. (AWC/Nov. '86)

Forgeron 1982 Cabernet Sauvignon, OR $8.95. (AWC/Nov. '86)

Franciscan 1980 Cabernet Sauvignon, Estate Bottled, Alexander Valley, CA $7.50. (AWC/Nov. '85)

Franciscan 1980 Cabernet Sauvignon, Estate Bottled, Napa Valley, CA $8.50. (AWC/Nov. '86)

Franciscan 1980 Cabernet Sauvignon, Private Reserve, Napa Valley, CA $10. (AWC/Nov. '86)

Freemark Abbey 1981 Cabernet Sauvignon, Napa Valley, CA $10.50. (AWC/Nov. '86)

Fulton Valley Cellars 1982 Cabernet Sauvignon, Steiner Vineyard, Sonoma Mountain, CA $12.50. (AWC/Nov. '86)

Gary Farrell 1983 Cabernet Sauvignon, Alexander Valley, Sonoma County, CA $12. (AWC/Nov. '86)

Gemello 1982 Cabernet Sauvignon, Alexander Valley, CA $10. (AWC/Nov. '85)

Geyser Peak 1981 Cabernet Sauvignon, Sonoma County, CA $6.95. (AWC/Nov. '85)

Girard 1981 Cabernet Sauvignon, Estate Bottled, Napa Valley, CA $14. High tannin, wood, acidity overwhelm fruit. (AWC/Nov. '85)

Giumarra 1984 Cabernet Sauvignon, CA $4.19. (AWC/Nov. '86)

Glen Ellen 1982 Cabernet Sauvignon, Glen Ellen Estate, Sonoma Valley, CA $9.75. (AWC/Nov. '86)

Golden Creek 1983 Cabernet Sauvignon, Sonoma County, CA $2.99. (AWC/Nov. '85)

Grand Cru 1982 Cabernet Sauvignon, Collector Series, Alexander Valley, CA $14.50. Lots of extract; ripe fruit, good varietal flavors, but too much oak and tannin. (AWC/Nov. '85)

Groth 1982 Cabernet Sauvignon, Napa Valley, CA $13. (AWC/Nov. '85)

Guenoc 1981 Cabernet Sauvignon, Lake County, CA $8.75. (AWC/Nov. '86)

Guenoc 1982 Cabernet Sauvignon, Lake County, CA $8.75. (AWC/Nov. '86)

Hacienda 1982 Cabernet Sauvignon, Sonoma Valley, CA $11. (AWC/Nov. '86)

Hargrave 1982 Cabernet Sauvignon, North Fork, Long Island, NY $9.95. (AWC/Nov. '85)

Hargrave 1982 Cabernet Sauvignon/Merlot, North Fork, Long Island, NY $10.99. (AWC/Nov. '85)

Haviland 1982 Cabernet Sauvignon, Estate Bottled, Haviland Vineyard, Yakima Valley, WA $16.95. (AWC/Nov. '86)

Haviland 1983 Cabernet Sauvignon, Estate Bottled, Haviland Vineyard, Yakima Valley, WA $12.95. (AWC/Nov. '86)

Hawk Crest (Stag's Leap Wine Cellars) 1982 Cabernet Sauvignon, North Coast, CA $5. (AWC/Nov. '85)

Haywood 1983 Cabernet Sauvignon, Estate Bottled, Sonoma Valley, CA $12.50. (AWC/Nov. '86)

Heitz 1980 Cabernet Sauvignon, Martha's Vineyard, Napa Valley, CA $45. (AWC/Nov.'85)

Heitz 1981 Cabernet Sauvignon, Martha's Vineyard, Napa Valley, CA $35. (AWC/Nov. '86)

Inglenook 1981 Cabernet Sauvignon, Estate Bottled, Napa Valley, CA $9. Sweet fruit. Light body. (AWC/Nov. '85)

Inglenook 1982 Cabernet Sauvignon, Estate Bottled, Napa Valley, CA $9. (AWC/Nov. '86)

Ivan Tamas 1983 Cabernet Sauvignon, Mendocino County, CA $5.99. (AWC/Nov. '86)

J. Carey 1981 Cabernet Sauvignon, Estate Bottled, Alamo Pintado Vineyard, Santa Ynez Valley, CA $8.75. (AWC/Nov. '85)

J. Lohr 1983 Cabernet Sauvignon, Napa Valley, CA $9. (AWC/Nov. '86)

J. Lohr 1984 Cabernet Sauvignon, CA $5. (AWC/Nov. '86)

J. Patrick Dore 1981 Cabernet Sauvignon, Signature Selection, Napa Valley, CA $3.95. (AWC/Nov. '86)

J. Patrick Dore Cabernet Sauvignon (nonvintage), Signature Selections, Limited Reserve, CA $5.95/1.5 liters. (AWC/Nov. '85)

J. W. Morris 1983 Cabernet Sauvignon, Alexander Valley, CA $7. (AWC/Nov. '86)

Jekel 1981 Cabernet Sauvignon, 65% Monterey County/35% San Luis Obispo County, CA $10. (AWC/Nov. '85)

Jordan 1981 Cabernet Sauvignon, Estate Bottled, Alexander Valley, CA $17. Very young, with promise, but weedy nose obscures fruit. (AWC/Nov. '85)

Kendall-Jackson 1983 Cabernet Sauvignon, Lake County, CA $7.50. (AWC/Nov. '86)

Kenwood 1982 Cabernet Sauvignon, Sonoma Valley, CA $10. (AWC/Nov. '86)

Konocti 1982 Cabernet Sauvignon, Lake County, CA $5.50. (AWC/Nov. '86)

Lambert Bridge 1982 Cabernet Sauvignon, Sonoma County, CA $9.50. (AWC/Nov. '86)

Laurel Glen 1983 Cabernet Sauvignon, Sonoma Mountain, CA $12.50. (AWC/Nov. '86)

Lenz 1983 Reserve, North Fork, Long Island, NY $9.75. (AWC/Nov. '85)

Llano Estacado 1983 Cabernet Sauvignon, Leftwich-Slaughter Vineyards, Lubbock County, TX $10.50. (AWC/Nov. '86)

Llano Estacado 1984 Cabernet Sauvignon, Slaughter-Leftwich Vineyards, Lubbock County, TX $10.50. (AWC/Nov. '86)

Louis M. Martini 1980 Cabernet Sauvignon, Sonoma Valley, CA $15. (AWC/Nov. '86)

Lower Lake 1980 Cabernet Sauvignon, Lake County, CA $11. (AWC/Nov. '85)

Lynfred (nonvintage) Cabernet Sauvignon, Bottled in 1983, Private Reserve, CA (winery in IL) $12. (AWC/Nov. '85)

M. G. Vallejo 1983 Cabernet Sauvignon, CA $4.50. (AWC/Nov. '86)

Marietta 1982 Cabernet Sauvignon, Sonoma County, CA $9. Sweet, plummy, cassis-like fruit. High acidity; rough tannins. (AWC/Nov. '85)

Mayacamas 1980 Cabernet Sauvignon, Napa Valley, CA $25. (AWC/Nov. '85)

McDowell Valley Vineyards 1981 Cabernet Sauvignon, Estate Bottled, McDowell Valley, CA $12.99. (AWC/Nov. '85)

McDowell Valley Vineyards 1982 Cabernet Sauvignon, Estate Bottled,

McDowell Valley, CA $10.85. (AWC/ Nov. '86)

Meier's 1983 Cabernet Sauvignon, Isle St. George, OH $6.99. (AWC/Nov. '86)

Meredyth 1983 Cabernet Sauvignon, VA $8.50. (AWC/Nov. '85)

Michael's (Artisan Wines) 1982 Cabernet Sauvignon, Napa Valley, CA $11.25. Full, rich wine marred by off flavors. (AWC/Nov. '85)

Michtom 1981 Cabernet Sauvignon, Alexander Valley, Sonoma County, CA $6. (AWC/Nov. '86)

Milano 1981 Cabernet Sauvignon, Sanel Valley Vineyard, Mendocino County, CA $18. (AWC/Nov. '85)

Montdomaine 1984 Cabernet Sauvignon, VA $12. (AWC/Nov. '86)

Monterey Peninsula 1982 Cabernet Sauvignon, Doctor's Reserve, Monterey, CA $14. (AWC/Nov. '86)

Monterey Peninsula 1982 Cabernet Sauvignon, Monterey County, CA $12. (AWC/Nov. '86)

Mount Veeder 1981 Cabernet Sauvignon, Mt. Veeder Vineyards, Napa County, CA $12.50. (AWC/Nov. '86)

Oasis 1983 Cabernet Sauvignon, VA $8. (AWC/Nov. '86)

Oasis 1984 Cabernet Sauvignon, VA $8. (AWC/Nov. '86)

Opus One 1981 Cabernet Sauvignon, Napa Valley, CA $52. Cherry and coffee nose. Light, lean fruit. (AWC/Nov. '85)

Pat Paulsen 1982 Cabernet Sauvignon, Estate Bottled, Alexander Valley, CA $10. Assertive, bell pepper shades into weedy astringency. (AWC/Nov. '85)

Paul Masson 1983 Cabernet Sauvignon, Sonoma County, CA $6.29. (AWC/Nov. '86)

Paul Thomas 1983 Cabernet Sauvignon, WA $13. (AWC/Nov. '86)

Pheasant Ridge 1984 Cabernet Sauvignon, Lubbock County, TX $11.99. (AWC/Nov. '86)

Pindar 1984 Cabernet Sauvignon, Long Island, NY $7.99. (AWC/Nov. '86)

Pine Ridge 1983 Cabernet Sauvignon, Rutherford Cuvee, Napa Valley, CA $13. (AWC/Nov. '86)

Preston Vineyards 1983 Cabernet Sauvignon, Estate Bottled, Dry Creek Valley—Sonoma County, CA $11. (AWC/Nov. '86)

Preston Wine Cellars 1979 Cabernet Sauvignon, WA $6.95. Soft, cassis fruit. Tannic bite in finish. (AWC/Nov. '85)

Preston Wine Cellars 1981 Cabernet Sauvignon, WA $7.95. (AWC/Nov. '86)

Quail Ridge 1982 Cabernet Sauvignon, Napa Valley, CA $13. Youthful. Light-to-medium body. Bordeaux-like. (AWC/Nov. '85)

Quilceda Creek 1982 Cabernet Sauvignon, WA $15.50. (AWC/Nov. '86)

R. H. Phillips 1983 Cabernet Sauvignon, CA $6. (AWC/Nov. '86)

Raymond 1981 Cabernet Sauvignon, Estate Bottled, Napa Valley, CA $12. (AWC/Nov. '86)

Ridge 1981 Cabernet Sauvignon, Monte Bello, CA $25. Bell peppers, black cherries, spice. Muscle without real power. (AWC/Nov. '85)

River Oaks 1982 Cabernet Sauvignon, Sonoma County, CA $5.95. Fresh, grapey. Somewhat flabby. (AWC/Nov. '85)

Robert Keenan 1982 Cabernet Sauvignon, Napa Valley, CA $12.50. (AWC/Nov. '85)

Robert Keenan 1983 Cabernet Sauvignon, Napa Valley, CA $10.50. (AWC/Nov. '86)

Robert Mondavi 1982 Cabernet

Sauvignon, Napa Valley, CA $10. (AWC/Nov. '86)

Rodney Strong 1980 Cabernet Sauvignon, Alexander's Crown Vineyard, Alexander Valley, CA $12. (AWC/Nov. '86)

Rodney Strong 1982 Cabernet Sauvignon, Sonoma County, CA $7. (AWC/Nov. '86)

Rombauer Vineyards 1982 Cabernet Sauvignon, Napa Valley, CA $12.50. (AWC/Nov. '86)

Rutherford Hill 1980 Cabernet Sauvignon, Napa Valley, CA $12. Metallic character in nose and flavor. (AWC/Nov. '85)

Rutherford Hill 1982 Cabernet Sauvignon, Napa Valley, CA $12. (AWC/Nov. '86)

Rutherford Vintners 1981 Cabernet Sauvignon, Napa Valley, CA $9.50. (AWC/Nov. '86)

San Saba (Smith & Hook) 1983 Cabernet Sauvignon, Monterey County, CA $15. (AWC/Nov. '86)

Santa Barbara Winery 1981 Cabernet Sauvignon, Reserve, Santa Ynez Valley, CA $12. (AWC/Nov. '86)

Sebastiani 1980 Cabernet Sauvignon, Proprietor's Reserve, Sonoma County, CA $13. Dark, intense; cassis, jammy, big alcohol. (AWC/Nov. '85)

Sebastiani 1981 Cabernet Sauvignon, Proprietor's Reserve, Sonoma Valley, CA $13. (AWC/Nov. '86)

Sebastiani 1982 Cabernet Sauvignon, Sonoma County, CA $7. Light body. Mild, up-front flavors. (AWC/Nov. '85)

Seghesio 1982 Cabernet Sauvignon, Estate Bottled, Northern Sonoma, CA $5. (AWC/Nov. '86)

Sequoia Grove 1982 Cabernet Sauvignon, Estate Bottled, Napa Valley, CA $14. (AWC/Nov. '86)

Shafer Vineyards 1982 Cabernet

Sauvignon, Napa Valley, CA $13. Sweet, lean fruit. Excellent balance. (AWC/Nov. '85)

Shafer Vineyards 1983 Cabernet Sauvignon, Hillside Select, Napa Valley, CA $20. (AWC/Nov. '86)

Shenandoah Vineyards 1982 Cabernet Sauvignon, Amador County, CA $8. (AWC/Nov. '86)

Silverado 1982 Cabernet Sauvignon, Napa Valley, CA $11. (AWC/Nov. '86)

Simi 1980 Cabernet Sauvignon, Reserve, Alexander Valley, CA $20. (AWC/Nov. '86)

Simi 1982 Cabernet Sauvignon, Sonoma County, CA $12. (AWC/Nov. '86)

Smith & Hook 1983 Cabernet Sauvignon, Monterey, CA $13. (AWC/Nov. '86)

Snoqualmie 1983 Cabernet Sauvignon, Yakima Valley, WA $10.89. (AWC/Nov. '86)

Souverain 1983 Cabernet Sauvignon, North Coast, CA $8. (AWC/Nov. '86)

St. Josef's Weinkeller 1983 Cabernet Sauvignon, OR $10. (AWC/Nov. '86)

Ste. Chapelle 1982 Cabernet Sauvignon, WA (winery in ID) $8.49. (AWC/Nov. '86)

Sterling 1982 Cabernet Sauvignon, Estate Bottled, Napa Valley, CA $12.50. (AWC/Nov. '86)

Stratford 1983 Cabernet Sauvignon, CA $8.50. (AWC/Nov. '86)

The Christian Brothers 1982 Cabernet Sauvignon, Napa Valley, CA $6.75. (AWC/Nov. '86)

Trentadue 1984 Cabernet Sauvignon, Estate Bottled, Alexander Valley, CA $7. (AWC/Nov. '86)

V. Sattui 1982 Cabernet Sauvi-

gnon, Napa Valley, CA $10.25. (AWC/Nov. '86)

Vichon 1982 Cabernet Sauvignon, Napa Valley, CA $11.25. (AWC/Nov. '86)

Whitehall Lane 1983 Cabernet Sauvignon, Napa Valley, CA $14. (AWC/Nov. '86)

Windsor Vineyards 1982 Cabernet Sauvignon, Vineyard Selection—Haehl Ranch Vineyards, Mendocino County, CA $10. (AWC/Nov. '86)

Windsor Vineyards 1982 Cabernet Sauvignon, Vineyard Selection—River West Estate, Russian River Valley, Sonoma County, CA $12. (AWC/Nov. '86)

Wm. Wheeler 1982 Cabernet Sauvignon, Dry Creek Valley—Sonoma County, CA $10. (AWC/Nov. '86)

Yakima River 1983 Cabernet Sauvignon, Mercer Ranch Vineyards, Columbia Valley, WA $9.89. (AWC/Nov. '86)

ZD 1982 Cabernet Sauvignon, CA $12. (AWC/Nov. '86)

OTHERS

Taltarni 1979 Cabernet Sauvignon, Victoria $7.99. Closed, yet shows ripe fruit and briary aromas. Very tannic, chewy. Flavors hint of cassis and blackberries, slightly smoky. (CR/Jan. '86) ★★1/2 (★★★1/2)

Seppelt 1980 Cabernet Sauvignon, Southeastern Australia $11.95. Lots of oak. Attractive, smoky quality fits well with vanilla and concentrated berry flavors. Smooth, elegant, full body. (CR/Jan. '86) ★★1/2

Gamla 1983 Cabernet Sauvignon, Israel $7.50. (Kosher and Kosher for Passover.) Ripe, fruity aromas: rich, herbaceous, banana-like. Full and berryish. Medium-full body. Soft tannins. (CC/Jan.'86) ★

Johnstone 1979 Cabernet Sauvignon, Special Reserve, Bin 444, Hunter River Valley, New South Wales $6.79. Light mustiness overlays fruit and oak. Acidity underscores fruit. (CR/Jan.'86) ★

Redbank 1984 Cabernet Sauvignon, Sally's Paddock, Victoria $13. Vegetal nose and flavor. Curious structure. Low alcohol; a bit flat. (JPN/Jan. '87) ★

ITALIAN

Italy makes more wine than any other country. The straw flasks of Chianti, jugs of Soave and Lambrusco are commonplace on American tables. But the focus of the reviews below is the little-known, top end of Italian wine.

In the last decade, more and more of Italy's better, limited-production wines have been exported to North America. They are primarily reds, and like all of the finest red wines, they require aging, sometimes long aging, to bring out their best. But Italy's best wines often spend more time in barrel and generally have more age and maturity when they are released onto the market compared to their French and American counterparts. With a few exceptions, they are also notably less expensive. Italy's best wines are even better bargains than its everyday wines.

The great grapes of Italy are the Nebbiolo, grown in the Piemonte district and most famous for the wines of Barolo and Barbaresco, and the Sangiovese, the principal grape of Chianti. They offer organoleptic adventures quite different from the more familiar varieties of France. The wines of Italy's venerable old cellars have a distinctive style, challenged in recent years by a trend in some quarters toward a more "international" style of winemaking stressing more direct, earlier-maturing fruit flavors and the use of French oak cooperage. Italian Cabernet Sauvignon and Merlot — particularly from Alto Adige and northeastern Italy — are rising stars.

The official label designation for Italy's better wines is "Denominazione di Origine Controllata" or "D.O.C.," similar to the French designation "Appellation Contrôlée," indicating the wine was grown within a defined, high quality vineyard district and made in accordance with certain fairly loose production guidelines. "D.O.C.G." or

"Denominazione di Origine Controllata e Garantita" is a higher-level designation given to Italy's very finest wines. But many of Italy's old guard winemakers have resisted the official classification system, believing it is too restrictive and arbitrary, and as a result it is not a foolproof guide to the best wines.

Giacosa 1978 Barbaresco, Santo Stefano $46. Expansive bouquet with notes of raspberries, flowers, mushrooms, truffles, leather, almonds, chestnuts, kirsch. Abundant flavor. Superb structure. One of the greatest wines we've ever tasted. (S&PW/Mar. '86) ★★★★

Moresco 1979 Barbaresco, Podere del Pajore $19.99. The best Barbaresco of this vintage. Enormous rich bouquet suggests ripe black cherries, tobacco, truffles. Fleshy. Explodes with sweet, ripe fruit. Complete, harmonious, still young, fabulously rich. Very long. (S&PW/Mar. '86) ★★★1/2 (★★★★)

Grai 1975 Cabernet dell'Alto Adige $12. Intensely rich nose of cassis and blueberries. Soft, round, velvety. Light tannin, lots of flavor, lots of style. Enormous length. Enjoyable now, with potential to improve. (S&PW/Mar. '86) ★★★1/2

Masi 1976 Amarone, Mazzano $12. Intensely perfumed, floral bouquet with licorice notes, peaches, a hint of Botrytis. Soft tannin. Richly flavored. Very long. (S&PW/ Mar. '86) ★★★1/2

Vietti 1979 Barolo, de Castiglione Falletto $12. Forward, rich, tobacco nose. Chocolate, licorice flavors. (JPN/Jan. '86) ★★★1/2

Bricco Rocche 1978 Barolo, Brunate $25. Intense aroma. Ripe fruit. Deep, profound. Enormous richness, exceptional balance. Not ready, but tempting. (S&PW/ Mar. '86) ★★★ (★★★★)

Conterno 1978 Barolo, Bussia Soprana $15. Enormously rich nose. Richly concentrated flavors. A lot of weight and extract. Needs another year at least. (S&PW/Mar. '86) ★★★ (★★★★)

Fattoria Montagliari 1975 Chianti Classico, Reserva, Vigna di Casaloste $13.75. Floral bouquet; refined, elegant. Stylish, flavorful, smooth textured. Raspberry-like fruit. A bargain. (S&PW/Mar. '86) ★★★ (★★★★)

Gaja 1982 Barbaresco, Sori Tildin $45. Oak obvious in the nose, some ripe fruit. Richly fleshed. Tastes of sweet, ripe fruit and oak. (S&PW/Mar. '86) ★★★ (★★★★)

Giuseppe Rinaldi 1978 Barolo $23.69. Rich, intense bouquet suggests cassis. Enormous core of rich, sweet, mouthfilling fruit seems very forward at first but recedes under tannic structure. Classic Barolo. Needs time. (S&PW/Mar. '86) ★★★ (★★★★)

Lungarotti 1975 Torgiano, Rubesco Monticchio, Riserva $15.87. Floral, cherry, spicy, peppery aroma. Exceptional balance. Mouthfilling flavor. Tempting now; will be superb in two to three years. (S&PW/Mar. '86) ★★★ (★★★★)

Marcarini 1978 Barolo, Brunate $18. Expansive aroma recalls raspberries and mushrooms. Well-structured wine with style, balance, flavor, elegance. Classic. (S&PW/Mar. '86) ★★★ (★★★★)

Martinenga 1982 Barbaresco $18.99. Tobacco, cherry aroma. Full of flavor. Extremely well-balanced, elegant. Long finish. (S&PW/Mar. '86) ★★★ (★★★★)

Monsanto 1975 Chianti Classico, Riserva, Il Poggio $21. Richly concentrated aroma. Lovely ripe fruit flavors fill the mouth. Enormous weight and extract. Considerable tannin is beginning to soften. Balanced. Enormous length. (S&PW/Mar. '86) ★★★ (★★★★)

Monsanto 1977 Chianti Classico, Riserva, Il Poggio $17.69. Big, rich-fruit bouquet; expansive, complex, nuances of flowers, blackberries, blueberries, apricots. Enormous extract and weight, exceptional balance. Quite tannic. (S&PW/Mar. '86) ★★★ (★★★★)

Montesodi 1978 Chianti Rufina $18.70. Richly fruited aroma with lots of depth, nuances of flowers, tobacco, oak. Enormous richness and weight, with concentration, extract, gobs of fruit, long finish. (S&PW/Mar. '86) ★★★ (★★★★)

Vietti 1978 Barolo, Rocche $20. Enormously rich bouquet of licorice, flowers, tea, tobacco, cherries. Incredible concentration of rich, ripe fruit flavors, so well balanced tannin hardly seems evident at first, but still very young. (S&PW/Mar. '86) ★★★ (★★★★)

Vietti 1982 Barbaresco, Masseria $19.75. Enormously rich nose. Big, rich, deep; the best Vietti Barbaresco to date. Superb. (S&PW/Mar. '86) ★★★ (★★★★)

Cantina Mascarello 1978 Barolo $20. Expansive bouquet fills the room. Enormous, concentrated fruit exudes style and elegance. Exceptional quality. (S&PW/Mar. '86) ★★★ (★★★1/2)

Castello di Neive 1978 Barbaresco, Riserva, Santo Stefano $18. Rich, intense, expansive bouquet; notes of hazelnuts and truffles. Enormous richness and concentration. Superbly structured. Needs 3-4 years. (S&PW/Mar. '86) ★★★ (★★★1/2)

Frescobaldi 1980 Chianti Rufina, Riserva $6. Complex bouquet, moderately intense, nuances of flowers, fruit, leather. Well balanced; moderate tannin. Flavorful. Some delicacy and style. Young. Fairly long finish. (S&PW/Mar. '86) ★★★ (★★★1/2)

Maculan 1983 Breganze Cabernet, Fratta $20. Incredibly rich nose of Cabernet fruit, oak. Enormous concentration and weight, well honed, supple. Very long, very young, very good. (S&PW/Mar. '86) ★★★ (★★★1/2)

Martinenga 1979 Barbaresco, Camp Gros $26.75. Floral, woodsy bouquet with a cherry-like note. Finely structured. Elegant, stylish. Long finish recalls licorice. Still young. (S&PW/Mar. '86) ★★★ (★★★1/2)

Masi 1979 Amarone, Serego Alighieri, Vaio Armaron $15. Complex bouquet: tobacco, tea, dried fruit. Enormous richness of flavor, dry with an impression of sweetness. Lots of style. Some tannin needs another two years. (S&PW/Mar. '86) ★★★ (★★★1/2)

Monte Vertine 1982 Le Pergole Torte $16.39. Beautiful, ruby robe. Expansive aroma of cherries, flowers, a touch of oak. Mouthful of intense, cherry-like, youthful fruit, with a firm, tannic vein. Soft centered. Finely honed. (S&PW/Mar. '86) ★★★ (★★★1/2)

Produttori del Barbaresco 1978 Barbaresco, Montefico, Riserva $20. Lovely, refined Nebbiolo bouquet. Well-structured, classic. (S&PW/Mar. '86) ★★★ (★★★1/2)

Scarpa 1978 Barolo, Le Coste $16. Complex bouquet suggests mint, green leaves, tar, resin, cherries. Mouthful of soft tannin, enormous fruit. Strikingly well balanced. Very tannic end. (S&PW/Mar. '86) ★★★ (★★★1/2)

Scarpa 1979 Barbaresco, Tetti di Neive $13. Deep, rich aroma suggests mint and pine. Fairly rich, sweet, ripe fruit flavors. Some tannin to lose. Fine balance. Lingering, raspberry finish. (S&PW/Mar. '86) ★★★ (★★★1/2)

Tenuta Carretta 1978 Barolo, Podere Cannubi. Intense aroma: tobacco, vaguely floral, cherries, and berry notes. Very well balanced. Masses of fruit, gobs of tannin. Years from ready, but everything is there. (S&PW/Mar. '86) ★★★ (★★★1/2)

Allegrini 1979 Amarone Classico, Vigna Fieramonte $14.29. Expansive aroma of almonds, flowers, figs, raisins, prunes. Robust, firm, full flavored, smooth textured. Very long finish with a touch of bitter almonds. (S&PW/Mar. '86) ★★★

Fattoria Selvapiana 1977 Chianti Rufina, Riserva $8.40. Woodsy, berrylike aroma; hint of peaches. Well balanced, soft, concentrated, tasty. Long, complex finish of raspberrries and blueberries. (S&PW/Mar. '86) ★★★

Francesco Rinaldi 1980 Barolo, Cannubio $13. Delicate perfume. Lots of style and elegance; perhaps the best Barolo of the vintage. (S&PW/Mar. '86) ★★★

Valentini 1974 Montepulciano d'Abruzzo $14.99. Intense, cherry-like aroma. Enormous weight and extract, intensely fruited. Fig-like note at the end. (S&PW/Mar. '86) ★★★

Vietti 1980 Barolo, Rocche $11. Good fruit in nose and mouth, but not showing Nebbiolo intensity. Good drinking now; should broaden with age. (JPN/Jan. '86) ★★★

Vietti 1982 Nebbiolo D'Alba, San Giacomo $6. Rich aroma and flavor redolent of tea, tobacco. Smooth, very drinkable. Amazing value. (JPN/Jan. '86) ★★★

E. Pira 1975 Barolo. Expansive, perfumed bouquet. Soft, round, very smooth. Tannin shows more in the finish. Still very good but approaching the end. (S&PW/Mar. '86) ★★1/2

Vietti 1983 Dolcetto D'Alba, Disa de Monforte $5. Attractive, cherry aroma, flavor. Medium-light wine. Slightly bitter finish. (JPN/Jan. '86) ★★1/2

Altesino 1979 Brunello di Montalcino, Riserva, Italy $17.99. Some oak, a lot of fruit, vaguely nutty note in the nose. Tannic with heaps of flavor to support it. Chewy. Needs four to five years to smooth out. (S&PW/Mar. '86) ★★ (★★★1/2)

Bricco Asili 1982 Barbaresco $34.99. Floral aroma. Loads of fruit; moderate tannin. Lots of potential. Still somewhat closed. (S&PW/Mar. '86) ★★ (★★★1/2)

Conterno 1974 Barolo, Riserva Speciale, Monfortino $22.50. Intense bouquet of tobacco and fresh fruit. A mouthful of tannin and immense fruit; hint of licorice. Long finish. Needs at least another four or five years. (S&PW/Mar. '86) ★★ (★★★1/2)

Produttori del Barbaresco 1979 Barbaresco, Rabaja, Reserva $16. Tobacco, cherries, strawberries under a woodsy aroma. Fullest body of the Produttori crus, one of the most tannic, but still some delicacy. (S&PW/Mar. '86) ★★ (★★★1/2)

Badia a Coltibuono 1980 Sanjoveto $16.49. Berries, flowers and oak aroma. Oak flavors on entry. Rich fruit, well knit. Long. (S&PW/Mar. '86) ★★ (★★★)

Costanti 1979 Brunello di Montalcino $17.25. Lovely bouquet of cherries, flowers, vanilla, berries. Delicate, well-balanced, almost sweet. Elegant. Long finish suggests nutmeg. (S&PW/Mar. '86) ★★ (★★★)

Giacosa 1980 Barolo, Vigna Rionda $15. Lots of fruit. Well balanced. Stylish. (S&PW/Mar. '86) ★★ (★★★)

Grai 1977 Cabernet dell'Alto Adige $10. Rich, fruity aroma; herbaceous touch, undertone of cassis. Fairly full bodied. Some tannin to soften. Supple center. Refined and stylish. (S&PW/Mar. '86) ★★ (★★★)

Il Poggione 1979 Brunello di Montalcino $19. Intense aroma hints of licorice, tar, spice. Tannic entry. Full-flavored fruit, soft centered. Needs three to four years. (S&PW/Mar. '86) ★★ (★★★)

Marcarini 1980 Barolo, Brunate $11.25. Lovely, cherry, tobacco, tarry aroma. Well balanced; lots of flavor. Some tannin to lose. Stylish. (S&PW/Mar. '86) ★★ (★★★)

Scarpa 1981 Barbaresco, Payore Barberis $11.20. Floral aroma. Rather sweet, round initial impression. Plenty of tannin and acid. Big fruit. Decidedly tannic finish. (S&PW/Mar. '86) ★★ (★★★)

Villa Cafaggio 1981 Solatio Basilica. Cherry, floral, berry aroma. Moderate tannin. Well balanced. Sweet, ripe fruit, rich and flavorful. (S&PW/Mar. '86) ★★ (★★★)

Sammicheli 1982 Chianti Classico, Italy $3.49. Lively, ripe fruit flavors. Light body. A little hot. (RF/Jan. '86) ★★

Cappellano 1980 Nebbiolo d'Alba $3.59. Light, jammy nose. Slightly cooked fruit. Lightish body. Past its prime. (RF/Jan. '86) ★1/2

MERLOT

Ten years ago there was almost no Merlot grown in American vineyards. Today it is one of the most exciting new American wines. It was initially planted for use in blending with Cabernet Sauvignon, which has become increasingly common. But with Merlot's increased availability, many wineries have begun producing it as a varietal. In 1985, 125 US wineries made a Merlot. In 1986 the number rose to 174.

The same vineyard areas and wineries producing California's best Cabernets appear to be the best bets for Merlot. The growing conditions and winemaking parameters for the two are closely linked, in this country as in their home in French Bordeaux. Outside California, Washington, Long Island, and Oregon Merlots have begun to distinguish themselves.

Being so new to American vineyards and wineries, Merlot shows little consistency of style from one brand to the next. One of the judges in the 1986 American Wine Competition identified at least three distinct styles among 52 Merlots tasted: "The Cabernet style: heavy oak, hard, structured. The spicy style, with loads of mint enclosed in a velvety texture. And Merlot as Merlot: softer and less dense than a Cab, velvety, refined, harmonious." Merlot is typically forward and fruity in the nose and, when fully ripe, has a fleshy, dense texture and a velvety finish. Its tannins are softer than Cabernet Sauvignon (to which it is often compared) and it is usually drinkable within a couple of years, but it also ages well.

Newton 1983 Merlot, Napa Valley, CA $12.50. Intense; loaded with fresh berries and spice. Deep, full flavors. Clean, tannic tightness. Harmonious. Built like Cabernet. Delicate but strong. Begs for five years cellaring. (AWC/Nov. '86) ★★★★

Lakespring 1983 Merlot, Napa Valley, CA $11. Ripe, currant-like flavors, round tannins, and a supple mouth-feel. (JDM/May '86) ★★★1/2 (★★★★)

Clos du Bois 1984 Merlot, Sonoma County, CA $9. Spicy, cedary, Bordeaux-like nose. Rich, chewy depth and intensity. Perfect balance. Classy. Short-term aging potential. (AWC/Nov. '86) ★★★1/2

Crystal Valley 1983 Merlot, Reserve Edition, Napa Valley, CA $10. Plummy, smoky nose. Good fruit concentration with healthy acid underpinning. Excellent structure promises development. (AWC/Nov. '86) ★★★1/2

Hogue 1983 Merlot, WA $8. Lush, minty aroma. Ripe, rich, smooth. (JPN/Jan.'86) ★★★1/2

Hogue 1984 Merlot, Reserve, WA $17.95. Exotic nose of coconut, currants, raisins, mint, camphor, black pepper, vegetables. Complex, multi-dimensional flavors. Well rounded, with harmony and finesse. Needs up to five years. (AWC/Nov. '86) ★★★1/2

Monterey Peninsula Winery 1983 Merlot, Monterey, CA $12. Assertive, herbal nose with volatile hints. Fleshy, rich flavors. Chocolate and licorice finish. Soft, harmonious style. (AWC/Nov. '86) ★★★1/2

Round Hill 1983 Merlot, Napa Valley, CA $7.50. Plummy aroma laced with toasty new wood. Youthful fruit. Medium-tannic structure. Good wood-fruit interplay. Could use five years. (AWC/Nov. '86) ★★★1/2

Silverado 1983 Merlot, Napa Valley, CA $12. Aromas of cedar, plum, cherry. Youthful, big, rich flavors with loads of

tannin. Good potential. (AWC/Nov. '86)
★★★1/2

St. Francis 1983 Merlot, Reserve, Sonoma Valley, CA $14. Rich, pruney nose with woody, vanilla-mint overtones. Full, creamy flavors with lots of stuffing. Stylish. Should improve for three to five years. (AWC/Nov. '86) ★★★1/2

Stag's Leap Wine Cellars 1977 Merlot, Stag's Leap Vineyard, Napa Valley, CA $25. Rich-fruit bouquet of cassis, tobacco, a touch of green olives, overlaid with vanilla-like oak and a hint of mint. Sweet, ripe, round, flavorful. Smooth texture. Very long finish. At its peak. (S&PW/Mar. '86) ★★★1/2

Wild Horse 1984 Merlot, Rancho Sisquoc Vineyards, Santa Maria Valley, CA $10.50. Stiff, tight nose belies big, jam-packed, highly extracted flavors. Cabernet-like. Somewhat tart, with firm tannins, muscular structure. Five-year ageability. (AWC/Nov. '86) ★★★1/2

Adelsheim 1983 Merlot, WA $9. Rich, fruity nose. Herbal-mint quality not overdone. Assertive acidity and tannin balance a fair amount of fruit. (JPN/Jan. '86) ★★★ (★★★1/2)

Arbor Crest 1983 Merlot, Bacchus Vineyard, WA $9. Mint, chocolate, and rich, berry-fruit flavor. Smooth, well balanced, substantial. (JPN/May '86) ★★★ (★★★1/2)

Columbia 1981 Merlot, WA $7. Beautiful mixed-fruit nose. Smooth but lively, complex fruit. (JPN/Jan.'86) ★★★ (★★★1/2)

Aquila 1981 Merlot, CA $22.50. Browning edges. Strong, minty-eucalyptus aromas. Opulent raspberry and cassis flavors. Great concentration. Soft tannins and low acidity; drink now. (AWC/Nov. '86) ★★★

Arbor Crest 1985 Merlot, Bacchus Vineyard, Columbia Valley, WA $9.25. Simple, fruity nose and candy-like, fruit flavors. Attractive and easy to drink. (AWC/Nov. '86) ★★★

Cain Cellars 1983 Merlot, Napa Valley, CA $12. Vibrant spice, cherry, and violet nose has a slight, dusty component. Fleshy, chocolate flavors with lively acidity. Needs a few years. (AWC/Nov. '86) ★★★

Ch. Ste. Michelle 1981 Merlot, WA $10. Sweet prune and cigar-box aroma. Licorice dominates ripe fruit flavors. (JPN/Jan.'86) ★★★

Clos du Val 1983 Merlot, Napa Valley, CA $14. Rich, mixed-fruit aroma. Sturdy, with rich fruit and oak in good balance. Tart acidity. Not overly tannic. (AWC/Nov. '86) ★★★

Columbia 1983 Merlot, WA $9. (AWC/Nov. '86) ★★★

Duckhorn 1983 Merlot, Three Palms Vineyard, Napa Valley, CA $17. Tight nose of earth and wood. Big, long flavors, with a lot of fruit. Moderately bitter finish. Needs three to five years. (AWC/Nov. '86) ★★★

Franciscan 1983 Merlot, Estate Bottled, Napa Valley, CA $8.50. Ripe cherry nose. Well-integrated, clean, soft flavors. Slightly bitter finish. (AWC/Nov. '86) ★★★

Inglenook 1982 Merlot, Limited Bottling, Napa Valley, CA $14. Pretty, mixed-fruit aroma and flavor. Soft but not flabby. Finishes with a hint of tar. (JPN/Jan. '87) ★★★

Inglenook 1983 Merlot, Estate Bottled, Reserve, Napa Valley, CA $11.50. Dense, spicy, chocolate nose. Long, fruity flavors, but with a very hard, tannic finish. Needs time. (AWC/Nov. '86) ★★★

Jaeger 1981 Merlot, Inglewood Vineyard, Napa Valley, CA $12.75. Browning edges. Ripe plum, chocolate, and tobacco nose with prominent oak that carries

through in fat, rich flavors. (AWC/Nov. '86)
★★★

Neuharth 1981 Merlot, WA $8. Herbaceous; hints of mint and oak. Sweet oak flavor. Attractive fruit. Great balance, not tannic. (JPN/Jan. '86) ★★★

Robert Keenan 1983 Merlot, Napa Valley, CA $15. Herbal, minty nose. Rich, earthy, intense flavors with sour cherry acidity and an austere, tannic finish. Needs five years cellaring. (AWC/Nov. '86) ★★★

Rutherford Hill 1982 Merlot, Napa Valley, CA $10. Fragrant, intense nose of raisins, meat, herbs, mint. Clean, ripe, mature flavors, though soft, somewhat low acid. Drink soon. (AWC/Nov. '86) ★★★

Rutherford Vintners 1981 Merlot, Napa Valley, CA $9. Fruity, smoky nose. Well-knit, rich, chewy flavors are almost overwhelmed by intense new oak. Needs short-term cellaring. (AWC/Nov. '86) ★★★

Shafer Vineyards 1984 Merlot, Napa Valley, CA $12.50. Reserved nose of herbs and pepper, with a dusty note. Long, clean, youthful flavors build in the mouth. Well balanced. Tannins are softening. Needs another two or three years. (AWC/Nov. '86) ★★★

St. Francis 1983 Merlot, Sonoma Valley, CA $10.75. Spicy nose with coconut and woody nuances. Clean, correct, Bordeaux-like structure. Rich, but not ponderous. Very tannic. (AWC/Nov. '86) ★★★

Waterbrook 1984 Merlot, WA $11. Lots of oak crowds rich, black cherry aromas. Deep, big, and chunky, with an astringent, chocolate finish. Noticeable residual sweetness. (AWC/Nov. '86) ★★★

Whitehall Lane 1984 Merlot, Knights Valley, CA $14. Complex scents of bramble fruits, cassis. Fresh, lively flavors of fruit and oak. Exuberant, youthful, with a little harshness in the aftertaste. Needs five years. (AWC/Nov. '86) ★★★

Newton 1982 Merlot, Napa Valley,

CA **$12.50.** Firmly structured in the style of a Cabernet. Earthiness and intensity. (JDM/May '86) ★★1/2 (★★★★)

Ch. Ste. Michelle 1982 Merlot, WA $8. Ripe fruit aroma. Fruity, soft, supple, approachable. (JPN/May '86) ★★1/2

Neuharth 1982 Merlot, WA $8. Berry nose with vegetative hints. Assertive, berry flavor. Good acidity. Fairly tannic. (JPN/Jan. '86) ★★ (★★★)

Snoqualmie 1984 Merlot, Signature Reserve, WA $10. Bitter chocolate, cherry nose. Lively, chocolate taste. (JPN/May '86) ★★ (★★1/2)

Bridgehampton 1984 Merlot, Long Island, NY $10.99. Straightforward raspberry and cassis nose. Supple, spicy, harmonious, with good acid structure. (AWC/Nov. '86) ★★

Carneros Creek Winery 1983 Merlot, Truchard Vineyards, Napa Valley, CA $10.50. Sharp, lean nose of mint, pepper, berries. Attractive, fairly tart flavors are quite woody. Tannic, green finish. (AWC/Nov. '86) ★★

Cosentino Select 1983 Merlot, The Poet, Napa Valley, CA $12.50. Smoky, plummy, aromatic nose. Fairly rich fruit taste with medium body. Big tannins call for cellaring. (AWC/Nov. '86) ★★

Glen Ellen 1983 Merlot, Proprietor's Reserve, CA $5.99. Jammy nose with dried oregano and black pepper nuances. Huge, concentrated, grape and cassis flavors. Dry, astringent finish. (AWC/Nov. '86) ★★

Lenz 1984 Merlot, Long Island— North Fork, NY $9.95. Youthful, floral, varietal nose. Big, mouthfilling attack, though flavors are simple and somewhat rough. Up to five years aging needed. (AWC/Nov. '86) ★★

Sokol Blosser 1981 Merlot, WA $7. Berry aroma and taste. Lively, medium-bodied. (JPN/Jan. '86) ★★

Ellendale 1982 Merlot, WA (winery

in OR) $8. Cigar, cherry, and smoke aromas. Approachable fruit flavors, but low acid. (JPN/Jan. '86) ★1/2

Haviland 1983 Merlot, WA $8. Overripe fruit; raisins and vanilla. Bing cherry flavor. Nice balance. (JPN/Jan. '86) ★1/2

Quail Run 1984 Merlot, Yakima Valley, WA $7. Minty nose with some asparagus, bell pepper. Hot and vegetal in the mouth. Olive, bell pepper flavors. (JPN/May '86) ★1/2

Leonetti Cellars 1983 Merlot, WA $11. Herbal and asparagus aromas dominate smoke and black cherry. Smooth, soft. (JPN/Jan. '86) ★

Angelo Papagni 1981 Merlot, Bonita Vineyard, Madera, CA $6. (AWC/Nov. '86)

Buena Vista 1983 Merlot, Private Reserve, Carneros, CA $14. (AWC/Nov. '86)

Ch. Biltmore 1983 Merlot, NC $14.95. (AWC/Nov. '86)

Ch. Julien 1983 Merlot, Bien Nacido Vineyard, Santa Barbara County, CA $12. Vegetal, cooked-green-bean aroma. (AWC/Nov. '86)

Ch. Ste. Michelle 1979 Merlot, WA $13. (AWC/Nov. '86)

Firestone 1982 Merlot, Santa Ynez Valley, CA $6.50. (AWC/Nov. '86)

Haviland 1983 Merlot, Columbia Valley, WA $12.95. (AWC/Nov. '86)

Haviland 1983 Merlot, Manor Reserve, Columbia Valley, WA $12.95. (AWC/Nov. '86)

L'Ecole No. 41 1983 Merlot, WA $10. (AWC/Nov. '86)

Lambert Bridge 1983 Merlot, Sonoma County, CA $9. (AWC/Nov. '86)

Louis M. Martini 1982 Merlot, Los Vinedos Del Rio Vineyard Selection, Russian River Valley, CA $10. Tart, berryish flavors. (AWC/Nov. '86)

Montdomaine 1984 Merlot, VA

$10. Off nose. Rich, intense fruit but extremely tannic. (AWC/Nov. '86)

Pindar 1984 Merlot, Long Island, NY $10. Tea-like, toasty aroma. Vegetal, stemmy finish. (AWC/Nov. '86)

Pindar 1985 Merlot, Long Island, NY $9.99. (AWC/Nov. '86)

Pine Ridge 1983 Merlot, Selected Cuvee, Napa Valley, CA $13. Dusty, stemmy nose. Tart cherry flavors. Astringent finish. (AWC/Nov. '86)

Preston Wine Cellars 1980 Merlot, WA $6.95. (AWC/Nov. '86)

Quail Run 1983 Merlot, Yakima Valley, WA $7.98. (AWC/Nov. '86)

Robert Young 1983 Merlot, Alexander Valley, CA $12. (AWC/Nov. '86)

Snoqualmie 1984 Merlot, Signature Reserve, Yakima Valley, WA $9.89. (AWC/Nov. '86)

Souverain 1983 Merlot, Sonoma County, CA $8. Light, lean, and clean. (AWC/Nov. '86)

Sterling 1983 Merlot, Estate Bottled, Napa Valley, CA $11. (AWC/Nov. '86)

Yakima River 1983 Merlot, Ciel du Cheval Vineyards, Yakima Valley, WA $9.89. (AWC/Nov. '86)

MISCELLANEOUS RED

The wines reviewed below include super-premium proprietary blends, varietals that do not fall under previous categories, and inexpensive reds for everyday use. They come from several different countries. Some are particularly good bargains.

AMERICAN

Sebastiani 1984 Gamay Beaujolais Nouveau, Sonoma County, CA $5.95. Light, fruity style. Serve slightly chilled with fruit and cheese. Delightful. Drink now. (DM/Jan. '86) ★★★

Adelsheim 1984 Merlot-Cabernet Sauvignon, OR-WA $9. Spicy, minty, some olive aromas. Youthfully fruity. A little rough. (JPN/May '86) ★★1/2 (★★★)

Cameron Winery 1985 Red Table Wine, OR $5. Fresh cherry aroma suggests carbonic maceration. Raspberry, cherry flavors. Beaujolais-like. Appealing; excellent value. (JPN/May '86) ★★1/2

Hawk Crest (Stag's Leap Wine Cellars) 1984 Gamay Beaujolais, Mendocino County, CA $4.25. Very fruity aroma. Cherry taste. Soft tannins. Delightful. (JPN/Jan. '87) ★★1/2

Hawk Crest (Stag's Leap Wine Cellars) 1985 Gamay Beaujolais, Mendocino County, CA $4.25. Light, soft, with dusty black cherry aroma and flavor. (JPN/Jan. '87) ★★1/2

Parducci 1979 Petite Syrah, Mendocino County, CA $4.99. Rhône-like nose. Very ripe, roasted fruit flavors. Medium weight. (RF/Mar. '86) ★★1/2

Souvin Rouge (Souverain) 1982 CA $3.99. Very light, floral fragrance. First-class red table wine, predominantly North Coast Cabernet and Zinfandel. Easy to drink. (DM/Jan. '86) ★★1/2

Worden's Washington Winery 1983

50% Cabernet/50% Merlot, WA $8. Veggie and minty aromas and tastes. Big, herbaceous, ripe, fruity, well balanced. (JPN/Jan. '86) ★★ (★★1/2)

Inglenook 1982 Napa Valley Red, Estate Bottled, CA $5. Berry-like fruit. Nicely balanced, flavorful. (JPN/May '86) ★★

Tepusquet 1982 Vineyard Reserve (65% Cabernet Sauvignon, 35% Merlot), Santa Maria Valley, CA $8.50. Low-key. Olive, cherry, and berry qualities emerge in the glass. Smooth, simple, quaffable, reasonably well-balanced. (JPN/Jan. '87) ★★

Charles Lefranc 1983 Red, CA $3.40. Cabernet fruit defines the aroma. Fruity. Easy to drink. Some tannin could use some softening. A true bargain. (S&PW/May '86) ★

The Monterey Vineyard 1981 Classic Red, CA $4.25. (78% Cabernet Sauvignon, 15% Zinfandel, 2% Pinot Noir, 2% Merlot.) Cabernet evident in the aroma. Soft and fruity, herbaceous character. Light tannin. (JPN/May '86) ★

Wente Bros. 1981 Petite Sirah, Special Selection, Livermore Valley, CA $8. Cooked, meaty, overripe aroma. Full, baked-fruit taste. Loose structure. Flat finish. (JPN/Jan. '87) 1/2

FRENCH
Ch. La Jaubertie 1982 Bergerac Rouge $6. Plummy aroma and taste. Fruity, rich. (JPN/Mar. '86) ★★★

Georges DuBoeuf 1983 Saint Amour, Beaujolais $3.99. Musty nose shows subdued, currant-like fruit. Lovely, ripe fruit flavors have surprising sweetness. Finishes dry. Soft, voluptuous. (RF/Jan. '86) ★★1/2

AUSTRALIAN

Johnstone 1979 Cabernet-Shiraz, Special Reserve, Hunter Valley, New South Wales $7.09. Fresh, raspberry aromas. Rich, ripe fruit flavors. Oak just complements. Acidity is adequate. (CR/Jan. '86) ★★★

Seppelt 1980 Cabernet-Shiraz, Southeastern Australia $8.95. No distinct varietal character, but pleasant, balanced, healthy fruit, and judicious oak. Soft, smooth, supple. (CR/Jan. '86) ★★1/2

Hardy's 1980 Nottage Hill Claret $4.95. Rich, plummy, ripe, with oaky overtones and lots of tannin. (CR/Jan. '86) ★★

Tyrrell's 1980 Long Flat Red, Hunter River, New South Wales $6.95. Full berry aromas and subtle, smokey, oak. Soft, medium bodied, balanced flavors. (CR/Jan.'86) ★★

Hill-Smith Estate 1978 Shiraz, Barossa Valley, South Australia $4.69. Subtle cherries and licorice. High alcohol, big body, lots of fruit, plenty of oak. (CR/Jan.'86) ★1/2

Redbank 1984 Mountain Creek Shiraz, Victoria $7. Grapey, eggy, carbonic aroma and taste. Spritzy, youthful. Low alcohol. Uncharacteristic Shiraz. (JPN/Jan. '87) 1/2

OTHER

Castillo de Pereleda 1974 Reserva, Girona, Spain $4.99. Slightly cooked fruit; scents of mushrooms. Medium bodied, very dry, peppery. Past its peak but still interesting, enjoyable. (RF/Jan. '86) ★★1/2

PINOT NOIR

Pinot Noir has become the Holy Grail of American wine. It is the most difficult of the great grapes — finicky about where it grows and how it is made. When all the pieces of the puzzle come together, American Pinot Noir can show the opulent, black-cherryish fruit, the nuances of earth and mushrooms, the complexity, depth, and softness of great French Burgundies, which set the standards for the variety. But it is all too easy for Pinot Noir to turn out thin and harsh, or ponderous and vegetal, or light and simple.

California winemakers have traditionally stuggled to make decent Pinot Noir. Too often the wines have been heavy and overripe. The vine prefers cooler, less sun-baked growing conditions. Within the last decade, the new wine districts of Oregon, particularly the Willamette Valley, have established a reputation for producing more supple, Burgundian-style wines. At the same time, California producers are homing in on certain cooler vineyard districts well-suited to the variety, notably the Carneros part of Napa and Sonoma, in the Santa Cruz Mountains, and in the lateral valleys of the Central Coast.

Pinot Noir is often ready to drink within two or three years but the bigger, better examples can take 5-10 years to mature.

AMERICAN

Arterberry 1983 Pinot Noir, Winemaker Reserve, Red Hills Vineyard, Yamhill County, OR $15. Deep, fruity nose. Nice structure; medium bodied, plenty of acid. Bitter cherry, black pepper, and smoky-sweet flavors. (JPN/Mar. '86) ★★★★

Byron 1984 Pinot Noir, Sierra Madre Vineyards, Santa Barbara County, CA $12. Perfumed, varietal nose shows earthiness laced with cherries and cinnamon. Exciting, vivid, youthful flavors of ripe cherries leave a sweet-sour, almost Beaujolais-like impression. Limited ★★★★

Mount Eden 1981 Pinot Noir, Santa Cruz Mountains, CA $15. Lovely, rich, ripe, maturing nose, with spice and smoke. Refined, complex, concentrated. Superb structure. Needs five years. (AWC/Nov. '85) ★★★★

Sanford 1983 Pinot Noir, Central Coast, CA $11. Top-notch, classic varietal nose: earthy, stemmy, herbal, floral, smoky, toasty. Attractive, approachable flavors. Good harmony. Some youthful, tannic bitterness. Needs five years. (AWC/Nov. '85) ★★★★

Sanford 1984 Pinot Noir, Central Coast, CA $12. Opulent, beautiful Burgundian nose has strawberry, cherry, stemmy, spicy, and dill-like hints. Many layers of round, delicious flavors. Excellent varietal definition. Aging potential up to five years. (AWC/Nov. '86) ★★★★

Yamhill Valley 1983 Pinot Noir, Hyland Vineyard, OR $17. Deep, black-cherry aroma and flavor, good structure, velvety. Excellent breed. (JPN/Mar.'86) ★★★★

Santa Cruz Mountain 1981 Pinot Noir, Estate Bottled, Santa Cruz Mountains, CA $15. Huge, intense, hard as nails; takes hours of aeration to open up. Must have more aging to bring out its abundant perfume of roses and spice. Seductive. Superb. (JDM/Mar. '86) ★★★1/2 (★★★★)

Amity 1982 Pinot Noir, Willamette Valley, OR $9. Muted, distinctive, Pinot Noir nose. Floral, low-key, cherry aromas. Well-made. Understated. (AWC/Nov. '85) ★★★1/2

Amity 1983 Pinot Noir, OR $14. Delicate nose of cherries, violets, and smoke. Pure, varietally correct flavors. Supple, with nice acid balance and no harsh tannins. Fine, delicate, lacey. Drink soon. (AWC/Nov. '86) ★★★1/2

Calera 1982 Pinot Noir, Reed, CA

$22.95. Opulent nose laced with mint, prune, and cassis. Round, gutsy, though still stylish and balanced. Needs two or three years. (AWC/Nov. '85) ★★★1/2

Joe Swan 1978 Pinot Noir, Sonoma Valley, CA $25. Expansive varietal bouquet of berries, spice, and mint. Rich flavors of sweet, ripe fruit. Velvet texture. Enormous length. Exudes class and style. Ready now. Should develop. (S&PW/Mar. '86) ★★★1/2

Knudsen Erath 1983 Pinot Noir, Vintage Select, Yamhill County, OR $9.95. Ripe, forward nose of cherries, almonds, berries, rose petals. Chewy, soft flavors linger. Needs short-term cellaring. (AWC/Nov. '85) ★★★1/2

Saintsbury 1984 Pinot Noir, Carneros, CA $12. Straightforward, plummy, peppery aromas. Lots of gutsy fruit matches earthy tannins and healthy acidity. Could use five years. (AWC/Nov. '86) ★★★1/2

Veritas 1983 Pinot Noir, OR $16. Lots of French oak balances berry-spicy-peppery fruit. Good depth. (JPN./Mar.'86) ★★★1/2

Whitehall Lane 1984 Pinot Noir, Napa Valley, CA $8.50. Pungent, spicy, sweet oak smells. Very ripe, rich, jammy fruit. Big and forward, but harmonious and not flabby. Nutty tannins in the finish. Typically Californian. (AWC/Nov. '86) ★★★1/2

Eyrie 1983 Pinot Noir, OR $15. Stinky at first, then becomes herbal-fruity. Firm, well structured, with delicate, complex fruit flavors. (JPN/Mar.'86) ★★★ (★★★★)

Saintsbury 1983 Pinot Noir, Carneros, Napa Valley, CA $12. Serious, medium-bodied Pinot just developing a crushed-rose bouquet. The flavor and aftertaste are full, intense, lingering. (JDM/Mar. '86) ★★★ (★★★1/2)

Adelsheim 1983 Pinot Noir, OR $12. Ripe, full nose. Herbal rather than fruity. Full, smoky-oaky flavors. (JPN/Mar. '86) ★★★

Alexander Valley Vineyards 1982 Pinot Noir, Estate Bottled, Alexander Valley, CA $6.50. Quiet but pretty nose of melon, dried flowers, minty eucalyptus. Rich, tannic, Cabernet-like. Five years in the cellar. (AWC/Nov. '85) ★★★

Amity 1982 Pinot Noir, Winemaker's Reserve, OR $16. Delicate nose of spice and cherries. Light, pleasant, Beaujolais style; broadens with airing. (AWC/Nov. '86) ★★★

Beaulieu (BV) 1984 Pinot Noir, Los Carneros Reserve, Napa Valley, CA $8. Pepper and ripe fruit nose. Tart berry and pepper taste, with slight mint. Delicate but strong. Excellent value. (JPN/Jan. '87) ★★★

Calera 1983 Pinot Noir, Jensen, CA $23. Excellent nose of Pinot Noir smokiness, cherries, violets, plus a little coconut, mint, and a sharp scent. Full, sour-cherry fruit, oaky, with ample tannin but no bitterness. Good potential for five years improvement. (AWC/Nov. '86) ★★★

Calera 1984 Pinot Noir, Selleck, CA $25. Ripe plum aroma backed by nuttiness and chocolate, plus a citrus note. Rounded, almost sweet, plummy flavors finish a little hot. Complex, powerful. (AWC/Nov. '86) ★★★

Cameron 1984 Pinot Noir, Reserve, OR $15. Cherry-berry fruit aroma and taste. Fairly rich. Solid structure. One of the best '84 Oregon Pinots. (JPN/Jan. '87) ★★★

Ch. Bouchaine 1982 Pinot Noir, Napa Valley, CA $12.50. Assertively herbal, spicy, with cherry and violet notes. Complex. Lovely balance. Light to medium bodied. (AWC/Nov. '85) ★★★

David Bruce 1982 Pinot Noir, Santa Cruz Mountains, CA $14. Lovely, earth-and-mushroom nose. Cinnamon and spice flavors. Medium-bodied. Long finish. (JPN/Jan. '86) ★★★

Davis Bynum 1983 Pinot Noir, Westside Road, Russian River Valley, CA $10. Restrained nose has damp earth and alfalfa notes. Medium-light body with tart cherry flavors accented by healthy acidity. Youthful, with some tannin for limited aging. (AWC/Nov. '86) ★★★

Edmeades 1982 Pinot Noir, Carney Vineyards, Anderson Valley, Mendocino, CA $10. Restrained, well-knit, strawberry, cherry, and herbal character. (AWC/Nov. '85) ★★★

Frick 1981 Pinot Noir, CA $12. Varietally correct, Pinot spice. Delicate but earthy. (AWC/Nov. '85) ★★★

Hanzell 1980 Pinot Noir, Sonoma Valley, CA $21.95. Rich cassis and raspberry nose. Not much like Pinot Noir. Huge fruit, firm flavor, hard tannins. Needs up to five more years aging. (AWC/Nov. '85) ★★★

Peter F. Adams 1984 Pinot Noir, Yamhill County, OR $10. Complex aroma and flavor of fresh cherries and spices. Medium body, approachable, well-balanced. (JPN/Jan. '87) ★★★

Robert Mondavi 1982 Pinot Noir, Reserve, Napa Valley, CA $18. Complex aroma of spices, fruit, smoke, toasty French oak. Flavors of spice, black pepper, plum skins, Bing cherry; ripe and rich. Fairly viscous and tannic. New French oak finish. (JPN/Jan. '87) ★★★

Saintsbury 1984 Garnet, Carneros, CA $8. Warm, roasted aromas of prunes, chocolate, coffee. Big, flavorful, tannic. (AWC/Nov. '86) ★★★

Sakonnet 1983 Pinot Noir, Southeastern New England, winery in RI $13.95. Pungent, young nose of beets with smoke and toast. Short-term cellaring. (AWC/Nov. '85) ★★★

Sanford 1982 Pinot Noir, Santa Maria Valley, CA $11. Vivid, geranium and earth nose. Ripe flavors with good fruit acid. (AWC/Nov. '85) ★★★

Smith-Madrone 1983 Pinot Noir, Estate Bottled, Napa Valley, CA $10. Cherry aroma with rose petal. Bright, black cherry flavor; nicely balanced fruit with some depth, no overripeness. (RF/Jan.'86) ★★★

Sokol Blosser 1983 Pinot Noir, Red Hills, Yamhill County, OR $10.95. Cassis and plum aromas. Almost Italian-style. Richness with grace. Needs five years. (AWC/Nov. '85) ★★★

Trefethen 1981 Pinot Noir, Napa Valley, CA $10. Austere earth and mushroom nose and taste followed by appealing hints of black cherry. (JPN/Jan.'86) ★★★

Tulocay 1982 Pinot Noir, Haynes Vineyard, Napa Valley, CA $12. Minty, eucalyptus, with a strong blast of French oak. Good depth of flavors. (AWC/Nov. '85) ★★★

Ventana 1980 Pinot Noir, Monterey County, CA $10. Lovely, berry-like, Pinot Noir nose with some cedar, pepper, and stemminess. Delightfully rich, creamy flavors have a sharp edge. (AWC/Nov. '86) ★★★

Wild Horse 1984 Pinot Noir, Santa Maria Valley, CA $11.50. Vivid, floral aroma is slightly green. Flavors are clean, rich, harmonious, varietal, but rather loosely knit. Needs a year or two to pull together. (AWC/Nov. '86) ★★★

ZD 1982 Pinot Noir, Napa Valley, CA $12.50. Very concentrated and firm. Long, vanilla-like aftertaste. Sassy fruit and hard tannins should come together in three to five years. (AWC/Nov. '86) ★★★

Amity 1981 Pinot Noir, OR $9. Substantial body but does not seem heavy. Earthy, complex, with hints of berries. (JPN/Jan. '86) ★★1/2 (★★★1/2)

Ponzi 1983 Pinot Noir, OR $15. Rich, deep, cherry aroma. Layers of fruit, with a fair amount of tannin. Very firm. (JPN/Mar. '86) ★★1/2 (★★★1/2)

Cecchetti-Sebastiani 1983 Pinot Noir, Reserve, Santa Maria Valley, CA $14. Roses and berries in the bouquet and flavor. Firm backbone. Full body. Pleasantly tart finish. Definite potential for improvement. ★★1/2 (★★★1/4)

Elk Cove 1983 Pinot Noir, Estate Bottled, Reserve, Willamette Valley, OR $16. Intense, smoky, herbal aromas. Full flavored. Somewhat alcoholic. (JPN/Mar.'86) ★★1/2 (★★★)

Mont St. John 1982 Pinot Noir, Carneros, Napa Valley, CA $9. Somewhat closed nose, but the flavor is generous with berry, cherry, faded-rose flavors and a touch of tart acidity. (JDM/Mar. '86) ★★1/2 (★★★)

Rex Hill 1983 Pinot Noir, Archibald Vineyard, Dundee Hills, OR $14. Ripe fruit and toasted barrel aromas. Full bodied. (JPN/Mar.'86) ★★1/2 (★★★)

Tualatin 1983 Pinot Noir, Estate Bottled, Willamette Valley, OR $10. Toasted French oak aroma. Broad, ripe cherry flavors. (JPN/Mar. '86) ★★1/2 (★★★)

Rex Hill 1983 Pinot Noir, Maresh Vineyard, OR $23. Sweet, almost stemmy nose. Full-bodied, cherry fruit. Finishes a little hot. (JPN/Mar.'86) ★★ (★★1/2)

Acacia 1983 Pinot Noir, St. Clair Vineyard, Napa Valley—Carneros, CA $14.99. Fat, spicy, raisiny aroma. Rich, broad, mature flavors, but there are still big, bitter tannins to be shed. (AWC/Nov. '86) ★★

Buena Vista 1981 Pinot Noir, Private Reserve, Carneros—Sonoma Valley, CA $14. Tight, intense nose of chocolate, tobacco, and anise. Stiff flavors show wood and sharply defined tannins. Excellent aging potential. (AWC/Nov. '86) ★★

Cameron 1984 Pinot Noir, OR $9. Melange of fruit aromas and flavors have delicacy, nice balance. (JPN/Mar.) ★★

Ch. Ste. Michelle 1983 Pinot

Noir, WA $10. Smoke and raspberry aroma. Smoky and spicy flavor with austere fruit and lots of French oak. Hot finish. (JPN/Jan. '87) ★★

Clos du Bois 1980 Pinot Noir, Proprietor's Reserve, Dry Creek Valley, CA $10.75. Herbal, licorice qualities with a hint of sharpness (volatile acidity). (AWC/Nov. '85) ★★

Columbia 1983 Pinot Noir, Otis Vineyard, Yakima Valley, WA $8. Lovely, open nose of strawberry and spice. Delicate, fruity taste, a trifle light. Tart, sour cherry finish. Drink now. (AWC/Nov. '86) ★★

David Bruce 1983 Pinot Noir, Estate Bottled, Santa Cruz Mountains, CA $10.20. Odd but pleasant nose of coconut oil, cedar, and licorice. Big, creamy flavors with perky acidity. Very tannic. (AWC/Nov. '86) ★★

Elk Cove 1982 Pinot Noir, Estate Bottled, Willamette Valley, OR $9. Lots of minty wood overlays berry aromas. Soft style, somewhat low in acid. Creamy texture and toasty oak. (AWC/Nov. '86) ★★

Elk Cove 1983 Pinot Noir, Reserve, Dundee Hills, Willamette Valley, OR $16. Ripe, cooked-fruit aroma. Big, full-bodied, rich; fairly tannic. (JPN/Mar. '86) ★★

J. Pedroncelli 1981 Pinot Noir, Sonoma County, CA $5.50. Pretty, dried-fruit nose. Pleasant, rich fruit. Awkward, tannic finish. (AWC/Nov. '85) ★★

Kenwood 1981 Pinot Noir, Jack London Vineyard, Sonoma Valley, CA $10. Big, minty, stemmy nose. Good, basic Pinot Noir flavors. Tannic, overripe finish. Needs up to five years. (AWC/Nov. '85) ★★

Mark West Vineyards 1983 Pinot Noir, Estate Bottled, Russian River Valley, CA $10. True Pinot Noir nose: cherries, raisins, chocolate, and tea-like facets. Well structured. Bitter tannins call for five years of cellaring. (AWC/Nov. '86) ★★

Oak Knoll 1983 Pinot Noir, OR $10. Ripe, plummy, smoky nose. Toast and cherry flavors. (JPN/Mar.'86) ★★

Peter F. Adams 1983 Pinot Noir, Yamhill County, OR $14. Rich fruit aroma. Full-bodied. (JPN/Mar. '86) ★★

Sokol Blosser 1983 Pinot Noir, Hyland Vineyards, Yamhill County, OR $9.95. Fairly big varietal nose of cassis, macaroon, cherry. Dried raspberry and pepper flavors. Needs a few years. (AWC/Nov. '85) ★★

Spring Mountain 1981 Pinot Noir, Napa Valley, CA $12. Sweet, jammy nose. Lots of wood flavor. Cabernet-like. Needs up to five years. (AWC/Nov. '85) ★★

Tulocay 1983 Pinot Noir, Haynes Vineyard, Napa Valley, CA $11. Pungent, tart-berry aromas have grassy and citric qualities. Straightforward fruit with a pronounced vegetal finish. Drink soon. (AWC/Nov. '86) ★★

Valley View 1982 Pinot Noir, OR $10. Ripe, pruney aroma. Smoky-sweet plum and cigar flavors. Good acidity. (JPN/Mar.'86) ★★

ZD 1981 Pinot Noir, Carneros, Napa Valley, CA $12.50. Closed, pungent, pruney, and minty nose. Slight dirty flavors dissipate with air. Up to five years age needed. (AWC/Nov. '85) ★★

Siskiyou 1983 Pinot Noir, OR $8. Closed, slightly veggie aroma. Medium body. Very pleasant cherry fruit. (JPN/Mar.'86)★1/2 (★★)

Bethel Heights 1984 Pinot Noir, OR $10. Berry aroma and flavor with pleasant earthiness. (JPN/Mar. '86) ★1/2

Salishan 1982 Pinot Noir, WA $10. A bit weedy. Light body and delicate cherry taste. Beaujolais style. Drink now. (JPN/Mar.'86) ★1/2

Sokol Blosser 1982 Pinot Noir,

Yamhill County, OR $8. Pleasant fruit aroma and taste. (JPN/Mar. '86) ★1/2

Elk Cove 1983 Pinot Noir, Reserve, Wind Hill, Willamette Valley, OR $16. Stemmy, beet-like aroma and flavor. (JPN/Mar. '86) ★

Hidden Springs 1983 Pinot Noir, OR $10. Fruity, with some dill-herbal notes. Firm structure. Tannic finish. (JPN/Mar. '86) ★

Hillcrest 1982 Pinot Noir, OR $10. Smoky, wet dog aroma. Thin, tannic. (JPN/Mar. '86) ★

Knudsen Erath 1982 Pinot Noir, Vintage Select, Yamhill County, OR $9. Pruney, slightly skunky. Tannic, hot, ripe fruit flavors verge on rubbery. (JPN/Mar. '86) ★

Acacia 1983 Pinot Noir, Winery Lake Vineyard, Carneros, Napa Valley, CA $15. Strong, bothersome, mint nose. Cherry-berry flavors. Modestly tannic. (AWC/Nov. '85)

Almaden 1982 Pinot Noir, San Benito County, CA $4.99. (AWC/Nov. '86)

Alpine 1983 Pinot Noir, Estate Bottled, Willamette Valley, OR $9. (AWC/Nov.'86)

Amity 1981 Pinot Noir, Estate Bottled, Willamette Valley, OR $10. Tanky, musty smells. (AWC/Nov. '85)

August Sebastiani Pinot Noir (nonvintage), Country, CA $5.75. (AWC/Nov. '85)

Bacigalupi (Belvedere Winery) 1982 Pinot Noir, Sonoma County, CA $12. Violet nose marred by high sulfur. Lovely, soft, generous flavors; nice balance. (AWC/Nov. '86)

Beringer 1980 Pinot Noir, Napa Valley, CA $6. (AWC/Nov. '85)

Bridgehampton 1984 Pinot Noir, The Hamptons—Long Island, NY $7.99. (AWC/Nov. '86)

Carneros Creek 1983 Pinot Noir, Carneros, Napa Valley, CA $17. (AWC/Nov. '85)

Ch. Benoit 1983 Pinot Noir, OR $12. Very closed, spicy, Rhône-like nose. Pleasant, light style. (AWC/Nov. '86)

Ch. Biltmore 1984 Pinot Noir, NC $17.95. (AWC/Nov. '86)

Ch. St. Jean 1983 Pinot Noir, McCrea Vineyards, Sonoma Valley, CA $12. (AWC/Nov. '86)

Ch. Ste. Michelle 1983 Pinot Noir, Limited Bottling, WA $11.50. (AWC/Nov. '86)

Charles Krug 1979 Pinot Noir, Napa Valley, CA $5.50. Pungent, spicy, with weedy or stemmy notes. (AWC/Nov. '85)

Cilurzo 1984 Pinot Noir, Temecula, CA $9.50. (AWC/Nov. '86)

Clos du Bois 1984 Pinot Noir, Sonoma County, CA $7.95. Toasty, cherry nose with yeasty overtones. Big, jammy flavor but very astringent. Should age well. (AWC/Nov. '86)

Clos du Val 1983 Pinot Noir, Napa Valley, CA $11.50. (AWC/Nov. '86)

Creston Manor 1983 Pinot Noir, San Luis Obispo County, CA $15. (AWC/Nov. '86)

Creston Manor 1985 Pinot Noir, November New, CA $7. (AWC/Nov. '86)

Davis Bynum 1982 Pinot Noir, Westside Road, Russian River Valley, Sonoma County, CA $10. (AWC/ Nov. '85)

De Loach 1981 Pinot Noir, Estate Bottled, Reserve, Sonoma Valley, CA $12. Strong, ripe, alcoholic, Cabernet-like aroma. Big, tannic. Slightly volatile finish. (AWC/Nov. '85)

De Loach 1983 Pinot Noir, Estate Bottled, Russian River Valley, CA $10. (AWC/Nov. '86)

Domaine Laurier 1981 Pinot Noir, Estate Bottled, Green Valley, Sono-

ma County, CA $10. (AWC/Nov. '85)

Elk Cove 1982 Pinot Noir, Reserve, Willamette Valley, OR $12. Tight nose has stemmy and earthy qualities. Flavors are clean, easy-drinking. Green, bitter finish. (AWC/Nov. '86)

Elk Cove 1983 Pinot Noir, Reserve, Willamette Valley, OR $15. Pungent, sweet nose of beets, pepper, and tea. Sharp, tart acidity. Low tannin calls for early drinking. (AWC/Nov. '86)

Eyrie 1984 Pinot Noir, Reserve, OR $18. Citric, cherry-like nose with floral complexity and ample wood. Sour-candy flavors improve substantially in the glass. Clean, short finish. (AWC/Nov. '86)

Felton-Empire 1982 Pinot Noir, Tonneaux Francais, Sonoma County, CA $11. (AWC/Nov. '86)

Forgeron 1983 Pinot Noir, OR $10. (AWC/Nov. '86)

Fulton Valley Cellars 1984 Pinot Noir, Russian River Valley, CA $7.50. (AWC/Nov. '86)

Gary Farrell 1982 Pinot Noir, Russian River Valley, Sonoma County, CA $10.50. (AWC/Nov. '85)

Gary Farrell 1983 Pinot Noir, Russian River Valley, CA $12. (AWC/Nov. '86)

Gary Farrell 1984 Pinot Noir, Russian River Valley, CA $12. (AWC/Nov. '86)

Geyser Peak 1981 Pinot Noir, Carneros, Sonoma County, CA $5.75. (AWC/Nov. '85)

Hacienda 1982 Pinot Noir, Sonoma Valley, CA $12. Spicy nose, sweet and toasty. (AWC/Nov. '85)

Hacienda 1983 Pinot Noir, Estate Bottled, Sonoma Valley, CA $12. (AWC/Nov. '86)

Henry Estate 1982 Pinot Noir, Estate Bottled, Umpqua Valley, OR $9.95. (AWC/Nov. '85)

Henry Estate 1983 Pinot Noir, Umpqua Valley, OR $12. Plywood aroma and flavor overwhelm fruit. (JPN/Mar. '86)

Husch 1981 Pinot Noir, Estate Bottled, Anderson Valley, CA $7. (AWC/Nov. '85)

Husch 1982 Pinot Noir, Estate Bottled, Anderson Valley, CA $9. (AWC/Nov. '86)

Inglenook 1983 Pinot Noir, Reserve-Estate Bottled, Napa Valley, CA $11.50. (AWC/Nov. '86)

Inglenook 1982 Pinot Noir, Estate Bottled, Napa Valley, CA $7.50. Musty, old wood nose. (AWC/Nov. '85)

Jekel 1980 Pinot Noir, Estate Bottled, Home Vineyard, Monterey County, CA $8.50. (AWC/Nov. '85)

Jekel 1982 Pinot Noir, Estate Bottled, Arroyo Seco, CA $9. (AWC/ Nov. '86)

Knudsen Erath 1981 Pinot Noir, Yamhill County, OR $7.95. Strong, cherry-fruit aroma. Beaujolais style. (AWC/ Nov. '85)

Knudsen Erath (non-vintage) Pinot Noir, Willamette Valley, OR $5.95. Elusive, cherry nose with some acetate. Undistinguished fruit. (AWC/Nov. '85)

La Crema Vinera 1983 Pinot Noir, CA $11. (AWC/Nov. '86)

Louis K. Mihaly 1982 Pinot Noir, Private Reserve, Napa Valley, CA $8. Pungent, barnyard aromas. Good concentration of sweet and sour fruit; Gamay-like. (AWC/Nov. '86)

Louis M. Martini 1980 Pinot Noir, Las Amigas, Vineyard Selection, Napa Valley, CA $10. (AWC/Nov. '86)

Mark West Vineyards 1979 Pinot Noir, Estate Bottled, Russian River Valley, CA $10. Initial off, musty, rubbery odor gives way to a raisiny, berry-like nose. (AWC/Nov. '85)

Mirassou 1981 Pinot Noir, Harvest

Reserve, Monterey County, CA $12. Off nose. (AWC/Nov. '86)

Montali 1982 Pinot Noir, Proprietor's Series, Santa Maria Valley, CA $10. (AWC/Nov. '85)

Oak Knoll 1983 Pinot Noir, Vintage Select, OR $15. (AWC/Nov. '86)

Paul Masson 1982 Pinot Noir, Sonoma County, CA $5.39. (AWC/Nov. '85)

Paul Masson 1984 Pinot Noir, Sonoma County, CA $5. (AWC/Nov. '86)

Ponzi 1982 Pinot Noir, Reserve, Willamette Valley, OR $10. (AWC/Nov. '86)

Ponzi 1983 Pinot Noir, Reserve, Willamette Valley, OR $15. (AWC/Nov. '86)

Ponzi 1983 Pinot Noir, Willamette Valley, OR $10. (AWC/Nov. '86)

Richardson 1983 Pinot Noir, Los Carneros, Sonoma Valley, CA $11.75. (AWC/Nov. '85)

Robert Mondavi 1981 Pinot Noir, Reserve, Napa Valley, CA $14.99. Oaky, butterscotch nose. Green, bitter flavors. (AWC/Nov. '86)

Robert Stemmler 1984 Pinot Noir, Sonoma County, CA $16. Slight acetate nose. Better on the palate. Rich underlying fruit. (AWC/Nov. '85)

Rodney Strong 1981 Pinot Noir, River East Vineyard, Russian River Valley, CA $8.50. (AWC/Nov. '86)

Sakonnet 1984 Pinot Noir, Southeastern New England, winery in RI $12.95. (AWC/Nov. '86)

San Pasqual 1984 Pinot Noir, Sierra Madre Vineyard, Santa Maria Valley, CA $10.50. (AWC/Nov. '86)

Schug 1981 Pinot Noir, Napa Valley, CA $10.75. (AWC/Nov. '86)

Schug 1982 Pinot Noir, Heinemann Vineyard, Napa Valley, CA $10.75.

Too woody. (AWC/Nov. '86)

Schug 1983 Pinot Noir, Beckstoffer Vineyard, Carneros—Napa Valley, CA $9.75. Cherry and bell-pepper nose with smoky oak. Astringent tannin. (AWC/Nov. '86)

Sea Ridge 1982 Pinot Noir, Sonoma County, CA $12. Heavy, toasty, smoky. (AWC/Nov. '85)

Sebastiani 1982 Pinot Noir, Tailfeathers, Sonoma Valley, CA $5. (AWC/Nov. '86)

Seghesio 1983 Pinot Noir, Estate Bottled, Northern Sonoma, CA $5. A chemical component mars an otherwise floral, cherry-berry bouquet. (AWC/Nov. '86)

Shafer Vineyard Cellars 1983 Pinot Noir, Estate Bottled, Willamette Valley, OR $13.50. (AWC/Nov. '86)

Simi 1981 Pinot Noir, North Coast, CA $7. (AWC/Nov. '85)

Simi 1982 Pinot Noir, North Coast, CA $7.50. (AWC/Nov. '86)

Siskiyou 1982 Pinot Noir, OR $8.25. Sweet grape candy aroma. Simple. (AWC/Nov. '85)

Trione (Geyser Peak Winery) 1980 Pinot Noir, Los Carneros, Sonoma County, CA $9.50. Ponderous, cooked fruit. (AWC/Nov. '85)

Ventana 1982 Pinot Noir, Estate Bottled, Monterey County, CA $10. (AWC/Nov. '86)

Weibel 1981 Pinot Noir, Proprietor's Reserve, Mendocino County, CA $8. (AWC/Nov. '85)

AUSTRALIAN

Johnstone 1979 Pinot Noir, Estate Bottled, Hunter River Valley $6.19. Big, clunky, high alcohol, with no varietal character. (CR/Jan. '86)

PORTUGUESE

Some of the finest buys in mature red wines today come from Portugal. Bargain prices aside, they deserve to be better known for their quality.

Some 180,000 growers cultivate 875,000 acres of vines in Portugal. Cooperatives process almost half of the grapes, and a scant 4% of Portugal's wineries bottle more than 3,000 cases. Consequently, merchants and brands are more important than growers.

The Douro region of northern Portugal, well known for the great, fortified wines of Porto, is also the source of medium-bodied, dry, fruity, red table wines. In the central part of the country, the Bairrada district is gaining a reputation for light-to-medium-bodied, dry reds, and the Dão is the source of many of Portugal's best reds. The latter tend to be medium-bodied and fruity, with an aroma reminiscent of kirsch. Though they have tannin, they are often supple, with up to 30% white grapes blended in.

In the southern part of Portugal, the Ribatejo district is the source of many good, inexpensive reds, and Colares, near the ocean, turns out full-bodied, rich, tannic reds that mature slowly and are long-lived.

Portugal grows its own family of wine grapes. The Periquita and Alvarinho are the most familiar on labels. "Garrafeira" is the term on labels indicating wine selected for special aging. "Garrafeira Particular" identifies wine reserved for still longer aging.

Ferreira 1978 Barca Velha, Douro $15. Rich fruit peeking out of a still-closed nose. Full, rich, mouth-filling flavors. Moderate tannin, some oak, loads of incredible flavors. Some firmness. Very long finish. (S&PW/Mar. '86) ★★★ (★★★1/2)

Carvalho, Ribeira & Ferreira 1955 Garrafeira Particular. Complex bouquet

suggests cherries and gingerbread. Soft, flavorful entry. Long, cherry-like, tannic finish.
Lovely now. (S&PW/Mar. '86) ★★★

**Carvalho, Ribeira & Ferreira 1979
Reserva, Douro $4.99.** Spicy, peppery
aroma. Big, full flavored. Very long, spicy
finish. Has class. (S&PW/Mar. '86) ★★★

**Caves Alianca 1964 Reserva, Dão
$11.33.** Rich, fruity aroma; tobacco and
cherry notes. Full bodied; full flavored. A
trace of drying out at the end. (S&PW/Mar.
'86) ★★★

**Caves Borlido 1966 Garrafeira Vel-
ho $8.32.** Refined, floral bouquet with a
vague, berry-like note. Full of flavor and
character. Velvet texture. Very long finish.
(S&PW/Mar. '86) ★★★

**Antonio Bernardino Paulo da Silva
1974 Chitas, Colares $6.75.** Deep,
rich, concentrated aroma of black peppers has
a sharp touch of volatile acidity. Full flavored, firm, tannic vein. Young, with a lot of
room for improvement. (S&PW/Mar. '86)
★★1/2 (★★★)

**Antonio Bernardino Paulo da Silva
1974 Garrafeira Particular, Reserva,
Colares $6.59.** Complex aroma suggests
black pepper and spice. Still some tannin to
lose. Richly flavored, similar to a very good
Côtes du Rhône. (S&PW/Mar. '86) ★★1/2

**Carvalho, Ribeira & Ferreira 1974
Garrafeira $5.25.** Rich aroma; cherry
notes, vaguely floral. Firm, tasty, well structured. Personality and length at a bargain
basement price. Ready. (S&PW/Mar. '86)
★★1/2

**Caves Alianca 1976 Garrafeira Par-
ticular, Bairrada $5.99.** Oak and fruit ar-
oma. Rich fruit flavors fill the mouth. Some
firmness. Well balanced. Long finish.
(S&PW/Mar. '86) ★★1/2

**Caves do Barroção 1970 Garrafeira
Particular $5.69.** Complex aroma shows
age and development. Mellow, soft-centered,
chewy; some tannin and character. Very nice

though somewhat rustic. (S&PW/Mar. '86)
★★1/2

Caves Velhas 1974 Romeira, Garrafeira, Ribatejo $5.99. Lovely, refined bouquet; fruit and floral notes, some spice. Soft, tasty, well balanced. Good quality, good value. (S&PW/Mar. '86) ★★1/2

Conde de Santar 1974 Reserva, Dão $5.49. Lovely bouquet; spicy, cherry notes, moderately intense. Some tannin up front, followed by smooth texture and full flavor. Finishes on a tannic note. (S&PW/Mar. '86) ★★1/2

João Pires 1983 Quinta da Bacalhoa, Cabernet Sauvignon, Azeitao $6.99. Aroma of new oak and Cabernet fruit. Well-balanced, full-flavored, some tannin, light finish. Ready now. (S&PW/Mar. '86) ★★1/2

Casa Ferreirinha 1980 Reserva Especial, Douro $8.99. Oak aroma up front; rich intense fruit in the back. Fairly tannic, well structured, richly flavored, somewhat closed. Very young, with intrusion of harsh tannins. (S&PW/Mar. '86) ★★ (★★★)

João Pires 1981 Anforas, Alentejo $2.99. Intense, concentrated aroma recalls cherries, tar, flowers, currants. Big, rich, full bodied, youthful, with some tannin. Lots of flavor makes it attractive now, but it should improve. (S&PW/Mar. '86) ★★ (★★1/2)

Antonio Bernardino Paulo da Silva 1974 Casal da Azenha, Chitas, Colares $5.49. Vaguely woody aroma, slight earthiness. Tasty. Light tannin. Some character. A bit short. (S&PW/Mar. '86) ★★

Carvalho, Ribeira & Ferreira 1980 Quinta da Folgorosa, Torres Vedras $5.99. Complex, cherry and spice bouquet. Full-bodied, soft, smooth, fruity, easy. Moderate length. Ready. (S&PW/Mar. '86) ★★

Caves Alianca 1975 Garrafeira, Bairrada $5.99. Richly fruited aroma, vaguely floral. Has character. Dry, some firmness, moderate length. (S&PW/Mar. '86) ★★

Caves Alianca 1980 Reserva **$2.99.** Spicy, fruity aroma. Fruity, well balanced, some character, moderate length. (S&PW/Mar. '86) ★★

Caves Borlido 1970 Bairrada **$5.30.** Cinnamon, ginger, bread-like aroma. Fruity, some firmness, tannic undertone, soft center. Ready. Fairly full bodied; some character. (S&PW/Mar. '86) ★★

Caves Borlido 1979 S. Vicente, Dao $2.59. Light, cherry aroma with black cherry nuances suggesting Côtes du Rhône. Soft, round, tasty, well balanced. Ready. Very good. (S&PW/Mar. '86) ★★

Caves do Grou 1965 Groval, Dão **$5.99.** Tawny rim. Some fruit in the nose. Caramel candy core. Showing a lot of age. Drinkable, very soft, no tannin left. (S&PW/ Mar. '86) ★★

Caves Velhas 1974 Garrafeira, Dão **$5.25.** Dried cherry aroma; vague raisin note. Some tannin, firmness, still soft; tasty. Finish is a bit tannic. (S&PW/Mar. '86) ★★

Caves Primavera 1970 Dão $4.37. Cherry aroma, some spice. Firm, flavorful, some harshness at the end. Quite enjoyable. (S&PW/Mar. '86) ★1/2

Caves Velhas 1980 Bairrada $2.49. Vaguely cherry, spicy aroma. Soft, flavorful, some tannin, could use more length and character. (S&PW/Mar. '86) ★1/2

Caves Velhas 1980 Dão $2.49. Spicy, cherry aroma. Well balanced, tasty, some character. (S&PW/Mar. '86) ★1/2

Adega Cooperativa do Cantanhede 1980 Reserva, Bairrada $2.99. Fruity aroma, black pepper note. Fruity, soft, ready, agreeable, simple. (S&PW/Mar. '86) ★

Carvalho, Ribeira & Ferreira 1980 Serradayres $2.99. Flavorful, soft, fruity, fairly well balanced. A tasty little agreeable wine. Some character. (S&PW/Mar. '86) ★

Caves Borlido 1970 Garrafeira **$5.30.** Spicy, cherry aroma; touch of black pepper. Beginning to dry out but still good.

Some decay in the finish. (S&PW/Mar. '86)
★

Caves do Barroção 1974 Garrafeira, Bairrada $5.31. Deep, Rhône-like aroma of black pepper, spice, cherries. Zippy acidity; a bit lean, firm. Nice fruit. Ready; old age creeping in. Drink up. (S&PW/Mar. '86) ★

Caves do Vale do Grou 1980 Gran Grou, Dão $3.49. Fresh, cherry-like aroma, hints of spice. Fruity, soft, easy to like, a bit simple. (S&PW/Mar. '86) ★

Caves Velhas 1968 Reserva, Dão $5.99. Slight nose. Firm acidity, fairly tannic, beginning to dry out. Still good; was better a few years ago. (S&PW/Mar. '86) ★

Caves Velhas 1976 Romeira, Garrafeira, Ribatejo $4.99. Cherry fruit, almond note. Oxidation and overripeness intrude. Still has flavor, but age beginning to show. (S&PW/Mar. '86) ★

Groval 1970 Garrafeira, Dão $5.99. Vaguely woodsy aroma; dried-fruit notes. Nice flavor, beginning to dry out, still agreeable. (S&PW/Mar. '86) ★

Conde de Santar 1978 Reserva, Dão $5.49. Oxidized. Barely drinkable. (S&PW/Mar. '86)

Monte Crasto (nonvintage) $2.99. Simple. Some tannin, some fruit, no character. Drinkable. (S&PW/Mar. '86)

ZINFANDEL

The origin of the Zinfandel grape is still a matter of debate. It was brought to California from somewhere in Europe (probably Italy) in the mid-1800s. By the 1880s it was an established feature of the west coast vineyard landscape and soon became a California specialty. Grown throughout the state, it is the most versatile of California grapes, used in blends for Central Valley jug reds, for premium varietals from prestigious wineries like Ridge and Sutter Home, and for the new generation of blush wines, the rosés of the 1980s *(see Rosé)*. Though it lacks the prestige of Cabernet Sauvignon, nearly twice as much Zinfandel is grown.

Premium-quality red Zinfandels typically have an assertive, raspberry or blackberryish character, often with a spicy, peppery note. Styles can range from light, Beaujolais-like, to big, dense, tannic wines requiring years to mature.

While the first half of this decade has been devoted to producing and marketing white Zinfandels, it appears that interest in the classic (red) Zinfandel is on the rise again. Zinfandel's popularity waned in the 1970s in the shadow of California Cabernet, but there has lately been a resurgence of interest in what winemaker Paul Draper of Ridge Vineyards calls "claret-style Zinfandel": mature, very dry, made from low-yield, unirrigated vineyards in the Coastal Range, aged in small cooperage and requiring several years of bottle age. Many of these wines bear vineyard designations. Expect to see more super-premium Zinfandels in the near future.

White Oak 1983 Zinfandel, Dry Creek Valley, Sonoma County, CA $7.50. Flavors are berryish with hints of spice, nicely oaked. Firm body and structure without abrasive tannins. Lovely now, it

should age for decades. (JDM/May '86)
★★★★

De Loach 1982 Zinfandel, Russian River Valley, CA $8. Raspberry aroma. Fairly intense flavors. Some tannin. (S&PW/May '86) ★★★

Konocti 1981 Zinfandel, Lake County, CA $4.99. Deep, blackberryish nose and flavor. Rich, very ripe, slightly roasted but without heaviness. (RF/Jan. '86) ★★★

Simi 1980 Zinfandel, Alexander Valley, CA $7.49. Lovely, blackberry-raspberry aroma. Soft and fruity, very easy to drink, with true Zinfandel character. (S&PW/Mar. '86) ★★★

Storybrook Mountain 1982 Zinfandel, CA $8.99. Lovely aroma of ripe fruit and Zinfandel berries. Heaps of flavor. Very long finish. (S&PW/Jan. '86) ★★★

Inglenook 1982 Zinfandel, Estate Bottled, Napa Valley, CA $9. Fresh berry aroma. Spicy fruit; oregano and pepper. Crisp. Should last and soften. (JPN/Jan. '87) ★★1/2 (★★★)

Preston Vineyards & Winery 1983 Zinfandel, Dry Creek Valley, CA $7.50. Rich, bramble-fruit aroma. Ripe, sweet fruit flavors fill the mouth. (S&PW/May '86) ★★1/2 (★★★)

Pedroncelli 1980 Zinfandel, Reserve, Sonoma County, CA $8. Richly fruited aroma suggests raspberries. Intensely flavored with a lot of extract and character. Rough, tannic finish calls for further aging. (S&PW/May '86) ★★ (★★★)

Hidden Cellars 1983 Zinfandel, Pacini Vineyard, Mendocino, CA $8.99. Fresh, raspberry aroma with a vague, pruney note. Balanced and fruity, with character. (S&PW/Mar. '86) ★★

Susine 1980 Zinfandel, Amador County, CA $5.50. Avoids pruney, raisiny quality, but just barely. Ripe and hearty. (JDM/Mar. '86) ★★

Wente Bros. 1981 Zinfandel, Special Selection, Livermore Valley, CA $8. Very ripe, dusty aroma. Big, full, cooked, raisiny taste. (JPN/Jan. '87) ★1/2

The Christian Brothers 1982 Zinfandel, Napa Valley, CA $6. Spicy, vanilla aroma. Oak masks reserved fruit. (JPN/Mar. '86) ★

WHITE WINES

ABBREVIATIONS & SYMBOLS

RATINGS

★★★★—Like extremely or Platinum Medal
★★★1/2—Like very strongly or Gold Medal
★★★—Like strongly or Silver Medal
★★—Like slightly or Bronze Medal
★—Neither like nor dislike, a useful wine
(★)—Estimated peak score with aging
No Star—A wine with no star is a wine that won no medal in competition or a wine that the reviewer disliked.

WHO WROTE THE DESCRIPTIONS

AWC—American Wine Competition Judges
BC—Bordeaux Classic Judges
JB—John Binder
CC—Carole Collier
RF—Richard Figiel
CG—Craig Goldwyn
JDM—Jerry D. Mead
DM—Denman Moody Jr.
JPN—Judy Peterson-Nedry
CR—Christina Reynolds
S&PW—Sheldon & Pauline Wasserman

PRICES. Prices are typical of those in major metropolitan markets for standard, 750-ml bottles *at the time the review was written* (note the date following the descriptions). The prices of some wines are likely to rise as time passes. Prices may also vary *significantly* from state to state and store to store.

AVAILABILITY. Some wines may be hard to find because they are produced in small quantities, and distribution methods often make wines that are bestsellers in one city unavailable in another. Even large stores can't carry more than a fraction of the thousands of wines sold in the US and Canada, so many merchants are happy to order wines for you. If can't find wines you want in your area, try to shop when you're in other major cities.

CHARDONNAY

More American wineries produce Chardonnay than any other varietal wine, red or white. California wineries have arguably been more successful with this variety than with any other, competing very successfully against the French classics from Burgundy.

Because of its short growing season and relative tolerance to cold weather, Chardonnay can be grown in a wide climatic range. In California it does best in the cooler regions. It has also proven its potential in Washington, Oregon, New York, Virginia, Maryland, Texas, and several other states.

In the cellar, Chardonnay is equally adaptable to a range of winemaking techniques, all of which adds up to a fascinating array of flavors and styles. The fruit flavors of wines grown in cool climates often suggest lemon, pineapple, green olive, and apple, while Chardonnays from warmer areas may recall melon, coconut, butterscotch, mango. The use of wooden cooperage for fermentation and/or aging can add qualities of vanilla, oak, toast, and smoke. Buttery scents and flavors are common, a result of one of the winemaker's most dramatic options: a secondary, malolactic fermentation.

US winemakers have generally moved away from the very ripe, high alcohol, buttery, oaky Chardonnays of the '70s to a more subdued, balanced style. The call for so-called "food wines" that don't overpower their culinary companions has been heeded, but there are already rumblings of reaction from those favoring the blockbusters. The whole gamut of styles is currently available. The consumer's best guide is tasting notes from reliable tasters.

Chardonnay is one white wine that can benefit substantially with some aging, though just how much is a delicate matter. California Chardonnays appear to peak within a few years, then decline somewhat more precipitously than white French Burgundies. Because of their higher acid levels, Chardonnays from other states may develop more slowly than their California counterparts, but their track records are not yet firmly established.

AMERICAN

Calera 1983 Chardonnay, Santa Barbara County, CA $10.75. Classic California style at its best. Seductive, toasty nose and lush flavors of mature fruit and oak. Not overstated. (AWC/Nov. '85) ★★★★

Ch. Potelle 1982 Chardonnay, Napa Valley, CA $13. Leans toward roasted coffee and butterscotch. Very complex. Like a good Meursault. (JDM/Jan. '86) ★★★★

Concannon 1984 Chardonnay, Selected Vineyards, 26% Santa Clara County/74% Santa Maria Valley, CA $9. Flawless, fresh, unembellished, varietal aromas. Supple, appley-lemony fruit, lightly spiced. Lean, stylish, crisp, perfectly balanced. (AWC/Nov. '85) ★★★★

Flora Springs 1984 Chardonnay, Barrel Fermented, Napa Valley, CA $18. Toasty, spicy, citrusy, and vanilla aromas. Flavors are rich, complex, and long, with a clean, refreshing finish. Chassagne-style Chardonnay with balance, structure, elegance. (AWC/Nov. '86) ★★★★

Inglenook 1984 Chardonnay, Estate Bottled, Reserve, Special Cuvee, Napa Valley, CA $18. Delicate, almost shy. Keeps revealing more. Lightly toasted oak just noted in a lovely bouquet; hints of nuts and allspice. Pear-like fruit with lemony edges. (AWC/Nov. '85) ★★★★

Joseph Phelps 1982 Chardonnay, Sangiacomo, CA $14. Voluptuous, barrel-fermented, with toasty notes. Wonderful depth of fruit intensity. Beautifully balanced and extracted. (JDM/Jan. '86) ★★★★

La Crema Vinera 1984 Chardonnay,

CA $11. Nutty, toasty aromas mingle with lush ripe fruit. Fat and buttery flavors with lowish acid but a firm oak structure. Long, complex finish. (AWC/Nov. '86) ★★★★

Landmark 1983 Chardonnay, Sonoma County, CA $9. Full, appley, with a touch of wood. Fruit impeccably balanced with solid acidity; firm structure. Should improve with another year or two. (AWC/Nov. '85) ★★★★

Acacia 1983 Chardonnay, Marina Estate Vineyard, Napa Valley-Carneros, CA $16. Very rich, very intense flavors with some toasty quality. Good acids, long finish. Slightly obtrusive alcohol in the finish. (JDM/Jan. '86) ★★★1/2

Adler Fels 1983 Chardonnay, Nelson Vineyard, CA $11. Lots of middle body, flavor intensity, complexity, oak influence, and length of aftertaste. (JDM/Jan. '86) ★★★1/2

Bargetto 1985 Chardonnay, Cypress, Santa Maria Valley, CA $7. Intense, ripe peaches, pineapples, and mangoes throughout, embroidered with oak. (AWC/Nov. '86) ★★★1/2

Byron 1984 Chardonnay, Reserve, Santa Barbara County, CA $13. Herbal, earthy aromas. Pineapple and pear-like fruit flavors. Round, viscous mouth feel. Warm finish. Character and sophistication. (AWC/Nov. '86) ★★★1/2

Byron 1985 Chardonnay, Central Coast, CA $9.50. Clean, varietal aroma. Subtle style with clean, delicate flavors, good balance. Toasty finish. (AWC/Nov. '86) ★★★1/2

Chalk Hill 1984 Chardonnay, Sonoma County, CA $8. Delicate, floral and citrusy aromas with a hint of oak. Trim and lean varietal flavors linger in the finish. Tight structure. (AWC/Nov. '86) ★★★1/2

Clos du Bois 1984 Chardonnay, Barrel Fermented, Alexander Valley, CA $9. Delicate nose of nuts, flowers, and apricots. Lemony fruit; clean and refreshing. Crisp, lingering finish. (AWC/Nov. '85) ★★★1/2

Clos du Bois 1984 Calcaire, Alexander Valley, CA $21. Subdued nose of fruit and oak. Rich fruit flavors with a good acid structure and slightly sweet vanilla finish. Potential for aging. (AWC/Nov. '86) ★★★1/2

Congress Springs 1985 Chardonnay, Santa Clara County, CA $12. Fruit aromas and flavors predominate throughout: melons, pears, pineapples, lemons, apples. Very clean, with good acid structure, lingering sweetness. Rich and lively. (AWC/ Nov. '86) ★★★1/2

Corbett Canyon 1984 Chardonnay, Coastal Classic, Central Coast, CA $7.99/liter. Melon-fruit nose. Light, toasty flavors with notable wood. Soft, easy to sip. (AWC/Nov. '85) ★★★1/2

Corbett Canyon 1985 Chardonnay, Coastal Classic, Central Coast, CA $6. Ripe fruit nose of honey, peaches, and spice with oaky overtones. Good extract gives a fat mouth feel. Long, slightly sweet finish. (AWC/Nov. '86) ★★★1/2

De Loach 1985 Chardonnay, Russian River Valley, CA $12.50. Straightforward Chardonnay highlighting ripe, complex fruit aromas and flavors, rich and well-integrated. Warm finish. (AWC/Nov. '86) ★★★1/2

Devlin 1984 Chardonnay, Sonoma, CA $7.50. Rich, almost oily. Spicy flavors, toasty. (JDM/May '86) ★★★1/2

Eberle 1983 Chardonnay, Paso Robles, CA $10. Intensely ripe style. Aromas of peaches and pineapples. Rich and supple mouth feel with some sweetness in the finish. (AWC/Nov. '86) ★★★1/2

Fetzer 1984 Chardonnay, Special Reserve, CA $12. Ripe fruit, vanilla, and caramel nose. Ripe fruit flavors balanced with a touch of oak. Lingering finish. (AWC/Nov.

'86) ★★★1/2

Franciscan 1983 Chardonnay, Vintner Grown, Alexander Valley, CA $9.50. Delicate, floral nose with spice and nuts. Soft fruit, silky texture, hints of French oak. (AWC/Nov. '85) ★★★1/2

Fulton Valley 1985 Chardonnay, Alexander Valley, CA $9.50. Classic, varietal Chardonnay nose. Lively, spicy flavors with crisp acidity, good balance and structure. Lovely, crisp finish and aftertaste. (AWC/Nov. '86) ★★★1/2

Guenoc 1984 Chardonnay, North Coast, CA $9.15. Rich, floral aroma of honeysuckle and lemongrass. Ripe fruit flavors of apples and pears with some oak complexity. Lovely finish. (AWC/Nov. '86) ★★★1/2

Hacienda 1983 Chardonnay, Clair de Lune, Sonoma Valley, CA $11. Alluring, complex aromas of lemons, quince, and pineapple. Lively, fruity flavors. Oaky finish. (AWC/Nov. '86) ★★★1/2

Husch 1984 Chardonnay, Estate Bottled, Mendocino, CA $9.75. Lemon, honey, green apple, vanilla, and oak aromas. Clean, round, supple style with nice balance and structure. Complex finish. (AWC/Nov. '86) ★★★1/2

Jekel 1982 Chardonnay, Private Reserve, Home Vineyard, Arroyo Seco, CA $14.50. Rich bouquet shows wisps of smoke and pine. Flavors of ripe fruit and toasty, vanilla-like oak, balanced with healthy acidity. A heavyweight. (AWC/Nov. '85) ★★★1/2

Karly 1985 Chardonnay, Santa Maria Valley, CA $12. Complex, rich, Burgundian nose shows fruit, oak, and floral components. Full, creamy flavors with a strong, acid backbone and long finish. (AWC/Nov. '86) ★★★1/2

Kendall-Jackson 1984 Chardonnay, Vintner's Reserve, CA $9.50. Complex nose, somewhat subdued fruit with spicy overtones and a hint of wood. Creamy, restrained texture. (AWC/Nov. '85) ★★★1/2

Louis M. Martini 1983 Chardonnay, North Coast, CA $8. Best Martini Chardonnay ever. Partial barrel-fermentation adds middle body. Crisp, Chablis style. Refreshing. (JDM/Jan. '86) ★★★1/2

Monticello 1984 Chardonnay, Corley Vineyard, Napa Valley, CA $12.50. Complex, ripe-fruit bouquet of apricots, ginger, other spices. Rich, unctuous texture but elegantly crafted with sufficient acid and oak. Warm, long finish. (AWC/Nov. '86) ★★★1/2

Obester 1984 Chardonnay, Mendocino County, CA $12. Full, almost sweet fruit with refreshing acidity. Good depth and balance. (AWC/Nov. '85) ★★★1/2

Raymond 1984 Chardonnay, Napa Valley, CA $12. Rich, intense nose of spicy wood, pineapple, and toasted coconut. Medium intense fruit flavors. Balanced, well-knit structure. Warm finish. (AWC/Nov. '86) ★★★1/2

Roudon-Smith 1984 Chardonnay, Nelson Ranch, Mendocino, CA $12.50. Very big wine with complex aromas and fleshy, rich, Burgundian character. (AWC/Nov. '86) ★★★1/2

Round Hill 1984 Chardonnay, Sonoma County, CA $5.35. Toasty oak, butterscotch, and vanilla aromas. Fresh but rich, complex flavors with good structure and acidity. Clean, balanced, Mâcon-like character. (AWC/Nov. '86) ★★★1/2

Rutherford Hill 1981 Chardonnay, Jaeger Vineyards, Cellar Reserve, Napa Valley, CA $14. Ripe Chardonnay aromas and flavors modulated with oak. Chewy, bold, powerful style. (AWC/Nov. '86) ★★★1/2

Saintsbury 1984 Chardonnay, Carneros, CA $11. Pronounced, oaky-buttery nose. Moderately complex flavors, good structure, rich finish. (AWC/Nov. '86)

★★★1/2
Sequoia Grove 1983 Chardonnay, Estate Bottled, Napa Valley, CA $14. Shy fruit-and-vanilla nose. Toasty, rich fruit with excellent acid support. (AWC/Nov. '85) ★★★1/2

Sequoia Grove 1983 Chardonnay, Sonoma County, CA $12. Lean, citrusy, tight structure, medium weight; in the Macon style. (AWC/Nov. '85) ★★★1/2

Shafer Vineyards 1983 Chardonnay, Napa Valley, CA $12. Toasty, solid fruit. Rich mouth feel, some complexity. Not quite filled out yet. Needs more time. (AWC/Nov. '85) ★★★1/2

Silverado 1984 Chardonnay, Napa Valley, CA $11. Light nose of fruit and toast. Ripe, lively, clean fruit flavors, moderately long. Crisp acidity. Understated. (AWC/Nov. '86) ★★★1/2

Sonoma-Cutrer 1984 Chardonnay, Russian River Ranches, Russian River Valley, CA. $11.99. Rich, varietal fruit flavors with lots of body and structure; toasty, nutty, powerful, with good aging potential. Meursault-like. (AWC/Nov. '86) ★★★1/2

Tualatin 1983 Chardonnay, Estate Bottled, OR $10. Lush fruit and French oak aroma and flavor. Very crisp, firm, complex. (JPN/Mar. '86) ★★★1/2

Wente Bros. 1984 Chardonnay, Reserve, Arroyo Seco, CA $8.95. Floral and spicy aromas of ginger, lemon, orange blossom, honeysuckle. Lively fruit flavors have good acid structure and a clean finish. (AWC/Nov. '86) ★★★1/2

White Oak 1984 Chardonnay, Sonoma County, CA $10. Tangy, lemony, peppery nose with oaky overtones. Clean, refined flavors. Tight structure. Crisp, oak-edged finish. (AWC/Nov. '86) ★★★1/2

ZD 1984 Chardonnay, CA $15. Complex, spicy aromas of vanilla, cinnamon, coconut, toasty oak. Big, lush, ripe-fruit style with length and power in the finish. (AWC/Nov. '86) ★★★1/2

Ste. Chapelle 1984 Chardonnay, 10th Anniversary Bottling, Symms Family Vineyard, ID $10. Reserved fruit aroma. Much more subdued than Ste. Chapelle's typically opulent Chardonnays, but classy and well composed. (JPN/Jan. '87) ★★★1/4

Iron Horse 1984 Chardonnay, Green Valley, Sonoma County, CA $12. Firm, lean, but with a layer of richness. Youthful, citric flavors, with oak complexity. (JDM/May '86) ★★★ (★★★★)

Bridgehampton 1984 Chardonnay, The Hamptons—Long Island, NY $8.99. Shy, refined nose. Lemony flavors with prominent, smoky-toasty and olive overtones. (RF/May '86) ★★★ (★★★1/2)

Ch. Potelle 1983 Chardonnay, Napa Valley, CA $13. Very complex. Entirely barrel-fermented. Firm, crisp. (JDM/Jan. '86) ★★★ (★★★1/2)

Heron Hill 1984 Chardonnay, Finger Lakes, NY $8.99. Firm, lean fruit. Tightly structured. Finesse; with a citrusy bite still to smooth out in the finish. Chablis style. (RF/May '86) ★★★ (★★★1/2)

Ingleside Plantation 1984 Chardonnay, VA $5.85. Aromatic, dark, varietal fruit overlayed with vanilla and wood. Silky, medium bodied, elegant. A prick of alcoholic heat. (RF/May '86) ★★★ (★★★1/2)

Newton 1983 Chardonnay, Turquon, Napa Valley, CA $14. Lean and crisp. Barrel-fermented, aged in heavily toasted, French oak. Intriguing, butterscotch quality. (JDM/May '86) ★★★ (★★★1/2)

Santa Cruz Mountain 1984 Chardonnay, Santa Cruz Mountains, CA $9.50. Barrel fermentation and oak aging contribute notes of butterscotch, fresh-roast coffee. (JDM/May '86) ★★★ (★★★1/2)

Acacia 1984 Chardonnay, Marina Estate Vineyard, Napa Valley—

Carneros, CA $18. Lush, tropical fruit mixed with toastiness. Good acidity, depth. Long, clean finish. (AWC/Nov. '85) ★★★

Adelsheim 1984 Chardonnay, Yamhill County, OR $10. Sweet, French oak aroma. Crisp, good melding of fruit and oak. (JPN/Mar. '86) ★★★

Bacigalupi (Belvedere Winery) 1983 Chardonnay, Sonoma County, CA $12. Rich bouquet matches generous, mature fruit and new oak flavors. Buttery. Substantial. (AWC/Nov. '85) ★★★

Bargetto 1984 Chardonnay, Cypress, CA $6. Much more taste and complexity than the price suggests. Attractive, vanilla quality in both bouquet and flavor. Citrusy. Fairly long finish. (JDM/Jan. '86) ★★★

Beaulieu (BV) 1984 Chardonnay, Los Carneros, Napa Valley, CA $13. Rich fruit aroma. Lots of austere, spicy fruit in the mouth. Toasty, oaky finish. Hefty but not overpowering. (JPN/Jan. '87) ★★★

Burgess 1984 Chardonnay, Vintage Reserve, Napa Valley, CA. $12. Tight structure. Ripe-fruit flavors. Medium body. (AWC/Nov. '86) ★★★

Calera 1984 Chardonnay, Santa Barbara County, CA $11.25. Buttery, caramel aromas of a mature wine. Generous fruit with significant oak. (AWC/Nov. '86) ★★★

Cameron 1984 Chardonnay, Willamette Valley, OR $8. Nice, pure fruit aroma. Spicy, French-oak flavor is a nice foil for the fruit. Perfectly balanced, some complexity. (JPN/May '86) ★★★

Cartlidge & Browne 1983 Chardonnay, Napa Valley, CA $11.50. Middleweight. Everything nicely proportioned and balanced. (AWC/Nov. '85) ★★★

Catoctin 1983 Chardonnay, Oak Fermented, MD $8.95. Restrained, Mâcon style. Lively fruit, toasty oak. (AWC/Nov. '85) ★★★

Ch. Potelle 1984 Chardonnay, Napa Valley, CA $11.75. Subdued nose. Tart and tangy fruit with significant acidity. Subtle, toasty. Somewhat short finish. (AWC/Nov. '86) ★★★

Corbett Canyon 1984 Chardonnay, Central Coast, CA $6. Light, varietal aroma. Clean, medium-bodied fruit flavors. Well made and satisfying. (AWC/Nov. '86) ★★★

Creston Manor 1984 Chardonnay, Edna Valley, CA $12. Ripe-fruit nose with piney accents. Lots of fruit on the palate with good acidity and medium complexity. (AWC/Nov. '86) ★★★

David S. Stare (Dry Creek Vineyard) 1983 Chardonnay, Dry Creek Valley, CA $13. Fruit overlaid with oaky vanilla. Richly flavored, firmly structured, very long finish. (S&PW/Jan. '86) ★★★

De Loach 1984 Chardonnay, Russian River, Sonoma County, CA $13.50. Perfumy, tropical fruit and vanilla aromas. Fruity. Full-bodied. Sweet oaky finish. (JPN/Jan. '87) ★★★

Dry Creek 1984 Chardonnay, Sonoma County, CA $10. Intense, complex aromas of vanilla, lemon, licorice. Rich style with lots of acidity, supple character. Warm finish. (AWC/Nov. '86) ★★★

Estancia 1985 Chardonnay, Alexander Valley, CA $6. Intensely fruity and floral bouquet. Straightforward, light-bodied fruit flavors have crisp acidity. (AWC/Nov. '86) ★★★

Estate William Baccala 1983 Chardonnay, Mendocino County, CA $11.50. Medium weight. Good complement of fruit, oak, acidity. (AWC/Nov. '85) ★★★

Felton-Empire 1984 Chardonnay, Tepusquet Vineyards, Santa Barbara County, CA $11. Flowery, rich, and sappy. Good acidity for development. (AWC/Nov. '85) ★★★

Felton-Empire 1985 Chardonnay, Tepusquet Vineyards, Santa Barbara

County, CA **$11.** Vanilla and butter nose. Expansive fruit in the mouth, with a full, viscous body. (AWC/Nov. '86) ★★★

Flora Springs 1985 Chardonnay, Napa Valley, CA $14. Citrusy, licorice nose is followed by clean, crisp flavors. Straightforward, well-knit style. (AWC/Nov. '86) ★★★

Franciscan 1982 Chardonnay, Estate Bottled, Napa Valley, CA $9.50. Burst of fruit up front, with toasty oak in balance. Fleshy, soft. (AWC/Nov. '85) ★★★

Grgich Hills 1984 Chardonnay, Napa Valley, CA $27.50. Pine, spice, and vanilla aromas. Fruit, oak, and acidity are well-balanced. Tight structure. (AWC/Nov. '86) ★★★

Groth 1983 Chardonnay, Napa Valley, CA $13. Stylish, light, vanilla nose. Soft fruit and spice. (AWC/Nov. '85) ★★★

Hogue 1984 Chardonnay, Yakima Valley, WA $9. Plenty of fruit but still lean, food oriented. Some melon in the nose and mouth. Crisp, clean finish. Hogue's best Chardonnay to date. Good value. (JPN/Jan. '87) ★★★

Inglenook 1984 Chardonnay, Reserve, Napa Valley, CA $13.50. Attractive, spicy nose. Medium-to-light intensity and finish. Very tart. (AWC/Nov. '86) ★★★

Ivan Tamas 1985 Chardonnay, Central Coast, CA $5.99. Subdued, ripe-fruit aromas with a touch of oak. Fruity flavors of medium intensity. Clean finish. (AWC/Nov. '86) ★★★

J. Lohr 1983 Chardonnay, Greenfield Vineyards, Monterey County, CA $9. Pineapple nose. Clean, moderately intense fruit. (AWC/Nov. '85) ★★★

Joe Swan 1982 Chardonnay, Sonoma Valley, CA $18. Golden color. Expansive aroma of fruit and oak. Full bodied and richly flavored. Very long finish. Fine character and large proportions; not for the timid. (S&PW/Mar. '86) ★★★

Kenwood 1984 Chardonnay, Yulupa Vineyard, Sonoma Valley, CA $12. Pineapple and melon nose with a touch of toast. Ripe, juicy flavors have medium body, a long finish. (AWC/Nov. '86) ★★★

Lambert Bridge 1983 Chardonnay, Estate Bottled, Sonoma County, CA $10. Lemony fruit. Nice oak finish. Some complexity. (AWC/Nov. '85) ★★★

Lambert Bridge 1984 Chardonnay, Sonoma County, CA $10. Light nose with fruity and floral overtones. Good varietal flavors with some complexity. Stylish. (AWC/Nov. '86) ★★★

Landmark 1983 Chardonnay, Alexander Valley, CA $12. Ripe, tropical fruit, with a distinct grapefruit note. Medium body, rich fruit. (AWC/Nov. '85) ★★★

Llano Estacado 1984 Chardonnay, Leftwich-Slaughter Vineyards, Lubbock County, TX $10.50. Lemongrass, apple blossom, and pear aromas. Lively, youthful, tangy flavors. Clean, well-balanced, fresh. (AWC/Nov. '86) ★★★

Mark West 1982 Chardonnay, Estate Bottled, Russian River Valley, CA $10. Flowery fruit, some nuttiness. Crisp acidity and high alcohol. (AWC/Nov. '85) ★★★

McDowell Valley 1983 Chardonnay, Estate Bottled, McDowell Valley, CA $12.99. Dark color shows a touch of oxidation. Fruit is soft and melony, with a buttery-oaky finish. Drink now. (AWC/Nov. '85) ★★★

McDowell Valley 1984 Chardonnay, Estate Bottled, McDowell Valley, CA $10.85. Big, complex bouquet of cinnamon, pear, and citrus. Rich, full flavors have lowish acidity, a slightly rough finish. (AWC/Nov. '86) ★★★

Morgan 1984 Chardonnay, Monterey County, CA $14. Rich, dense, complex nose. Lush, ripe fruit flavors have a twinge of high acidity in the finish. (AWC/ Nov. '86) ★★★

Newton 1984 Chardonnay, Napa Valley, CA $14. Clean, varietal fruit with some complexity in a tightly structured wine. Needs time. (AWC/Nov. '86) ★★★

Quail Run 1983 Chardonnay, Yakima Valley, WA $7.50. Light, lemony fruit with aggressive acidity. Clean. (AWC/ Nov. '85) ★★★

Raymond 1983 Chardonnay, Napa Valley, CA $12. Toasty, aromatic, sweet oak. Big fruit dominated by oak. Fat finish. (AWC/Nov. '85) ★★★

River Oaks 1984 Chardonnay, Sonoma County, CA $5.95. Flowery, refreshing, citrus character. Lean, youthful. (AWC/Nov. '85) ★★★

Round Hill 1984 Chardonnay, North Coast, CA $6. Subtle, toasty complexity. (JDM/May '86) ★★★

Round Hill 1985 Chardonnay, House, CA $5. Fresh, lively fruit aromas and clean varietal flavors. Crisp acidity. Well balanced. (AWC/Nov. '86) ★★★

Schug 1982 Chardonnay, Napa Valley, CA $14.69. Big nose, full of fruit and oak. Flavorful, well balanced, with a lot of character. Some firmness and grip at the end. (S&PW/Mar. '86) ★★★

Silverado 1983 Chardonnay, Napa Valley, CA $11. Fresh, floral nose. Spritz works well with bright, spicy fruit. (AWC/ Nov. '85) ★★★

Simi 1982 Chardonnay, Sonoma County, CA $11.50. Shy, camphor-fruit nose. Lots of oak showing. (AWC/Nov. '85) ★★★

Simi 1983 Chardonnay, Mendocino-Sonoma, CA $12. Ripe-fruit nose. Crisp acidity and solid oak structure. Big yet controlled style with a long, warm finish and good balance. (AWC/Nov. '86) ★★★

Sonoma-Cutrer 1983 Chardonnay,

Les Pierres Vineyard, Sonoma Valley, CA $18. Pineapple and apple aroma, with a buttery note. Well balanced, complex, with a creamy texture. Quite long. (S&PW/ Mar. '86) ★★★

Sterling 1984 Chardonnay, Estate Bottled, Napa Valley, CA $14. Subdued nose. Light body. Clean and well-balanced style. (AWC/Nov. '86) ★★★

The Monterey Vineyard 1982 Chardonnay, CA $5.99. Slight sulfide funk adds complexity to delicate fruit. Creamy texture. Acidity keeps it fresh. (AWC/Nov. '85) ★★★

Ultravino 1983 Chardonnay, Napa Valley, CA $8. Clean, Chardonnay nose and flavors with good acidity and length. (AWC/Nov. '85) ★★★

Ventana 1985 Chardonnay, Gold Stripe Selection, Monterey, CA $8. Expansive, floral and citrus nose with hints of peach. Rich, soft flavors in the mouth, with lowish acidity. (AWC/Nov. '86) ★★★

Wagner 1984 Chardonnay, Estate Bottled, Finger Lakes, NY $10.80. Aggressive, ripe-fruit aromas of mango, papaya, coconut, vanilla. Rich, buttery flavors with enough acidity for a clean finish. (AWC/ Nov. '86) ★★★

Wente Bros. 1982 Chardonnay, CA $5.50. Restrained, clean, citrusy fruit. Oak is present but acidity predominates. (AWC/ Nov. '85) ★★★

Wm. Wheeler 1984 Chardonnay, Sonoma County, CA $11. Spice and citrus nose. Nicely balanced fruit flavors of medium intensity. (AWC/Nov. '86) ★★★

ZD 1983 Chardonnay, CA $14. Powerful bouquet. Ripe flavors of melon, banana, vanilla. A blockbuster that could kill a Soave drinker. Heavily wooded. (AWC/Nov. '85) ★★★

Cameron 1984 Chardonnay, Reserve, Willamette Valley, OR $12. Butter, barrel-toast, ripe apples, butterscotch aroma. French-oak masks fruit flavor. Smooth, lingering, oaky finish. (JPN/May '86) ★★1/2 (★★★)

Amity 1983 Chardonnay, OR $13. Slight off-odor followed by vanilla scent. Light body. Reminiscent of Chablis. Crisp, restrained, delicate. (JPN/May '86) ★★1/2

Liberty School 1985 Chardonnay, Lot 7, CA $6. Very crisp and lively with fresh citrus notes. Some oak complexity and vanilla. (JDM/May '86) ★★1/2

Peter F. Adams 1983 Chardonnay, Yamhill County, OR $11. Rich, herbal, sagey, toasty aroma. Full, viscous, buttery, with plenty of acid to hold it together. (JPN/Jan. '87) ★★1/2

Rodney Strong 1982 Chardonnay, Chalk Hill Vineyard, Sonoma County, CA $10. Pineapple aroma with a nice touch of oak. Round, lush fruit flavors. Nicely balanced. A bargain. (S&PW/May '86) ★★1/2

Ultravino 1984 Chardonnay, Napa Valley, CA $9. Very approachable, citrus style, charmingly highlighted by vanilla and spice. (JDM/May '86) ★★1/2

Valley View 1984 Chardonnay, OR $8. Closed, vaguely apple nose. Straightforward, mineral, apple taste. Simple, understated, appealing; lemony finish. (JPN/May '86) ★★1/2

Veritas 1984 Chardonnay, OR $8. Quite oaky. Good body and flavor. Plenty of fruit. (JPN/Mar. '86) ★★1/2

Yamhill Valley 1983-84 Chardonnay, OR $11. French oak, juniper aromas. Light, crisp; good food wine. (JPN/May '86) ★★1/2

Beaulieu (BV) 1984 Pinot Chardonnay, Beaufort, Estate Bottled, Napa Valley, CA $9. Sweet vanilla aroma. Crisp and fruity with some peach and apple flavors. (JPN/Jan. '87) ★★1/4

Alexander Valley 1984 Chardonnay, 10th Anniversary Release, Al-

exander Valley, CA $10.50. Light oak adds complexity to an aroma of butterscotch and apples. Some firmness. Well balanced. Flavorful. Has elegance and length. (S&PW/ May '86) ★★

Ch. Julien 1983 Chardonnay, Private Reserve, Cobblestone Vineyard, Monterey County, CA $17. Candied-fruit style. Soft, well balanced. (AWC/Nov. '85) ★★

Ch. Montelena 1984 Chardonnay, Napa Valley, CA $18. Subdued fruit and oak on the nose. Medium-bodied flavors with a clean finish. (AWC/Nov. '86) ★★

Ch. St. Jean 1984 Chardonnay, Robert Young Vineyards, Alexander Valley, CA $18. Closed-in nose. Light, clean, fruity flavors. Fresh and lively. (AWC/ Nov. '86) ★★

Ch. St. Jean 1984 Chardonnay, Sonoma County, CA $11. Subdued, floral nose. Clean fruit with some oak. Light body. (AWC/Nov. '86) ★★

Corbett Canyon 1984 Chardonnay, Winemaker's Reserve, Edna Valley, CA $10. Subdued, butterscotch nose. Good varietal fruit flavors with a soft finish. (AWC/Nov. '86) ★★

Davis Bynum 1984 Chardonnay, Reserve Bottling, Sonoma County, CA $12.50. Subdued grapefruit and green apple nose. Interesting if not complex flavors. (AWC/Nov. '86) ★★

Davis Bynum 1984 Chardonnay, Sonoma County, CA $12.50. Grapefruit and melon, with crisp acidity. Lean, clean, green. (AWC/Nov. '85) ★★

De Moor 1984 Chardonnay, Napa Valley, CA $10. Caramel and butter aromas. Lush, intense flavors and imposing style, but short and hot in the finish. (AWC/ Nov. '86) ★★

Eberle 1982 Chardonnay, Paso Robles, CA $12. Rich aroma of olives and herbs. Toasty barrel flavors. Lemony finish.

(JPN/Jan. '87) ★★

Fetzer 1984 Chardonnay, Barrel Select, CA $8.50. Pineapple nose. Simple, prominent fruit. (AWC/Nov. '85) ★★

Forgeron 1983 Chardonnay, OR $10.50. Earthy aroma. Medium bodied. Fairly rich fruit taste. Well balanced. Sweetish, toasty finish. (JPN/May '86) ★★

Groth 1984 Chardonnay, Napa Valley, CA. $13. Ripe fruit and spicy oak nose. Pleasant, straightforward fruit flavors. (AWC/Nov. '86) ★★

Jekel 1982 Chardonnay, Home Vineyard, Arroyo Seco, CA $10. Big, rich, with lots of vanilla. Intense fruit, acidity, viscosity. A heavy hitter. (AWC/Nov. '85) ★★

Joseph Phelps 1983 Chardonnay, Napa Valley, CA $12.75. Well-structured wine with lemon, peach, and licorice aromas. Simple, straightforward, attractive. (AWC/Nov. '86) ★★

Kendall-Jackson 1983 Chardonnay, Royale, California $11. Intense, spicy, gingery nose and rich, viscous fruit in the mouth. Somewhat hot finish. (AWC/Nov. '86) ★★

La Reina 1984 Chardonnay, Monterey, CA $10. Ripe, melony, fleshy fruit aromas. Medium-bodied with lowish acid and some sweetness in the finish. (AWC/Nov. '86) ★★

M. G. Vallejo 1985 Chardonnay, CA $4.50. Fruity, almost Riesling-like, honeyed nose. Clean, simple flavors have medium intensity. (AWC/Nov. '86) ★★

Mark West 1983 Chardonnay, Estate Bottled, Russian River Valley, CA $10. Sweet, ripe-fruit and vanilla nose. Creamy, ripe flavors with a slightly hot finish. A little awkward at this stage. (AWC/Nov. '86) ★★

Mirassou 1984 Chardonnay, Harvest Reserve, Monterey County, CA $12. Fruity, varietal nose. Somewhat sweet, appley fruit flavors have good acidity. Easy drinking. (AWC/Nov. '86) ★★

Newton 1983 Chardonnay, Napa Valley, CA $14. Good fruit-acid balance. Citrusy. Clean, lemony finish. (AWC/Nov. '85) ★★

Rex Hill 1984 Chardonnay, Willamette Valley, OR $9. Sweet, oaky aroma. Medium body with full, oak-and-cloves taste. A bit short on fruit in the middle. (JPN/Jan. '87) ★★

Robert Keenan 1984 Chardonnay, Estate, Napa Valley, CA $12.50. Green apple and lemon grass aromas. Lively, tangy fruit flavors leave a balanced, clean finish. (AWC/Nov. '86) ★★

Rombauer 1984 Chardonnay, Napa Valley, CA $14.50. Subdued nose. Interesting, ripe fruit on the palate. (AWC/Nov. '86) ★★

Rutherford Vintners 1984 Chardonnay, Napa Valley, CA $12. Rieslinglike, apricot and peach aromas. Simple fruit flavors with a slightly sweet, soft finish. (AWC/Nov. '86) ★★

Santa Barbara 1985 Chardonnay, Santa Ynez Valley, CA $8.50. Rich, oaky bouquet with tropical fruit aromas. Noticeable oak and acid on the palate. Warm finish. Age may smooth the rough edges. (AWC/Nov. '86) ★★

Stag's Leap Wine Cellars 1983 Chardonnay, Napa Valley, CA $13.50. Green apple nose. Fresh, clean, tasty. (AWC/Nov. '85) ★★

Tepusquet 1985 Chardonnay, Reserve, Santa Maria Valley, CA $8.50. Smoky, toasty aroma shows little fruit. Smooth and viscous. Rich, ripe fruit flavor comes out after a while in the glass. Hot finish. Good value. (JPN/Jan. '87) ★★

Tepusquet 1985 Chardonnay, Santa Maria Valley, CA $6. Ripe melon, some vanilla, and a dirty note in the nose. Fruity, smooth but fairly lively flavors. Background oak. Excellent value. (JPN/Jan. '87) ★★

The Merry Vintners 1984 Chardonnay, Sonoma County, CA $13.75. Delicate, subdued nose. Tightly wrought structure with crisp acidity. Opens up in the glass. Good potential for development with age. (AWC/Nov. '86) ★★

Woodward Canyon 1984 Chardonnay, WA $13.50. Viscous. Floral nose, appley flavor with buttery quality. Pleasant, barrel toast; alcoholic finish. Pleasant by itself; not as good with food. (JPN/May '86) ★★

Zaca Mesa 1984 Chardonnay, Santa Barbara County, CA $9.75. Delicate, citrus and vanilla aromas. Ripe fruit flavors of medium weight. Simple and clean. (AWC/Nov. '86) ★★

Pat Paulsen 1983 Chardonnay, Sonoma County, CA $11. Appley aroma with an overlay of oak. Round, fruity, balanced. (S&PW/May '86) ★3/4

Raymond 1983 Chardonnay, Private Reserve, Napa Valley, CA $18-19. Oak up front gives way to a Chardonnay fruit nose. Well balanced. Dry. Good acidity, almost crisp. Full bodied. A touch of alcohol mars the finish. (S&PW/May '86) ★3/4

Bethel Heights 1984 Chardonnay, Willamette Valley, OR $10. Some sulfur in nose. Viscous, oaky in mouth. Smooth. One-dimensional. (JPN/May '86) ★1/2

Northwest Daily 1984 Chardonnay, Yakima Valley First Edition, WA $5. Nice fruit, slight oak aroma. Shy fruit in mouth. Well balanced; crisp. Good value. (JPN/May '86) ★1/2

F. W. Langguth 1983 Chardonnay, WA $7. Ripe fruit aroma and flavor. Not enough acid. (JPN/May '86) ★

Grgich Hills 1983 Chardonnay, Napa Valley, CA $17.50. Resinous, oaky aroma. Big, fat, smooth, oaky. Finishes hot. (JPN/Jan. '87) ★

Adelaida 1983 Chardonnay, Paso

Robles, CA **$9.75.** Light, spritzy, with a rope-like woodiness. Needs more fruit. (AWC/ Nov. '85)

Adelaida 1984 Chardonnay, Paso Robles, CA $8.75. (AWC/Nov. '86)

Alexander Valley 1983 Chardonnay, Estate Bottled, Alexander Valley, CA $10. (AWC/Nov. '85)

Alexander Valley 1984 Chardonnay, Estate Bottled, Alexander Valley, CA $10.50. Neutral, light, somewhat sweet. (AWC/Nov. '86)

Allegro 1983 Chardonnay, York County, PA $9.90. (AWC/Nov. '86)

Allegro 1984 Chardonnay, York County, PA $9.90. (AWC/Nov. '86)

Almaden 1983 Chardonnay, San Benito County, CA $4.99. (AWC/Nov. '85)

Almaden (nonvintage) Chardonnay, CA $6.99/liter. (AWC/Nov. '85)

Amity 1982 Chardonnay, Winemaker's Reserve, OR $15. (AWC/Nov. '86)

Amity 1983 Chardonnay, Estate Bottled, Willamette Valley, OR $12. (AWC/Nov. '86)

Angelo Papagni 1982 Chardonnay, Estate Bottled, Bonita Vineyard, Madera, CA $7.20. Weak, fat fruit. Low acid. High alcohol. (AWC/Nov. '85)

Angelo Papagni 1983 Chardonnay, Bonita Vineyard, Madera, CA $7.20. (AWC/Nov. '86)

Arbor Crest 1983 Chardonnay, Sagemoor Vineyards, Columbia Valley, WA $15. Subdued nose opens with airing. A little too subtle. (AWC/Nov. '86)

Arbor Crest 1983 Chardonnay, Sagemoor Vineyards, WA $9.25. (AWC/Nov. '85)

Arbor Crest 1984 Chardonnay, Columbia Valley, WA $9.75. (AWC/Nov. '86)

August Sebastiani 1984 Chardonnay, Sonoma Valley, CA $7. (AWC/

Nov. '85)

Bandiera 1984 Chardonnay, Sonoma County, CA $6. Riesling-like nose and grapey flavors. (AWC/Nov. '86)

Bargetto 1983 Chardonnay, Tepusquet Vineyard, Santa Maria Valley, CA $9.50. Overripe nose with some oxidation. Strong, ripe fruit flavors show excessive oak. (AWC/Nov. '86)

Bedell 1985 Chardonnay, Long Island, NY $8.99. (AWC/Nov. '86)

Belvedere 1984 Chardonnay, Winery Lake Vineyards, Los Carneros, CA $12. (AWC/Nov. '86)

Beringer 1983 Chardonnay, Barrel Fermented, Gamble Vineyard, Napa Valley, CA $13.50. Something awry in the nose and flavor. (AWC/Nov. '85)

Beringer 1983 Chardonnay, Estate Bottled, Napa Valley, CA $14.50. Tastes more like Riesling than Chardonnay, with Botrytised, apricot flavors. Overripe and fading. (AWC/Nov. '86)

Beringer 1983 Chardonnay, Gamble Vineyard, Napa Valley, CA $12. (AWC/Nov. '86)

Beringer 1983 Chardonnay, Private Reserve, Napa Valley, CA $15.50. (AWC/Nov. '85)

Beringer 1984 Chardonnay, Napa Valley, CA $10. (AWC/Nov. '86)

Black Mountain 1984 Chardonnay, Gravel Bar, Alexander Valley, CA $18. (AWC/Nov. '86)

Bridgehampton 1984 Chardonnay, Long Island, NY $8.99. (AWC/Nov. '86)

Bridgehampton 1985 Chardonnay, Estate Reserve, The Hamptons—Long Island, NY $10.99. Tart, tight flavors with high acidity. Simple and short. (AWC/Nov. '86)

Buena Vista 1982 Chardonnay, Private Reserve, Carneros—Sonoma Valley, CA $16.50. Ripe, slightly candied bouquet. Somewhat flat finish. (AWC/ Nov. '86)

Buena Vista 1984 Chardonnay, Sonoma Valley—Carneros, CA $10.75. Floral, fruity nose. Ripe and fleshy. Short, hot finish. (AWC/Nov. '86)

Buena Vista 1984 Chardonnay, Vineyard Selection, Jeannette's Vineyard, Carneros—Sonoma Valley, CA $12.50. Sweet, overripe nose. Better flavors. (AWC/Nov. '86)

Burgess 1983 Chardonnay, Vintage Reserve, Napa Valley, CA $11.95. (AWC/Nov. '85)

Byrd 1984 Chardonnay, Estate Bottled, Catoctin, MD $8.75. (AWC/ Nov. '86)

Cain 1984 Chardonnay, Napa Valley, CA $10. Dry, nutty, green apple aromas. Citrusy flavors have a bitter note. Lean, tight structure. Chablis style. (AWC/Nov. '86)

Callaway 1984 Chardonnay, Temecula, CA $9. (AWC/Nov. '86)

Carneros Creek 1983 Chardonnay, Napa Valley, CA $10. Faint, lean, lemony fruit. One-dimensional. (AWC/Nov. '85)

Catoctin 1983 Chardonnay, MD $8.95. (AWC/Nov. '85)

Catoctin 1984 Chardonnay, MD $8.95. Weak, Sauvignon-type aroma. Good acid structure. Somewhat lacking in fruit. (AWC/Nov. '86)

Caves Laurent Perrier 1982 Chardonnay, Blanc de Blancs, CA $8.69. (AWC/Nov. '85)

Ch. Benoit 1983 Chardonnay, OR $9.95. Strange, resinous nose. Fruit is attractive. (AWC/Nov. '85)

Ch. Bouchaine 1983 Chardonnay, Los Carneros, Napa Valley, CA $14.50. (AWC/Nov. '85)

Ch. Bouchaine 1983 Chardonnay, Napa Valley, CA $12.50. (AWC/Nov. '85)

Ch. Diana 1985 Chardonnay, Dawn Manning Selection, Monterey, CA $5.50. (AWC/Nov. '86)

Ch. Georges 1985 Chardonnay, NY $6. Peculiar, perfumed note in the nose. Thin, short flavors. (AWC/Nov. '86)

Ch. Grand Traverse 1982 Chardonnay, MI $8.99. (AWC/Nov. '85)

Ch. Grand Traverse 1983 Chardonnay, MI $10.99. (AWC/Nov. '86)

Ch. Julien 1983 Chardonnay, Paraiso Springs Vineyard, Monterey County, CA $15. (AWC/Nov. '86)

Ch. Lagniappe 1983 Chardonnay, OH $12. (AWC/Nov.'86)

Ch. Morrisette 1984 Chardonnay, VA $9. (AWC/Nov. '85)

Ch. Potelle 1985 Chardonnay, CA $5.50. (AWC/Nov. '86)

Ch. Ste. Michelle 1983 Chardonnay, Ch. Reserve, River Ridge Vineyards, WA $19.50. (AWC/Nov. '86)

Ch. Ste. Michelle 1982 Chardonnay, WA $7.95. Light, citric. Not much varietal interest. (AWC/Nov. '85)

Ch. Ste. Michelle 1983 Chardonnay, WA $8.95. (AWC/Nov. '86)

Chalone 1983 Chardonnay, CA $22. (AWC/Nov. '85)

Chappellet Winery 1983 Chardonnay, Napa Valley, CA $12.50. (AWC/Nov. '85)

Charles Krug 1983 Chardonnay, Napa Valley, CA $10. (AWC/Nov. '85)

Charles Lefranc 1983 Chardonnay, San Benito County, CA $7.99. (AWC/Nov. '85)

Charles Lefranc 1984 Chardonnay, Monterey County, CA $8.49. (AWC/Nov. '86)

Charles Lefranc 1984 Chardonnay, Sage Ranch, San Benito County, CA $9.49. (AWC/Nov. '86)

Charles Lefranc 1984 Chardonnay, Tepusquet Vineyards, Santa Barbara

County, CA $10.59. (AWC/Nov. '86)

Chase Creek 1985 Chardonnay, Napa Valley, CA $7. (AWC/Nov. '86)

Christian Brothers 1984 Chardonnay, Napa Valley, CA $7.99. (AWC/Nov. '86)

Christophe 1984 Chardonnay, CA $4.99. (AWC/Nov. '85)

Cilurzo 1983 Chardonnay, Temecula, CA $9.50. (AWC/Nov. '86)

Clos du Bois 1985 Chardonnay, Barrel Fermented, Alexander Valley, CA $9. (AWC/Nov. '86)

Clos du Val 1983 Chardonnay, CA $11.50. (AWC/Nov. '85)

Clos du Val 1984 Chardonnay, CA $11.50. Subdued bouquet of toast, lemons, and spice. Lean, tight structure. Somewhat simple and thin. (AWC/Nov. '86)

Columbia 1983 Chardonnay, Barrel Fermented, Wyckoff Vineyards, Yakima Valley, WA $16. (AWC/Nov. '85)

Columbia 1983 Chardonnay, Wyckoff Vineyards, Yakima Valley, WA $9. (AWC/Nov. '85)

Commonwealth Winery 1984 Chardonnay, Dana Vineyard, MA $7.95. (AWC/Nov. '85)

Commonwealth Winery (nonvintage) Chardonnay, American (winery in MA) $7.95. (AWC/Nov. '85)

Commonwealth Winery (nonvintage) Chardonnay, Quail Hill Vineyard, American (winery in MA) $7.95. (AWC/Nov. '85)

Conn Creek 1982 Chardonnay, Napa Valley, CA $14. (AWC/Nov. '86)

Cuvaison 1983 Chardonnay, Napa Valley, CA $10.95. Simple. Monodimensional. (AWC/Nov. '86)

David Bruce 1984 Chardonnay, CA $8.20. (AWC/Nov. '86)

David S. Stare (Dry Creek Vineyard) 1982 Chardonnay, Estate Bottled, Dry Creek Valley, CA $15.

(AWC/Nov. '85)

De Loach 1983 Chardonnay, Russian River Valley, CA $12.50. (AWC/Nov. '85)

Debevc 1982 Chardonnay, OH $6.95. (AWC/Nov. '85)

Delicato 1984 Chardonnay, CA $7. (AWC/Nov. '85)

Delicato 1984 Chardonnay, Golden Anniversary, Napa Valley, CA $12. (AWC/Nov. '86)

Domain San Martin 1985 Chardonnay, Central Coast, CA $7.25. Peach aroma. Medium-light flavor and body. Short finish. Simple. (AWC/Nov. '86)

Domaine Laurier 1983 Chardonnay, Sonoma Valley, CA $13. (AWC/Nov. '85)

Domaine St. George 1984 Chardonnay, Sonoma County, CA $4.99. (AWC/Nov. '85)

Domaine St. George 1985 Chardonnay, Sonoma County, CA $5.99. (AWC/Nov. '86)

Dry Creek 1983 Chardonnay, Sonoma County, CA $10. (AWC/Nov. '85)

Elk Cove 1983 Chardonnay, Willamette Valley, OR $12. (AWC/Nov. '86)

Estate William Baccala 1984 Chardonnay, Mendocino, CA $8.50. (AWC/Nov. '86)

Estrella River 1983 Chardonnay, Estate Bottled, Paso Robles, CA $9. (AWC/Nov. '85)

Estrella River 1984 Chardonnay, Estate Bottled, Paso Robles, CA $9. (AWC/Nov. '86)

Fairmont 1983 Chardonnay, Private Selection, Napa Valley, CA $10.50. Tropical fruit flavors. (AWC/Nov. '85)

Farview Farm 1985 Chardonnay, Barrel Fermented, San Luis Obispo County, CA $10. (AWC/Nov. '86)

Fetzer 1985 Chardonnay, Sundial,

Mendocino County, CA $6.50. Floral, fruity aromas. Full fruit flavors in a tight structure. Somewhat monodimensional. (AWC/Nov. '86)

Finger Lakes 1985 Chardonnay, Finger Lakes, NY $8.99. (AWC/Nov. '86)

Firelands 1985 Chardonnay, Lake Erie, OH $5.95. (AWC/Nov. '86)

Fisher 1983 Chardonnay, Sonoma County, CA $14. (AWC/Nov. '85)

Flora Springs 1983 Chardonnay, Barrel Fermented, Napa Valley, CA $18. Strong, wild fruit flavors. (AWC/Nov. '85)

Flora Springs 1983 Chardonnay, Napa Valley, CA $13. (AWC/Nov. '85)

Franciscan 1984 Chardonnay, Oakville Estate, Napa Valley, CA $8.50. (AWC/Nov. '86)

Franciscan 1982 Chardonnay, Estate Bottled, Reserve, Oakville Vineyard, Napa Valley, CA $12. (AWC/Nov. '85)

Freemark Abbey 1983 Chardonnay, Napa Valley, CA $14. (AWC/Nov. '86)

Frick 1984 Chardonnay, Santa Maria Valley, CA $12. (AWC/Nov. '85)

Gainey 1982 Chardonnay, CA $10. Fruit fades fast, leaving too much acid. (AWC/Nov. '85)

Giumarra 1985 Chardonnay, Proprietor's Reserve, Central Coast, CA $6.50. (AWC/Nov. '86)

Glen Ellen 1984 Chardonnay, Sonoma Valley, CA $7.99. Simple, clean varietal aromas and flavors. Slightly harsh finish. Some bitterness. (AWC/Nov. '86)

Glenora 1983 Chardonnay, Finger Lakes, NY $7.99. (AWC/Nov. '85)

Glenora 1984 Chardonnay, Finger Lakes, NY $7.99. (AWC/Nov. '86)

Grgich Hills 1979 Chardonnay, Napa Valley, CA $30. (AWC/Nov. '85)

Guenoc 1982 Chardonnay, CA

$9.15. Rich, nutty nose, but spritz, flabby fruit, and strong oak don't mesh. (AWC/Nov. '85)

Guenoc 1982 Chardonnay, Lake County—Mendocino County, CA $9.15. Apricot aromas. Ripe, flabby flavors are short. (AWC/Nov. '86)

Guenoc 1983 Chardonnay, North Coast, CA $9.15. (AWC/Nov. '86)

Hargrave 1985 Chardonnay, Reserve, NY $11. Odd nose of wet wool or cardboard. Overripe, flabby flavors. (AWC/Nov. '86)

Haviland 1983 Chardonnay, Barrel Fermented, Columbia Valley, WA $12.95. (AWC/Nov. '86)

Haviland 1984 Chardonnay, Barrel Fermented, Columbia Valley, WA $12.95. (AWC/Nov. '86)

Haywood 1983 Chardonnay, Estate Bottled, Sonoma Valley, CA $11. (AWC/Nov. '85)

Haywood 1984 Chardonnay, Estate Bottled Reserve, Sonoma Valley, CA $12.50. (AWC/Nov. '86)

Haywood 1984 Chardonnay, Sonoma Valley, CA $9.50. (AWC/Nov. '86)

Henry Estate 1981 Chardonnay, Vintage Select, Umpqua Valley, OR $9.95. (AWC/Nov. '85)

Heron Hill 1985 Chardonnay, Nevers Reserve, Finger Lakes, NY $10.49. (AWC/Nov. '86)

Hogue 1985 Chardonnay, WA $9.95. (AWC/Nov. '86)

Hood River 1983 Chardonnay, OR $9.95. (AWC/Nov. '85)

Husch 1983 Chardonnay, Estate Bottled, Mendocino, CA $9.75. (AWC/Nov. '85)

Inglenook 1984 Chardonnay, Estate Bottled, Napa Valley, CA $9. (AWC/Nov. '86)

Innisfree 1985 Chardonnay, Napa Valley, CA $9. (AWC/Nov. '86)

Ivanhoe 1985 Chardonnay, TX **$7.99.** (AWC/Nov. '86)

J. Lohr 1984 Chardonnay, Greenfield Vineyards, Monterey County, CA **$9.** (AWC/Nov. '86)

J. Patrick Dore 1982 Chardonnay, Signature Selection, Napa Valley, CA **$6.95.** (AWC/Nov. '86)

J. Patrick Dore 1984 Chardonnay, Signature Selections, CA **$3.95.** (AWC/Nov. '86)

J. Patrick Dore 1984 Chardonnay, Signature Selections, Santa Maria Valley, CA **$5.49.** Light. More body than flavor. (AWC/Nov. '86)

J. Patrick Dore (nonvintage) Chardonnay, Signature Selections, Limited Reserve, CA **$5.95/1.5 liter.** (AWC/Nov. '85)

Jekel 1984 Chardonnay, Arroyo Seco, CA **$10.50.** (AWC/Nov. '86)

Jordan 1982 Chardonnay, Estate Bottled, Alexander Valley, CA **$16.** Nothing amiss, but not much intensity. (AWC/Nov. '85)

Joseph Phelps 1983 Chardonnay, Sangiacomo Vineyard, Carneros, CA **$14.** Nose is sweet, ripe, and hot. Ripe fruit flavors balanced somewhat uneasily by high acids and significant oak. High-strung. (AWC/Nov. '86)

JW Morris 1984 Chardonnay, Alexander Valley, CA **$7.** (AWC/Nov. '86)

Kendall-Jackson 1984 Chardonnay, Dennison Vineyard, Anderson Valley, Mendocino, CA **$12.** (AWC/Nov. '86)

Kendall-Jackson 1984 Chardonnay, Proprietor's Reserve, CA **$13.50.** Light, Chablis-style. Sharp up front, followed by full fruit. (AWC/Nov. '85)

Kendall-Jackson 1985 Chardonnay, Vintner's Reserve, CA **$9.50.** (AWC/Nov. '86)

Kenwood 1983 Chardonnay, Beltane Ranch, Sonoma Valley, CA **$14.** (AWC/Nov. '85)

Kiona 1984 Chardonnay, Estate Bottled, Yakima Valley, WA $8.95. (AWC/Nov. '86)

Kistler 1984 Chardonnay, Dutton Ranch, CA $15. (AWC/Nov. '86)

Knapp 1985 Chardonnay, Finger Lakes, NY $8.95. (AWC/Nov. '86)

Knudsen-Erath 1983 Chardonnay, Yamhill County, OR $7.95. Off odors of the nail polish variety. Tannic, acidic. Hollow. (AWC/Nov. '86)

La Crema Vinera 1984 Chardonnay, Reserve, CA $15. Off flavors. Oaky and acidic. (AWC/Nov. '86)

Landmark 1982 Chardonnay, Sonoma County, CA $9. (AWC/Nov. '85)

Landmark 1984 Chardonnay, Sonoma County, CA $9. Coconut and pineapple aromas. Thin flavors. Somewhat acidic despite slightly sweet finish. (AWC/Nov. '86)

Landmark 1985 Chardonnay, Cypress Lane, CA $6. (AWC/Nov. '86)

Latah Creek 1984 Chardonnay, WA $8.49. (AWC/Nov. '86)

Liberty Tavern 1984 Chardonnay, MD $8.95. (AWC/Nov. '86)

Llano Estacado 1985 Chardonnay, Slaughter-Leftwich Vineyards, Lubbock County, TX $10.50. (AWC/Nov. '86)

Llords & Elwood 1984 Chardonnay, The Rare, Napa Valley, CA $8. (AWC/Nov. '86)

Louis Facelli 1983 Chardonnay, WA (winery in ID) $9.99. (AWC/Nov. '85)

Louis J. Foppiano 1984 Chardonnay, Sonoma County, CA $5.85. Easy to drink: light, pleasant, lacking distinction or complexity. (AWC/Nov. '86)

Louis K. Mihaly 1983 Chardonnay, Special Reserve, Napa Valley, CA $10. (AWC/Nov. '86)

Louis M. Martini 1983 Chardonnay, Las Amigas Vineyard Selection, Los Carneros, CA $12. (AWC/Nov. '86)

M. Marion 1984 Chardonnay, CA $5.50. Faint nose. Clean, pleasant, simple. (AWC/Nov. '86)

Markham 1982 Chardonnay, Napa Valley, CA $11. Acetone nose. Overblown, late-harvest character. (AWC/Nov. '86)

Martin Brothers 1984 Chardonnay, Central Coast, CA $10. (AWC/Nov. '86)

Matanzas Creek 1984 Chardonnay, Sonoma County, CA $15. (AWC/Nov. '86)

Meier's 1985 Chardonnay, Isle St. George, OH $4.99. (AWC/Nov. '86)

Meredyth 1983 Chardonnay, VA $9.50. (AWC/Nov. '85)

Merry Vintners 1985 Chardonnay, Vintage Preview, Sonoma County, CA $9.75. (AWC/Nov. '86)

Michael's (Artisan Wines) 1983 Chardonnay, Napa Valley, CA $15. (AWC/Nov. '85)

Michtom 1983 Chardonnay, Vintner Grown, Alexander Valley, CA $6. (AWC/Nov. '85)

Michtom 1984 Chardonnay, Vintner Grown, Alexander Valley, CA $7. (AWC/Nov. '86)

Milano Winery 1984 Chardonnay, California Reserve, CA $6. Weak, flat fruit. (AWC/Nov. '85)

Mirassou 1983 Chardonnay, Harvest Reserve, Monterey County, CA $11. (AWC/Nov. '85)

Mirassou 1984 Chardonnay, Monterey County, CA $8. (AWC/Nov. '85)

Montali 1984 Chardonnay, Reserve, Santa Maria Valley, CA $9.50. (AWC/Nov. '86)

Montdomaine 1984 Chardonnay, Albemarle County, VA $7. (AWC/Nov. '86)

Subscribe now to

Monticello 1983 Chardonnay, Barrel Fermented, Napa Valley, CA $14.50. Unripe apple character. Weak fruit, high acidity. (AWC/Nov. '85)

Morgan 1983 Chardonnay, Monterey County, CA $12.50. Lacks fruit. (AWC/Nov. '85)

Mount Veeder 1984 Chardonnay, Napa County, CA $13.50. (AWC/Nov. '86)

Mountain View 1985 Chardonnay, Monterey County, CA $4.99. (AWC/Nov. '86)

Navarro 1983 Chardonnay, Mendocino, CA $8.85. Ripe fruit aroma; some apricots. Low acid with a bit of residual sweetness. Short finish. (AWC/Nov. '86)

Oak Knoll 1984 Chardonnay, OR $8. (AWC/Nov. '86)

Oakencroft 1985 Chardonnay, VA $8. Grapefruit, apple, and vegetal aromas. Moderately clean, fresh flavors compromised by a strongly astringent, bitter finish. (AWC/Nov. '86)

Oakencroft 1984 Chardonnay, VA $7. (AWC/Nov. '85)

Obester 1985 Chardonnay, Mendocino County, CA $12. (AWC/Nov. '86)

Otter Spring (Heron Hill Winery) 1983 Chardonnay, Estate Bottled, Free Run, Finger Lakes, NY $9.49. (AWC/Nov. '86)

Paul Masson 1983 Chardonnay, Estate Bottled, Pinnacles Selection, Monterey, CA $8.50. (AWC/Nov. '85)

Paul Masson 1985 Chardonnay, Monterey County, CA $6.29. (AWC/Nov. '86)

Peconic Bay 1985 Chardonnay, North Fork—Long Island, NY $8.99. (AWC/Nov. '86)

Pindar 1984 Chardonnay, Green Label, Long Island, NY $8.99. (AWC/Nov. '86)

Pindar 1984 Chardonnay, Long Is-

land, NY $7.99. (AWC/Nov. '86)

Pindar 1985 Chardonnay, Green La-bel, Long Island, NY $8.99. (AWC/Nov. '86)

Pine Ridge 1984 Chardonnay, O.K. Cuvee, Napa Valley, CA $13. (AWC/Nov. '86)

Plam 1984 Chardonnay, Napa Val-ley, CA $12. (AWC/Nov. '86)

Plane's 1983 Chardonnay, Signa-ture Reserve, Finger Lakes, NY $12. (AWC/Nov. '85)

Ponzi 1984 Chardonnay, Willa-mette Valley, OR $10. (AWC/Nov. '86)

Preston Wine Cellars 1981 Char-donnay, WA $7.95. (AWC/Nov. '85)

Prince Michel 1985 Chardonnay, VA $7. (AWC/Nov. '86)

Quail Ridge 1983 Chardonnay, Na-pa Valley, CA $14. (AWC/Nov. '85)

Quail Run 1984 Chardonnay, Yaki-ma Valley, WA $9.49. (AWC/Nov. '86)

R. H. Phillips 1984 Chardonnay, Reserve, CA $6. Light nose. Soft, neutral flavors. (AWC/Nov. '86)

R. H. Phillips 1985 Chardonnay, CA $6. Ripe, tropical fruit aromas and fla-vors. Somewhat low in acidity and soft in the finish. (AWC/Nov. '86)

Richardson 1984 Chardonnay, Napa Valley, CA $10. (AWC/Nov. '85)

Ridgemont 1984 Chardonnay, American, winery in WA $8.50. (AWC/Nov. '86)

River Oaks 1985 Chardonnay, So-noma County, CA $5.95. (AWC/Nov. '86)

Robert Keenan 1983 Chardonnay, Napa Valley, CA $12.50. (AWC/Nov. '85)

Robert Keenan 1984 Chardonnay, Napa Valley, CA $10.75. Lemon and oak aromas have off elements. Slightly thin fruit. (AWC/Nov. '86)

Robert Mondavi 1984 Chardonnay,

Napa Valley, CA $10.99. Ripe fruit aromas and flavors. Soft, with too much oak in the finish. (AWC/Nov. '86)

Robert Stemmler 1981 Chardonnay, Sonoma County, CA $14. (AWC/Nov. '85)

Rodney Strong 1983 Chardonnay, Chalk Hill Vineyard, Sonoma County, CA $10. Late-harvest Riesling character. (AWC/Nov. '86)

Rodney Strong 1984 Chardonnay, River West Vineyard, Russian River Valley, CA $10. (AWC/Nov. '86)

Rodney Strong 1984 Chardonnay, Sonoma County, CA $7.50. (AWC/Nov. '86)

Round Hill 1984 Chardonnay, House, CA $4.65. (AWC/Nov. '85)

Round Hill 1984 Chardonnay, Napa Valley Reserve, CA $7.50. (AWC/Nov. '86)

Rutherford Hill 1983 Chardonnay, Jaeger Vineyards, Napa Valley, CA $10.75. (AWC/Nov. '85)

Rutherford Ranch Brand 1984 Chardonnay, Reese Vineyard, Napa Valley, CA $10. (AWC/Nov. '86)

S. Anderson 1984 Chardonnay, Estate Bottled, Napa Valley, CA $12.50. (AWC/Nov. '86)

Sakonnet 1984 Chardonnay, Southeastern New England, winery in RI $9.95. (AWC/Nov. '85)

Sakonnet 1985 Chardonnay, Estate Grown & Barrel Fermented, Southeastern New England, winery in RI $10.95. (AWC/Nov. '86)

Sanford 1983 Chardonnay, Central Coast, CA $12.50. (AWC/Nov. '85)

Sanford 1984 Chardonnay, Central Coast, CA $12.50. Oxidized. Out of whack. (AWC/Nov. '85)

Sanford 1985 Chardonnay, Santa Barbara County, CA $12. (AWC/Nov. '86)

Santa Barbara 1985 Chardonnay, Reserve, Santa Ynez Valley, CA $15. (AWC/Nov. '86)

Schug 1983 Chardonnay, Beckstoffer Vineyard, Carneros—Napa Valley, CA $11.75. (AWC/Nov. '86)

Schug 1984 Chardonnay, Ahollinger Vineyard, Carneros—Napa Valley, CA $9.75. (AWC/Nov. '86)

Sebastiani 1983 Chardonnay, Proprietor's Reserve, Sonoma Valley, CA $12. (AWC/Nov. '86)

Sebastiani 1983 Chardonnay, Sonoma Valley, CA $8. (AWC/Nov. '85)

Seghesio 1985 Chardonnay, CA $5. (AWC/Nov. '86)

Sequoia Grove 1983 Chardonnay, Napa Valley, CA $10. (AWC/Nov. '85)

Sequoia Grove 1984 Chardonnay, Estate Bottled, Napa Valley, CA $14. (AWC/Nov. '86)

Sequoia Grove 1984 Chardonnay, Napa Valley, CA $12. Pungent, oaky bouquet. Big, clumsy fruit with a hot finish. (AWC/Nov. '86)

Sequoia Grove 1984 Chardonnay, Sonoma County, CA $12. (AWC/Nov. '86)

Shafer Vineyard Cellars 1983 Chardonnay, Willamette Valley, OR $11. Not much fruit. Tight. Uninteresting. (AWC/Nov. '85)

Shafer Vineyard Cellars 1984 Chardonnay, Willamette Valley, OR $10.50. (AWC/Nov. '86)

Shafer Vineyards 1984 Chardonnay, Napa Valley, CA $12. (AWC/Nov. '86)

Simi 1982 Chardonnay, Reserve, Sonoma County, CA $25. (AWC/Nov. '86)

Siskiyou 1983 Chardonnay, OR $8.25. (AWC/Nov. '85)

Snoqualmie 1983 Chardonnay, Yakima Valley, WA $7.99. Stingy, green fruit. High acidity. (AWC/Nov. '85)

Snoqualmie 1984 Chardonnay, Early Release, Yakima Valley, WA $5.99. (AWC/Nov. '85)

Snoqualmie 1984 Chardonnay, Yakima Valley, WA $7.89. Overripe, boiled fruit aromas. Tart, quince-like flavors. Hollow. Out of balance. (AWC/Nov. '86)

Sokol Blosser 1981 Chardonnay, Reserve, Yamhill County, OR $11.95. (AWC/Nov. '85)

Sokol Blosser 1982 Chardonnay, Reserve, Yamhill County, OR $11.95. (AWC/Nov. '85)

Sokol Blosser 1983 Chardonnay, Reserve, Yamhill County, OR $11.95. (AWC/Nov. '86)

Sokol Blosser 1983 Chardonnay, Yamhill County, OR $8.95. (AWC/Nov. '86)

Souverain 1984 Chardonnay, Sonoma County, CA $8. (AWC/Nov. '86)

Spring Mountain 1983 Chardonnay, Napa Valley, CA $14. (AWC/Nov. '85)

Ste. Chapelle 1982 Chardonnay, Reserve, Symms Family Vineyard, Old Block, ID $12.09. (AWC/Nov. '85)

Ste. Chapelle 1983 Chardonnay, Blanc, ID $5.99. (AWC/Nov. '85)

Ste. Chapelle 1983 Chardonnay, Blanc, Idaho—Washington, winery in ID $6.95. (AWC/Nov. '86)

Ste. Chapelle 1983 Chardonnay, Symms Family Vineyard, ID $9.39. (AWC/Nov. '85)

Sterling 1983 Chardonnay, Diamond Mountain Ranch, Napa Valley, CA $15. Off odors and flavors. (AWC/Nov. '86)

Sterling 1983 Chardonnay, Estate Bottled, Napa Valley, CA $14. (AWC/Nov. '85)

Stevenot 1984 Chardonnay, CA $6. (AWC/Nov. '85)

Stevenot 1984 Chardonnay, Proprietor's Reserve, Calaveras County, CA $10. (AWC/Nov. '85)

Stewart 1984 Chardonnay, Wahluke Slope, Columbia Valley, WA $8. (AWC/Nov. '86)

Stony Hill 1983 Chardonnay, Napa Valley, CA $24. (AWC/Nov. '86)

Stratford 1983 Chardonnay, CA $8.50. (AWC/Nov. '85)

Stratford 1984 Chardonnay, CA $8.50. Not much aroma. Flavors are delicate, lemony, somewhat thin. Lacks character. (AWC/Nov. '86)

Tabor Hill 1983 Chardonnay, Winemaster Selection, Lake Michigan Shore, MI $12.95. (AWC/Nov. '85)

Taylor California Cellars (nonvintage) Chardonnay, CA. (AWC/Nov.' 85)

Tepusquet 1984 Chardonnay, Vineyard Reserve, Santa Maria Valley, CA $8.50. (AWC/Nov. '85)

The Monterey Vineyard 1984 Chardonnay, Monterey County, CA $7. (AWC/Nov. '86)

Thomas Fogarty 1984 Chardonnay, Ventana Vineyards, Monterey, CA $15. Complex nose. Ripe fruit, buttery, and oaky flavors. Somewhat soft in the middle. (AWC/Nov. '86)

Thomas Fogarty 1984 Chardonnay, Winery Lake Vineyard, Napa Valley—Carneros, CA $15. (AWC/Nov. '86)

Trentadue 1984 Chardonnay, Private Reserve, Alexander Valley, CA $9.50. (AWC/Nov. '86)

Trione (Geyser Peak Winery) 1983 Chardonnay, Alexander Valley, CA $9.50. (AWC/Nov. '85)

Tucker 1983 Chardonnay, Yakima Valley, WA $7.39. (AWC/Nov. '86)

V. Sattui 1984 Chardonnay, Napa Valley, CA $10.75. (AWC/Nov. '86)

Valfleur 1983 Chardonnay, Alexander Valley, CA $10.50. (AWC/Nov. '86)

Valfleur 1984 Chardonnay, Jimtown Ranch, Alexander Valley, CA $10.50. (AWC/Nov. '86)

Ventana 1982 Chardonnay, Barrel Fermented, Monterey County, CA $14. (AWC/Nov. '85)

Ventana 1984 Chardonnay, Barrel Fermented, Monterey, CA $14. (AWC/Nov. '86)

Vichon 1984 Chardonnay, Napa Valley, CA $12. Earthy, mushroomy nose. Undistinguished flavors. Bitter finish. (AWC/Nov. '86)

Walker Valley 1983 Chardonnay, NY $8.99. (AWC/Nov. '85)

Waterbrook 1985 Chardonnay, WA $9. Good but not exciting. (AWC/Nov. '86)

Weibel 1984 Chardonnay, Proprietor's Reserve, Mendocino County, CA $8. (AWC/Nov. '85)

Wente Bros. 1984 Chardonnay, Arroyo Seco, CA $5.50. (AWC/Nov. '86)

Whitehall Lane 1983 Chardonnay, Cerro Vista Vineyard, Napa Valley, CA $14. (AWC/Nov. '86)

William Byrd 1984 Chardonnay, California Cuvee, Napa Valley, CA (winery in MD) $5. Subdued nose with some fruit and wood showing. Light Mâcon style with medium body. Pleasant. (AWC/Nov. '86)

Windsor 1984 Chardonnay, Estate Grown, Vineyard Selection, Russian River Valley, CA $10. (AWC/Nov. '86)

Wm. Wheeler 1983 Chardonnay, Sonoma County, CA $11. (AWC/Nov. '85)

GERMAN

The vineyards of Germany are the most northerly of all the world's major winegrowing areas. They drape the valley walls of the Rhine, Mosel, Saar, and Ruwer Rivers, especially the south-facing slopes that soak up a maximum of sunshine. Vintages vary dramatically according to how ripe the grapes get each year.

All the important wines of Germany are white, and all the best are made from the Riesling grape, the other principal varieties being Sylvaner, Gewürztraminer, and Müller-Thurgau. The latter share some of German Riesling's lively fruit, and may have their own charms, but they never achieve the depth, the melding of flowers, steel, spice, appley acidity and honeyed sweetness of Riesling.

The Mosel-Saar-Ruwer valleys are lumped into one appellation, known for wines of delicacy yet depth, full of flowers and fruit. The Rheingau district of the lower Rhine Valley produces firmer wines with more richness, spice, and minerally flavors. Wines from further up the Rhine River Valley in the Rheinhessen and Pfalz are usually softer and fuller.

German labels are the most informative of any wine. A wine's name generally consist of two words: first the name of the nearest town to its vineyard, then the name of the vineyard itself or vineyard area. This may be followed by the varietal, then the grade of the wine. The Kabinett grade is the driest; Spätlese is fuller and may show some sweetness; Auslese is made from selected grapes yielding sweeter dessert wine. Beerenauslese, Trockenbeerenauslese, and Eiswein are very sweet, succulent, concentrated wines made only in the most favorable years, carrying high price tags for the experience of some of the world's greatest sweet wines.

Dr. Burklin Wolf 1971 Wachen-heimer Gerumpel, Riesling, Trocken-beerenauslese, Pfalz $75-100. Complex bouquet suggests apricots, flowers, honey. Intense, rich, thick, luscious, sweet. Still quite young, with the sweetness showing a bit too much. Needs a few years. (S&PW/May '86) ★★★★

Friedrich-Wilhelm-Gymnasium 1983 Graacher Himmelreich, Riesling, Auslese, Mosel-Saar-Ruwer $12. Fragrant, flowery. Impeccable structure. Not very sweet for Auslese. Clean as a whistle. Steely finish. (JB/May '86) ★★★★

Dr. Pauly Bergweiller 1985 Graacher Himmelreich, Riesling, Kabinett, Mosel-Saar-Ruwer $7.99. Fat, tutti-frutti nose. Crisp acids, 2.6% residual sweetness, appley finish. Round, a bit earthy. (JB/May. '86) ★★★1/2 (★★★★)

Elisabeth Christoffel-Berres 1983 Ürziger Würzgarten, Riesling, Spätlese, Mosel-Saar-Ruwer $8.50. Luscious, fruit-salad nose. Deeply flavored, fresh, clean, sweet. (JB/May '86) ★★★1/2

Schloss Vollrads 1976 Riesling, Auslese, Wiesgold, Rheingau $16.99. Classic. Honey-scented. (JB/Jan. '86) ★★★1/2

Schloss Groenesteyn 1983 Rüdesheimer Bischofsburg, Riesling, Kabinett, Rheingau $5.49. Fruity, flowery, luscious, ripe, perfectly structured, great depth, touch of spritz. Classic. (JB/Jan. '86) ★★★ (★★★★)

Friedrich Altenkirch 1983 Lorcher Kröne, Riesling, Kabinett, Rheingau $5.99. Ripe, with vanilla, spice. (JB/Jan. '86) ★★★ (★★★1/2)

Fürst Löwenstein 1983 Hallgarten-er Hendelberg, Riesling, Spätlese, (Pink & Silver Capsule), Halbtrock-en, Rheingau $8.99. Peachy nose. Big, round body. 1.38% RS. (JB/Jan. '86) ★★★ (★★★1/2)

Schöll and Hillebrand 1983 Rüdesheimer Berg Roseneck, Riesling, Kabinett, Rheingau $6.99. Round, ripe, with pineapple, banana, notes. Fleshy, long finish. Drier than most. (JB/Jan. '86) ★★★ (★★★1/2)

Staatsweingüter 1983 Steinberger, Riesling, Kabinett, Rheingau $6.99. Fresh nose of apples, peaches, and strawberries. Full bodied, but finishes steely and dry. First-rate. (JB/Jan. '86) ★★★ (★★★1/2)

Fürst Löwenstein 1983 Hallgartner Schönhell, Riesling, Spätlese, (Pink & Gold Capsule), Rheingau $9.99. Not as sweet as many Spätlesen. Peachy nose, hint of honey. (JB/Jan. '86) ★★★ (★★★1/2)

Friedrich-Wilhelm-Gymnasium 1983 Falkensteiner Hofberg, Riesling, Kabinett, Mosel-Saar-Ruwer $7. Ripe apple nose. Bright, focused flavors. Crisp, clean. (JB/May '86) ★★★

Langwerth von Simmern 1983 Eltviller Sonnenberg, Riesling, Kabinett, Halbtrocken, Rheingau $5.99. Spicey, Alsatian-style nose. Full bodied and soft, but finishes crisp. Not quite totally dry. (JB/Jan. '86) ★★★

Rudolf Müller 1983 Deidesheimer Hofstück, Spätlese, Rheinpfalz, $5.50. Lovely, peach and apricot aromas and flavors. Light, clean, lively. Smooth finish. Super value. (JPN/Jan. '87) ★★★

G. Breuer 1983 Rüdesheimer Kirchenpfad, Riesling, Kabinett, Rheingau $5.99. Nose and flavors tightly packed together. Spectacular balance and weight bode well for the future. (JB/Jan.'86) ★★1/2 (★★★★)

Landgraflich Hessiches 1983 Winkeler Hasensprung, Riesling, Kabinett, Rheingau $5.49. Reticent nose with vanilla hints. Superb structure. Steely, dry finish. Begs for food. (JB/Jan. '86) ★★1/2 (★★★★)

Schloss Vollrads 1983 Kabinett, Blausilber, Halbtrocken, Rheingau $6.49. Closed nose with a hint of slate. Clean, delicate, impeccably balanced. (JB/Jan. '86) ★★1/2 (★★★★)

Friedrich Altenkirch 1984 Lorcher Pfaffenweis, Riesling, Kabinett, Rheingau $5.49. Forward nose of melon and strawberry. Ripe, fruit flavors, nice acid backbone. (JB/Jan. '86) ★★1/2 (★★★1/2)

Fürst Löwenstein 1983 Hallgartner Jungfer, Riesling, Kabinett, (Blue & Silver Capsule), Rheingau $6.99. Forward bouquet of peaches and strawberries. Dry, fruity finish. (JB/Jan. '86) ★★1/2 (★★★1/2)

Friedrich Altenkirch 1981 Lorcher Kapellenberg, Riesling, Kabinett, Rheingau $5.49. Clean, appley scents and flavor carry through to finish. Slightly angular acids. (JB/Jan. '86) ★★1/2 (★★★)

Friedrich Altenkirch 1982 Lorcher Pfaffenweis, Riesling, Kabinett, Rheingau $6.99. Delightful, fresh, grape nose. Soft but still focused. (JB/Jan.'86) ★★1/2 (★★★)

Friedrich Altenkirch 1984 Lorcher Kapellenberg, Riesling, Qualitätswein, Rheingau $4.99. Closed nose hints at pineapples. Very well balanced. Finishes a bit dry. Ripe for the vintage. ★★1/2 (★★★)

Schloss Vollrads 1983 Riesling, Kabinett, (Blue & Gold Capsule), Rheingau $6.49. Clean, peachy. On the sweet side, but well balanced by acidity. (JB/Jan. '86) ★★1/2 (★★★)

Friedrich-Wilhelm-Gymnasium 1979 Trittenheimer Apotheke, Riesling, Auslese, Mosel-Saar-Ruwer $8.37. Lovely, characteristic Riesling fruit and flowers, with a slate-like note. Very well balanced. (S&PW/Jan. '86) ★★1/2

Gustav A. Schmitt 1983 Niersteiner Rehbach, Riesling, Spätlese,

Rheinhessen $7. Varietal aroma. Flavorful, well balanced, with a long finish. Lovely, and a bargain. (S&PW/Jan. '86) ★★1/2

Peter Nicolay Berres-Erben 1985 Ürziger Goldwingert, Riesling, Auslese, Mosel-Saar-Ruwer $17.99. Honey-like Botrytis nose. Round, ripe, peachy flavors. Finishes soft. (JB/May '86) ★★1/2

Dr. Pauly Bergweiller 1985 Bernkasteler Badstube, Riesling, Spätlese, Mosel-Saar-Ruwer $8.99. Strawberry jumps from the glass. Round, balanced, sumptuous. (JB/May '86) ★★ (★★★1/2)

Friedrich Altenkirch 1983 Lorcher Kapellenberg, Riesling, Kabinett, Rheingau $6.99. Very tight nose. Slight spritz. Flavors are bunched up tight, but has beautiful balance. Clean. Finishes dry. (JB/Jan. '86) ★★ (★★★1/2)

Landgraflich Hessiches 1983 Johannisberger Klaus, Riesling, Kabinett, Rheingau $5.99. Very light, pure, grapey nose with a whiff of honey and vanilla. Light-bodied wine for the vintage. Clean. (JB/Jan. '86) ★★ (★★★)

Peter Nicolay Berres-Erben 1985 Ürziger Wurzgarten, Riesling, Kabinett, Mosel-Saar-Ruwer $8.49. Strawberry-apple nose. Full blown ripeness. Acids a bit soft. (JB/May '86) ★★ (★★★)

Reichsgraf Von Kesselstatt 1981 Graacher Josephshoffer, Riesling, Spätlese, Mosel-Saar-Ruwer $8.99. Very shy, tight nose. Crisp, almost tart acids. Relatively lightweight, lots of zip. (JB/May '86) ★★ (★★★)

Schloss Vollrads 1983 Riesling, Kabinett, (Blue Capsule), Rheingau $5.49. Quite dry, even austere. Very tightly closed. Steely finish. (JB/Jan. '86) ★★ (★★★)

Weinbauschüle & Forschungsanstalt 1983 Geisenheimer Fuchsburg, Riesling, Kabinett, Rheingau $5.49.

Quiet, with flavors very tightly bunched. Overall weight and structure promises a good future. (JB/Jan. '86) ★★ (★★★)

Rudolf Müller 1983 Piesporter Goldtropfchen, Riesling, Spätlese, Mosel-Saar-Ruwer $11. Apple aroma and taste somewhat masked by salty character. Smooth, mineral finish. (JPN/Jan. '87) ★★ (★★1/2)

Rudolf Müller 1983 Deidesheimer Hofstück, Kabinett, Rheinpfalz $4.50. Nice aroma and taste. Lively, fairly sweet. Very good value. (JPN/Jan. '87) ★★

Friedrich-Wilhelm-Gymnasium 1984 Trittenheimer Apotheke, Riesling, Qualitätswein, Mosel-Saar-Ruwer $6.24. Appley aroma and flavor. A tart edge adds zest and balances sweetness. (S&PW/Jan. '86) ★1/2

Reichsgraf von Kesselstatt 1982 Piesporter Goldtröpfchen, Riesling, Spätlese, Mosel-Saar-Ruwer $8.99. Rich, fresh nose shows just a hint of Botrytis. Bright, grapey aromas, but rich flavors quickly diffuse. Not enough acid. (JB/May '86) ★1/2

Reichsgraf von Kesselstatt 1983 Scharzhofberger, Riesling, Auslese, Mosel-Saar-Ruwer $12.99. Shy, tightly knit. Lightweight, almost delicate, only hints of flowery perfume. (JB/May '86) ★ (★★★)

Zach-Bergweiler-Prüm Erben Dr. Heidemanns-Bergweiler 1983 Bernkasteler Lay, Riesling, Spätlese, Mosel-Saar-Ruwer $8. Slight mustiness. Otherwise ripe, spicy, appley. Nice balance; on the dry side. Steely finish. (JB/May '86) ★ (★★1/2)

Rudolf Müller 1983 Piesporter Treppchen, Kabinett, Mosel-Saar-Ruwer $5. Delicate, appley aroma and taste. Smooth texture. (JPN/Jan. '87) ★

GEWURZTRAMINER

Originally a German variety, Gewurztraminer has made its reputation in the Alsace region of France. In the late 1970s it caught the fancy of California winemakers and today ranks fourth in production among California white varietals. The most distinctive wines of this variety come from cool vineyard areas, including some in the Northwest and New York.

The very distinctive aroma of Gewurztraminer is related to Muscat grapes: perfumy, flowery, and spicy. Alsace Gewurz is most often made completely dry, with the spicy element dominating the aroma and flavor, leaving a crisp, tangy, sometimes slightly bitter finish. Even late-harvest Gewurz from Alsace, labeled "Vendage Tardive," can be relatively dry or it may have residual sweetness.

Occasional examples of the dry Alsace style are produced in the US, but American Gewurztraminer is more often made in a German style: semi-dry, with more floral, perfumy aromas and a softer finish. Some late-harvest wines are also made from Gewurztraminer in Alsace, the US, and Germany.

Gewurztraminer has never achieved widespread acceptance in this country, in part because it is hard to prounounce (Guh-*vurts*-truh-mee-ner) and hard to mate with food (try it with Oriental dishes). As a cocktail wine, however, it is a natural with intriguing scents and flavors that can be savored on their own.

AMERICAN
Yamhill Valley Vineyard 1985 Gewurztraminer, OR $7.50. Floral aroma and flavor, pleasantly spicy. Dry, tart, well balanced. No bitterness in finish. (JPN/May '86) ★★★ (★★★1/2)
De Loach 1984 Gewurztraminer, Late Harvest, Russian River Valley, CA $10. Lovely, floral bouquet of citrus and

spice. Delicacy and sweetness well balanced by acidity. Long, spicy finish has a liquorice nuance. (S&PW/Jan. '86) ★★★

Henry 1984 Gewurztraminer, Estate Bottled, OR $6. Full, pretty, spice and floral aroma. Excellent balance. Off dry. (JPN/Mar. '86) ★★★

Hinman 1983 Gewurztraminer, OR $7.35. Slight sulfur followed by complex range of spice, fruit, and flower aromas and flavors. Sophisticated. (JPN/Mar. '86) ★★★

Tualatin Vineyards 1983 Gewurztraminer, Estate Bottled, Willamette Valley, OR $7. Fresh spice, apple, and floral. Spicy with a bit of spritz. Threshold sweetness, lively acidity. (JPN/Mar. '86) ★★★

Amity 1984 Gewurztraminer, OR $7. Delicate, powdery-sweet perfume. Light, delicate, even a little thin. Dry. (JPN/Mar. '86) ★★1/2

Crosswood 1984 Gewurztraminer, CT $7.50. Shy, pretty, musky fruit nose. Varietal, fruit-and-spice flavors. Refined, dry, brisk acidity. (RF/Mar.'86) ★★1/2

Dr. Konstantin Frank 1983 Gewurztraminer, Finger Lakes, NY $8.99. Perfumed bouquet with characteristic spicy overlay. Well balanced. Smooth texture. Fruity. Light sweetness. Lively acidity. Fairly long, spicy finish. (S&PW/May '86) ★★1/2

Hacienda 1984 Gewurztraminer, Sonoma County, CA $7. Delicate, floral nose. Smooth and delicate in the mouth; some spice. Off dry, well balanced. (JPN/May '86) ★★1/2

Valley View 1982 Gewurztraminer, OR $7. Delicate, floral aroma. Nice, clean, spice flavor. Dry, well-balanced. (JPN/Mar. '86) ★★1/2

Columbia 1985 Gewurztraminer, WA $6. Powdery, perfumy, floral and musk aroma. Intense spice in the mouth; peppery, slightly bitter, dry, and quite acidic. Good intensity but rough; needs bottle aging. (JPN/

Jan. '87) ★★ (★★★)

Ch. Benoit 1984 Gewurztraminer, OR $7.50. Delicate, floral aroma. Spicy, slightly spritzy, semi-sweet. (JPN/Mar. '86) ★★

Ernest & Julio Gallo 1983 Gewurztraminer, Limited Release, CA $4. Spicy varietal aroma. Semi-sweet. Medium body. (JPN/Mar. '86) ★★

Hillcrest 1982 Gewurztraminer, OR $5.70. Pleasantly spicy nose. Subdued fruit. Clean and delicate. (JPN/Mar. '86) ★★

Shafer Vineyard Cellars 1984 Gewurztraminer, Willamette Valley, OR $7. Musky, rose-petal nose. Delicate musk and spice flavors. Semi-sweet. (JPN/Mar. '86) ★★

Alexander Valley Vineyards 1984 Gewurztraminer, Alexander Valley, CA $6.50. Light spice and floral aroma. Fresh and clean. Touch of sweetness balanced with nice acidity. Spicy finish. Good value. (S&PW/May '86) ★3/4

Parducci 1984 Gewurztraminer, Mendocino County, CA $7-8. Varietal spice on the nose. Clean and fresh, with light, balanced sweetness. Fruity. Nice by itself or with food. (S&PW/May '86) ★3/4

Finger Lakes Wine Cellars 1984 Gewurztraminer, Finger Lakes, NY $4.99/375ml. Delicate nose. Bright flavors. Light, spicy fruit and candy quality offset prickly acidity. (RF/Jan. '86) ★1/2 (★★)

Bethel Heights Vineyard 1984 Gewurztraminer, Willamette Valley, OR $6. Faintly grassy and appley aromas. Lemony-herbal taste. (JPN/Jan. '86) ★1/2

Oak Knoll 1983 Gewurztraminer, OR $6.50. Slightly stinky, salt water aroma. Moderate floral-and-spice taste. No depth. Off-dry. (JPN/Mar. '86) ★

Siskiyou Vineyards 1983 Gewurztraminer, OR $7. Musk and ripe-fruit aroma. A bit clumsy. Off-dry. (JPN/Mar. '86) ★

Worden's 1985 Gewurztraminer, WA

$6.50. Floral aroma. Spritzy. Sweet, flat, watery middle. (JPN/May '86) ★

E. B. Foote 1982 Dry Gewurztraminer, WA $6. Gardenia and spice aroma becomes stinky . (JPN/Mar. '86)

Elk Cove 1984 Gewurztraminer, Estate Bottled, Willamette Valley, OR $7. Pronounced sulfur dioxide. Watery, off dry, flat. (JPN/Mar. '86)

Ellendale 1983 Gewurztraminer, WA (winery in OR) $6. Strange, sauerkraut aroma. Watery, sweet-and-sour taste. (JPN/Mar. '86)

Garden Valley Winery 1984 Gewurztraminer, OR $7. Vague fruit and stinky aromas. Caramelized, somewhat bitter. Off dry. (JPN/Mar. '86)

Hoodsport Winery 1984 Gewurztraminer, WA $6. Sweet, smoky, slightly skunky, non-varietal aromas. (JPN/Mar. '86)

Mont Elise Vineyards 1984 Gewurztraminer, WA $6.50. Skunky. Lemon water taste. Thin and insipid. (JPN/Mar. '86)

Sokol Blosser 1983 Gewurztraminer, WA $7.50. Heavy, old-flower aroma. Somewhat sour, flat, old tasting. Off-dry. (JPN/Mar. '86)

Tucker Cellars 1983 Gewurztraminer, Yakima Valley, WA $6.50. Skunky, sulfurous. (JPN/Mar. '86)

FRENCH

Willm 1983 Gewurztraminer, Cuvée Emile Willm, Alsace $10.75. Delicate, pineapple scent opens into intense, varietal character with amazing length. Great fullness, depth, subtlety, power. Will continue to improve. (CC/March '86) ★★★★

Landmann Ostholt 1983 Gewurztraminer, Vendange Tardive, Zinnkoepfle, Alsace $12/500 ml. Lush, silky texture. Rich, spicy, varietal flavors. Bouquet sweetly scented with cloves and nutmeg. Dry.

(CC/Mar. '86) ★★★ (★★★★)

Klug 1983 Gewurztraminer, Réserve, Alsace $7.99. Delightful perfume and flavors held in check by powerful structure. Elegant. Silky finish. (CC/Mar. '86) ★★★ (★★★1/2)

Dopff 1983 Gewurztraminer, Réserve, Alsace $6.50. Moderately intense perfume of lychees and candied citrus peel. Just enough crisp acidity to balance a trace of residual sweetness. (CC/Mar. '86) ★★★

Jean Geiler 1983 Gewurztraminer, Cuvée Prestige, Alsace $6.99. Medium-intense nose of coriander, nutmeg, and jasmine. Ripe, very rich, with complex, buttery notes. (CC/Mar. '86) ★★★

Klug 1983 Gewurztraminer, Alsace $5.50. Packed with such intense varietal aromas and flavor that it verges on overwhelming. (CC/Mar. '86) ★★★

Preiss-Henny Ch. de Mittelwihr 1983 Gewurztraminer, Alsace $7. Dry yet intensely fruity. Lychees and rose petals follow through in smooth, lingering finish. (CC/Mar. '86) ★★

MISCELLANEOUS WHITE

Many of the wines reviewed below might be called "country wines," made to be drunk when young and full of freshness and fruit. Chenin Blanc is a good example. Made from the grape used to produce French Vouvray, it has not been one of California's more successful varietals, but the wines are getting much better, and Chenin Blanc is establishing an excellent track record in Washington State, where higher acid levels work well to balance the residual sweetness common in this varietal.

Seyval Blanc is a similar success story in New York and other eastern states. An exceptionally versatile grape, it usually makes light, generously fruity wines with a touch of sweetness, but it can also be dry and full with oak overtones in the style of a Chardonnay.

Like Sauvignon Blanc, Semillon has been reincarnated from an anonymous partner in sweet California Sauterne to a serious, dry varietal from wineries in the Northwest as well as California.

The other wines reviewed below — from the US and other countries — carry ratings and tasting notes that make a strong argument for wine drinkers to shop with an adventurous spirit. Beyond the most popular and best-known wines lie countless other vinous treasures.

AMERICAN CHENIN BLANC
Hogue Cellars 1984 Chenin Blanc, Yakima Valley, WA $6. Delicate, true varietal aroma. A little spritz. Lively, lovely tartness. (JPN/Jan. '86) ★★★★
Christian Brothers 1985 Chenin Blanc, Napa Valley, CA $7. Sweet, powdery aroma. Pineapple and fruity chewing gum taste. Tart, crisp, lively. (JPN/Jan. '87) ★★★

Simi 1984 Chenin Blanc, Mendocino County, CA $6.50. Melony aroma and flavor. Rich texture. Slightly sweet but lively. (JPN/Mar. '86) ★★★

Staton Hills 1984 Chenin Blanc, WA $6.50. Sweet nose of herbs and cheese. (JPN/Jan. '86) ★★★

Bookwalter 1984 Chenin Blanc, WA $6. Delicate fruit. True Chenin flavor. (JPN/Jan. '86) ★★1/2

Northwest Daily 1984 Chenin Blanc, Yakima Valley, WA $4.50. Fresh, crisp, peach-apricot aroma, taste. Clean, refreshing. Excellent value. (JPN/May '86) ★★1/2

Paul Thomas 1984 Chenin Blanc, WA $6. Grapefruit and melon nose. Spritzy. Refreshing, with good balance. (JPN/Jan. '86) ★★1/2

Pontin Del Roza 1984 Chenin Blanc, Yakima Valley, WA $6.50. Herbs and a little pineapple. Lively flavors, fair amount of residual sweetness balanced by acidity. (JPN/Jan. '86) ★★1/2

Preston Vineyards & Winery 1984 Dry Chenin Blanc, Dry Creek Valley, CA $6. Fresh, grassy aroma with a peach-like component and a touch of oak. Dry, with some softness from the oak. Round, fresh, clean. (S&PW/Jan. '86) ★★1/2

Worden's Washington Winery 1984 Chenin Blanc, WA $6. Grassy aroma with a tinge of bitterness, refreshing crispness. (JPN/Jan. '86) ★★1/2

Bethel Heights Vineyard 1984 Chenin Blanc, Willamette Valley, OR $6. Fresh, herbal-grassy aromas and flavors. Almost dry and fairly acidic. (JPN/Jan. '86) ★★

Ch. Maja (Conn Creek) 1983 Chenin Blanc, Napa Valley, CA $6. Fairly dry, quite fruity, full bodied, soft. Well made and tasty. (S&PW/Jan. '86) ★★

Dry Creek 1985 Dry Chenin Blanc,

Sonoma County, CA $6. Fresh, fruity varietal aroma with a suggestion of grass. Very light sweetness. Clean and fresh. Well balanced, firm, lively. Slight tartness at the end. (S&PW/Jan. '86) ★★

The Christian Brothers 1984 Chenin Blanc, Napa Valley, CA $6. Melony aroma and flavor; soft but appealing. Semi-sweet. (JPN/Mar. '86) ★★

Worden's Washington Winery 1985 Chenin Blanc, WA $6. Sweet, talcum powder aroma. Citrusy taste. Lively, good acid, balanced. (JPN/May '86) ★1/2

AMERICAN SEMILLON

Congress Springs 1984 Semillon, Estate, Santa Cruz, CA $8. No grassy character. Cigar box aroma and fig flavors. Richer than most. Low acidity. (JDM/Jan. '86) ★★★1/2

Ch. Ste. Michelle 1982 Semillon, Chateau Reserve, Lot Selected, French Oak Aged, WA $13. Very smoky, rich, ripe nose. Aroma and flavors suggest figs, grass, cheese. Rich, smooth, radically different from other Washington Semillons. (JPN/Jan. '87) ★★★

Columbia 1985 Semillon, WA $6. Delicate herb and smoke aromas with some sweet vanilla and grassiness. Tart, almost citric, very fruity, with a clean, herb-and-spice finish. (JPN/Jan. '87) ★★★

Ch. Ste. Michelle 1985 Semillon-Blanc, WA $5. Fresh, lemon grass aroma. Nice, citric character in the mouth. Grapefruit finish with threshhold residual sweetness. (JPN/Jan. '87) ★★1/2

Columbia 1984 Semillon, WA $7. Figs. Firm, fresh, clean, and fruity. Light bodied. (S&PW/Mar. '86) ★★

Snoqualmie 1983 Semillon, Yakima Valley, WA $7. Fig-like aroma with a lanolin note. Smooth in texture with a firm, acid vein that adds zest. Balanced. Moderately long finish. (S&PW/Mar. '86) ★

AMERICAN SEYVAL BLANC

Woodbury 1984 Proprietor's Seyval, NY $5.29. Brisk, spicy grapefruit nose. Rich grapefruit-apricot flavors perfectly balanced with acidity. Refreshing, generous, with a note of sweetness. (RF/Mar. '86) ★★★

Wagner 1984 Seyval Blanc, Barrel Fermented, Finger Lakes, NY $4.94. Intriguing, aromatic nose. Rich, smooth, wood-and-fruit flavors. A hot edge needs to smooth out. (RF/Mar. '86) ★★1/2 (★★★)

Glenora 1984 Seyval Blanc, Finger Lakes, NY $7.49/1.5 liter. Crisp, slightly grapefruity nose. Full, orange-citrus flavor. Good value. (RF/Mar. '86) ★★1/2

Walker Valley Vineyards 1984 Seyval Blanc, Hudson River Region, NY $4.99. Delicious, deep fruit. Well balanced and clean. Off-dry. (RF/Mar. '86) ★★1/2

Heron Hill 1985 Seyval, Finger Lakes, NY $5.49. Once sulfur blows off, a quaff for hot afternoons. Refreshing thirst-quencher, orangey-appley fruit, lots of spritz, low alcohol. (RF/May '86) ★★

Great Western 1984 Seyval Blanc, Finger Lakes, NY $4.49. Mellow, orangey-fruit flavors and a nice note of wood. Lively acid. (RF/Mar.'86) ★1/2

Finger Lakes Wine Cellars 1983 Seyval, Finger Lakes, NY $4.99. Bright, pineappley fruit. Semi-sweet; a bit cloying. (RF/Mar. '86) ★

Bully Hill 1985 Seyval Blanc, Finger Lakes, NY $4.99. Fruit somewhat thin, and the acid way too high. Sulfur also shows. (RF/May '86)

OTHER AMERICAN VARIETALS AND BLENDS

Chanticleer 1984 Colombard, CA $3.75. Dry, with unobtrusive fruit notes.

Crisp, light, delicate. (JDM/May '86) ★★★★

Eberle 1985 Muscat Canelli, Paso Robles, CA $8. Pale silvery grey color. Very sweet, powdery aroma. Spritzy. Ripe peach flavor. Very sweet, but balanced by high acidity. Finishes crisp and refreshing. Luscious. (JPN/Jan. '87) ★★★1/2

Ponzi 1985 Pinot Gris, Willamette Valley, OR $7.50. Smoky, herbal aroma; fruity, underripe banana character. Not oak aged, but has richness of Chardonnay. Rich, crisp finish. Serve with salmon. (JPN/May '86) ★★★1/2

Bully Hill 1984 Ravat Blanc, NY $4.99. Intense, tart grapefruit flavors. Lots of acidity offsets residual sweetness. Refreshing. (RF/Mar. '86) ★★★

Chinook 1984 Topaz, WA $9. Blend of Sauvignon Blanc and Semillon. Fruity, herbal nose and mouth. Crisp, perfectly balanced. (JPN/May '86) ★★★

Heron Hill (nonvintage) White Table Wine, Finger Lakes, NY $5.69/1.5 liter. Clean, citrusy, refreshing. Acidity balanced by touch of sweetness. Lovely, herbal nose. Charming. (RF/Jan. '86) ★★★

Louis M. Martini 1983 Sauvignon Blanc-Semillon, CA $6.80. Approximately two-thirds Sauvignon to one-third Semillon. Avoids grassiness. Totally dry, perfect balance. Complex aftertaste, flinty hints. (JDM/Jan.'86) ★★★

Boordy 1984 Maryland Premium White Wine, MD $3.99. Fruit is subdued behind a smoky-earthy character. Assertive food wine. (RF/May '86) ★★1/2

Ch. Benoit 1985 Muller-Thurgau, OR $5. Fresh, lively, Riesling aroma. Delicate flavor. Very lively, spritzy. Semi-sweet. (JPN/May '86) ★★1/2

Columbia Crest 1985 White, Vineyard Reserve, Columbia Valley, WA $5. Musky nose and flavors. Crisp, nicely balanced, just barely sweet. (JPN/Jan. '87) ★★1/2

Plane's Cayuga Vineyard 1985 Trio, Finger Lakes, NY $4.49. Forceful, pineapple-grapefruit flavors have lots of acidity but sweetness still shows. Lush fruit. (RF/May '86) ★★1/2

Poplar Ridge 1985 Vidal Blanc, Finger Lakes, NY $4.99. Bright, lush, orangey fruit. Semi-sweet, with prominent acidity in balance. Simple, delicious. (RF/May '86) ★★1/2

Sokol Blosser 1985 Muller-Thurgau, Yamhill County, OR $5. Sweet, tropical fruit, musk aromas. Clean, floral taste. Light, semi-sweet, some spritz. Bracing finish. (JPN/May '86) ★★1/2

Plane's Cayuga Vineyard 1984 Duet, Finger Lakes, NY $3.75. Impetuous, citrus nose. Strong, grapefruit flavors. Sweetness almost erased by high acidity. (RF/Jan.'86) ★★ (★★★)

Bridgehampton 1984 Premiere Cuvee Blanc, The Hamptons, Long Island, NY $6.99. Attractive hints of earth, spice, smokiness. Smooth fruit flavors, good length. (RF/Jan. '86) ★★

Otter Spring (Heron Hill) 1985 Cayuga White, Finger Lakes, NY $5.49. Intriguing, aromatic nose. Almost dry, with a touch of wood. Pineapple-orange flavor. (RF/May '86) ★★

Wagner (nonvintage) White Table Wine, Finger Lakes, NY $2.79. Clean, light, refreshing. Lively acidity. Dry, pineappley fruit. (RF/May '86) ★★

Widmer (nonvintage) Rhine Wine, NY $3.29. Perfumed nose. Very pleasant, semi-dry sipper. (RF/Mar.'86) ★★

Wiemer (nonvintage) Estate White, Finger Lakes, NY $4.99. Delicious, mouthfilling, fruit flavors. Slightly bitter vein. (RF/Mar.'86) ★★

Inglenook 1984 Napa Valley White, Estate Bottled, CA $5. Herbaceous, floral aroma and taste. Light, clean, dry. (JPN/May '86) ★1/2

AUSTRALIAN

Hill-Smith Estate 1984 Varietal White, Barossa Valley, South Australia $3.79. Light, pretty, floral, fruity aroma. Fairly full, crisp, clean, ripe grapefruit flavors; undertones of pears. Quite dry. (CR/ Jan. '86) ★★★

Michelton 1983 Marsanne, Wood Matured, Victoria $8. Fresh hay aroma and taste. Excellent balance on the rich, smooth side. (JPN/Jan. '87) 3/4

Brown Brothers 1980 Semillon, Milawa, Victoria $7.99. Dominant, woody bouquet hides varietal character. Enough oak for a sawmill. Lacks body; flat. (CR/Jan.'86)

FRENCH

Martin Schaetzel 1983 Tokay d'Alsace (Pinot Gris), Alsace $6.99. Huge, rich, concentrated, with oodles of fruit. Great length and plenty of sprightly acidity. (CC/Mar. '86) ★★★ (★★★1/2)

Trimbach 1982 Pinot Blanc, Alsace $5.69. Very fresh, light nose. Bright, clean, lemony flavors set off nicely with lively acidity. Beautifully proportioned, stylish. (RF/Jan. '86) ★★★

Bouchard Père et Fils 1983 Aligoté, Bouzeron, Domaine Carnot, Burgundy $6. Nice nose, fresh and fruity. Ripe, clean, fresh, flavorful, with well balanced acidity. (S&PW/Jan. '86) ★★

Schlumberger 1983 Pinot Blanc, Cuvée des Princes Abbes, Alsace $4.99. Delicate aroma of glacéed pineapple and cotton candy. Clean, fresh, dry. (CC/Mar. '86) ★★

Ch. La Jaubertie 1984 Bergerac Sec $5.50. Sweet, herbal-grassy aroma. Pleasant, peach taste. (JPN/Mar.'86) ★1/2

Klug 1983 Sylvaner, Alsace $4.99.

Delicate, simple, but refreshing. (CC/Mar. '86) ★1/2

Klug 1983 Tokay d'Alsace, Alsace $4.99. Restrained nose and bland flavors, but dry, clean. (CC/Mar. '86) ★

Léon Beyer 1983 Pinot Blanc de Blancs, Alsace $4.99. Cheesy, off-putting aromas give way to light, toasty scent. Pleasant, lemony, cardamom-like notes. Acidity is too soft. (CC/Mar. '86) ★

Preiss-Henny 1983 Sylvaner, Ch. de Mittelwihr, Alsace $4.75. Delicate almond aroma and flavor. Fresh, dry, light-bodied. (CC/Mar. '86) ★

Valbon White (nonvintage) $3.49. Toastiness, with a hint of olives. Suggests a nice white Burgundy, but fruit and acid are both low. (RF/Jan. '86) ★

Klug 1983 Edelzwicker, Alsace $4.99. Pineapple nuances. Dry, simple, dull, and short. (CC/Mar. '86)

Klug 1983 Muscat, Alsace $4.99. Herbaceous, grassy, minty nose. Off-dry, light-bodied. (CC/Mar. '86)

ITALIAN

Collavini 1984 Chardonnay, Estate Bottled, Delle Tre Venezie $4.99. Light, lemony nose. Some sulfur showing. Tart with green olive accents. Long, mild fruit finish. (RF/Jan. '86) ★★

Folonari (nonvintage) Tura $2.99. Clean, light, with slightly sudsy spritz. (RF/Jan. '86) ★

PORTUGUESE

Casa do Landeira 1984 Vinho Verde, Adamado $5.49. Fresh fig, green apple aroma. Dry, smooth flavors. Delicate, spearmint accents in the finish. (CC/Jan. '86) ★★★

Palacio da Brejoerira 1983 Alva-rinho, Moncão $17.49. Ripe pear aroma. Rich flavor, lively, zesty acidity.

Smooth textured, very long finish. As good as it is rare. (S&PW/Mar. '86) ★★★

Casa de Compostela 1984 Vinho Verde $5.99. Mellow, fruity nose, hints of pineapple. Good spritz. Bone dry. Tangy, lemon flavors; crisp, bracing finish. (CC/Jan. '86) ★★1/2

Quinta do Tamariz 1984 Vinho Verde $4.99. Flowery, fig-like nose. Restrained flavors. Bone dry. Tart and tangy; adequate spritz. Clean, sharp style. (CC/Jan. '86) ★★

Tormes 1983 Vinho Verde $4.99. Vanilla, figs, and quince nose. Medium-bodied. Tart, tangy, acid-edged finish. Snappy, bone-dry wine. (CC/Jan. '86) ★★

Tormes 1984 Vinho Verde $5.49. Fresh, fruity, melon and pineapple nose. Lively spritz. Tart, refreshing acidity. Ultra-dry wine with brisk finish. (CC/Jan. '86) ★★

RIESLING

Johannisberg Riesling is the name most often used on American wines made from Germany's great white variety, paying homage to the famous Rhine Valley wine estate Schloss Johannisberg. But White Riesling is an alternate name gaining acceptance, and a simple Riesling label is also sometimes used.

Riesling is the world's premier cool-climate varietal wine. The right vineyard site and a long, cool fermentation bring out a charming, floral scent and appley, citrusy fruit character, delicate but with depth. Prominent acidity (from cool growing conditions) is a key element, brightening fruit flavors and balancing any residual sweetness. Although Riesling can be successful as a dry wine, it is usually made with at least a hint of sweetness and ranges up to intensely sweet, concentrated wines.

Labels are getting better about letting consumers know how much sweetness to expect, often indicating "Dry" or "Early Harvest" for the more food-oriented wines and almost always saying "Late Harvest" for the very sweet, dessert wines. Check any small print, too, for a listing of the residual sweetness percentage (about 1-2% indicates slight sweetness). When the sweetness level is known for wines reviewed below, it is listed with the tasting notes.

"Botrytis" is a word often encountered in connection with Riesling. It refers to a type of mold that, given favorable ripening weather, can dehydrate the grapes and produce especially concentrated, late harvest wine with a characteristic honey-and-almond quality.

Although its total US acreage is less than half that of Chardonnay or Cabernet Sauvignon, Riesling is more widely grown. New York (especially the Finger Lakes), Washington, and Oregon have gained recognition for producing some of the best American Rieslings, and excellent wines have also come out of Idaho, Michigan, and a number of other states. California's best Rieslings come from its coolest districts, notably the Russian River Valley, Santa Inez, Santa Maria, Lake County, Mendocino, and Monterey County.

AMERICAN

Ch. Ste. Michelle 1977 Johannisberg Riesling, WA $15-20. Luscious, enticing bouquet. Like a first-rate German Beerenauslese. Just about perfect balance. Incredible. (DM/Mar.'86) ★★★★

Elk Cove Vineyards 1985 Riesling, Late Harvest, Willamette Valley, OR, $10. 5.9% Residual Sweetness. Concentrated, spicy, lemony nose. Sweet and luscious with excellent acid backbone. Perfectly balanced and harmonious. A long, crisp, green-apple finish invites the next sip. (AWC/Nov. '86) ★★★★

Hidden Cellars 1984 Johannisberg Riesling, Botrytised Late Harvest, Bailey J. Lovin Vineyard, Mendocino County, CA $10/375 ml. 11.6% Residual Sweetness. Beautiful, honeyed nose. Opulent, luscious, raisiny flavors. Long, lemony finish. Well balanced; not overpowering. Should continue improving. (AWC/Nov. '86) ★★★★

Joseph Phelps 1982 Johannisberg Riesling, Special Select Late Harvest, Napa Valley, CA $45. Intense, concentrated, honey nose laced with fruit and vanilla. Lots of Botrytis. Round, full, harmonious. (AWC/Sept. '85) ★★★★

Kenwood 1984 Johannisberg Riesling, Estate Grown, Late Harvest, Sonoma Valley, CA $7.50/375ml. Intense peach and honey scents with some juniper spice. (AWC/Sept. '85) ★★★★

Konocti 1984 White Riesling, Lake County, CA $5. Lively, lemony; sturdy, solid wine. Well made. (AWC/Nov.

'85) ★★★★

Robert Mondavi 1981 Johannisberg Riesling, Botrytised, Napa Valley, CA $25/375 ml. Rich, apricot and honey aroma. Lush apricot fruit enhanced by flavors of cream, treacle, burnt sugar. Refreshing. Slightly smoky. Should age beautifully. (JPN/Jan. '87) ★★★★

Susine 1982 Johannisberg Riesling, Late Harvest, El Dorado County, CA $15/375ml. An experience. Essence of apricot and honey so intense it almost resembles butterscotch. Very complex, very sweet, very long. More liqueur than wine. (JDM/Mar. '86) ★★★★

Windsor 1985 Johannisberg Riesling, Select Late Harvest, Russian River Valley, Sonoma County, CA $15. 11.8% Residual Sweetness. Deep gold color heralds an intense, honey-Botrytis nose. Deep, lip-smacking fruit flavors are sweet and long. Complex. Magnificent. (AWC/Nov '85) ★★★★

Bargetto 1984 White Riesling, Late Harvest, Santa Maria Valley, CA $10. 9.0% Residual Sweetness. Intensely Botrytised nose laced with apricot and pineapple aromas. Opulently ripe, full fruit flavors and soft acids. (AWC/Nov. '86) ★★★1/2

Ch. St. Jean 1984 Johannisberg Riesling, Robert Young Vineyards, Select Late Harvest, Alexander Valley, CA $15/375 ml. 18.4% Residual Sweetness. Delicate, charming nose shows some Botrytis. Extremely concentrated, ripe fruit flavors have hints of cinnamon and spice. Well balanced. (AWC/Nov. '86) ★★★1/2

Ch. St. Jean 1985 Johannisberg Riesling, Select Late Harvest, Russian River Valley, CA $12. 15.3% Residual Sweetness. More fruit than Botrytis in a lovely, lemony-citric nose. Great sugar-acid balance, with tangy fruit surging past the sweetness. Should age well up to five years. (AWC/Nov. '86) ★★★1/2

Clos du Bois 1984 Johannisberg Riesling, Early Harvest, Alexander Valley, CA $6.50. Forward. Citrusy. Good balance and varietal character. Will improve for a few years. (AWC/Nov. '85) ★★★1/2

Debevc 1985 Johannisberg Riesling, American (winery in OH) $6.95. 1.9% Residual Sweetness. Fine, bright, ultra-clean nose. Rich flavors of fresh fruit are well balanced by crisp acids. (AWC/Nov. '86) ★★★1/2

F. W. Langguth 1983 Johannisberg Riesling, Select Harvest, Columbia Valley, WA $11. Very Botrytised aroma. Somewhat Botrytized, crisp, restrained flavors. Doesn't taste as sweet as it is — 7.5%. A steal. (JPN/May '86) ★★★1/2

Fetzer 1985 Johannisberg Riesling, CA $6. 3.1% Residual Sweetness. Spicy, peachy nose. Round, grapey flavors, on the soft side. Long, lemony finish shows persistent ripeness. (AWC/Nov. '86) ★★★1/2

Firestone 1985 Johannisberg Riesling, Santa Ynez Valley, CA $6.50. 2.5% Residual Sweetness. Spicy, honey-and-apricot nose. Ripe, rich mouth feel balanced by refreshing acidity. Elegant. (AWC/Nov. '86) ★★★1/2

Gabriele y Caroline 1982 Riesling, Late Harvest, Monterey, CA $24. Honey and apricot and toast nose. Sweet, luscious. (AWC/Sept. '85) ★★★1/2

Kendall-Jackson 1985 Johannisberg Riesling, Monterey County, CA $7.50. 3.8% Residual Sweetness. Fragrant, honey and wildflower nose blossoms with airing. Rich in the mouth, embroidered with light spritz. Long, full, peachy flavors. (AWC/Nov. '86) ★★★1/2

Mark West Vineyards 1983 Johannisberg Riesling, Late Harvest, Estate Bottled, Russian River Val-

ley, CA **$10/375 ml.** 10.1% Residual Sweetness. Strong, raisiny, caramel-laced nose is full of Botrytis. Fat and honey-rich in the mouth. (AWC/Nov. '86) ★★★1/2

Preston Wine Cellars 1984 Johannisberg Riesling, WA $5.75. 2.25% Residual Sweetness. Plump but clearly etched nose of peaches, melons, and lychee nuts. Luscious, forward flavors well balanced with tangy acids. (AWC/Nov. '86) ★★★1/2

Rutherford Vintners 1982 Johannisberg Riesling, Napa Valley, CA $7.50. Deep, ripe nose of apricots, honey, and more than a little Botrytis. (AWC/Nov. '85) ★★★1/2

Santa Barbara Winery 1985 Johannisberg Riesling, Santa Ynez Valley, CA $6.50. 2.2% Residual Sweetness. Light, floral nose. Tastes less sweet than the nose promises. Elegant, lemony fruit. Crisp, tasty, tart finish. (AWC/Nov. '86) ★★★1/2

Stewart 1985 White Riesling, Select Late Harvest, Columbia Valley, WA $14. 8.1% Residual Sweetness. Flowery, peachy nose. Endless fruit nectar flavors. Tart, clean finish. Short-term aging potential. (AWC/Nov. '86) ★★★1/2

The Hogue Cellars 1984 Johannisberg Riesling, Markin Vineyard, Yakima Valley, WA $6.99. Fresh Riesling bouquet of pineapple, grapefruit, and lemon. (AWC/Nov. '85) ★★★1/2

Wagner 1985 Johannisberg Riesling, Estate Bottled, Finger Lakes, NY $6.98. 0.6% Residual Sweetness. Big, ripe, melony nose, followed by crisp, green-apple flavors. Clean, balanced, elegant. (AWC/Nov. '86) ★★★1/2

Winterbrook 1985 Riesling, Select Late Harvest, Santa Barbara County, CA $12/375 ml. 18.3% Residual Sweetness. Gentle, floral nose. Elegant style. Ripe fruit, not overpowering, prevails over honeyed, Botrytis flavors. Should improve for up to five years. (AWC/Nov. '86) ★★★1/2

Columbia 1985 Johannisberg Riesling, Late Harvest (Botrytis Affected), Red Willow Vineyard, WA $15. Fresh, citric aroma. Intense, burnt sugar, orange peel, and apricot flavors. Very clean and lively. Needs time. (JPN/Jan. '87) ★★★ (★★★★)

Arterberry 1985 White Riesling, Vintage Select, Yamhill County, OR $7.50. 4% Residual Sweetness. Sweet, appley aroma and flavor with hints of musk. Good body, complexity, delicacy. Clean, acidic finish. (JPN/Jan. '87) ★★★ (★★★1/2)

Poplar Ridge 1984 Johannisberg Riesling, Finger Lakes, NY $6.79. Light spice nose. Soft entry, with nice, spicy fruit, dry finish. Orange-apricot fruit. (RF/May '86) ★★★ (★★★1/2)

Alexander Valley Vineyards 1984 Johannisberg Riesling, Estate Bottled, Alexander Valley, CA $6. Flowery with hints of smoke. Full flavored, rich. (AWC/Nov. '85) ★★★

Alpine 1985 White Riesling, Estate Bottled, Willamette Valley, OR $7. 1.0% Residual Sweetness. Closed nose, but nice fruit in the mouth. Sweet entry, with a spicy, lingering finish. (AWC/Nov. '86) ★★★

Barboursville 1984 Riesling, Monticello, VA $6. Fragrant, simple, light, and clean. (AWC/Nov. '85) ★★★

Congress Springs 1985 Johannisberg Riesling, Santa Clara County, CA $7.50. 4.5% Residual Sweetness. Nose starts off peachy, then becomes nutty. Sweet and rich, almost heavy in the mouth. Soft, sweet finish. (AWC/Nov. '86) ★★★

F. W. Langguth 1984 Johannisberg Riesling, Late Harvest, Columbia Valley, WA $5.99. Full, flowery, ripe nose (AWC/Nov. '85) ★★★

Hidden Cellars 1985 Johannisberg Riesling, Potter Valley, Mendocino County, CA $7.50. 4.8% Residual Sweetness. Faint, sharp smells air out, uncovering apricot and apple aromas. Rich fruit and honey flavors are almost thick, could use a bit more acid. (AWC/Nov. '86) ★★★

J. Lohr 1984 Johannisberg Riesling, Greenfield Vineyards, Monterey County, CA $6. Pear aromas. Crisp, citric, grapefruit flavors. (AWC/Nov. '85) ★★★

J. Lohr 1985 Johannisberg Riesling, Greenfield Vineyards, Monterey County, CA $6. 2.4% Residual Sweetness. Shy, peachy, melony nose. Delicious, round, and fruity, with sweetness perhaps a bit high for the acidity to support. (AWC/Nov. '86) ★★★

Joseph Phelps 1983 Johannisberg Riesling, Special Select Late Harvest, Napa Valley, CA $25/375 ml. 23.6% Residual Sweetness. Rich nose of very ripe apricots. Very rich, sweet, honey flavors linger in the finish. (AWC/Nov. '86) ★★★

Kendall-Jackson 1985 Johannisberg Riesling, Lake County, CA $8. 2.9% Residual Sweetness. Melony nose tinted with clove-like spice. Slightly spritzy in the mouth. Clean and refreshing. Long, citric finish. (AWC/Nov. '86) ★★★

Kenwood 1984 Johannisberg Riesling, Estate Grown, Sonoma Valley, CA $8.50/375 ml. Subdued character. Pleasing fruit. (AWC/Nov. '85) ★★★

Kenwood 1985 Johannisberg Riesling, Late Harvest, Estate Grown, Sonoma Valley, CA $10/375 ml. 11.35% Residual Sweetness. Pleasantly pungent nose of clove and honey. Simple, sweet-fruit flavors. (AWC/Nov. '86) ★★★

Kiona 1985 White Riesling, Estate Bottled, Yakima Valley, WA $5.95. 3.0% Residual Sweetness. Clean, shy, but charming, apple-vanilla nose. Bright, high acid, lemony fruit flavors. Restrained style. (AWC/Nov. '86) ★★★

Konocti 1985 White Riesling,

Lake County, CA $5. 3.3% Residual Sweetness. Clear, ripe, varietal nose, fragrant and spicy. Light, sweet, citric flavors linger. (AWC/Nov. '86) ★★★

Louis Facelli 1984 Johannisberg Riesling, ID $7. Lovely, peach aroma and flavor. Light body. High acidity. (JPN/Jan. '86) ★★★

Mulhausen 1983 Riesling, Estate Bottled, Willamette Valley, OR $6.75. Complex aromas of fruit, cheese, herbs, flowers. Complex flavors of musk, salt water, apples. Moderate sweetness masked by lively acidity. (JPN/Jan. '87) ★★★

Obester 1984 Johannisberg Riesling, Mendocino County, CA $6.95. Clean, fruity nose. Well balanced; with substance. (AWC/Nov. '85) ★★★

Obester 1985 Johannisberg Riesling, Monterey County, CA $6.95. 1.5% Residual Sweetness. Short, apricoty nose. Lovely, mouth-filling fruit flavors, backed up by just enough acid. (AWC/Nov. '86) ★★★

Quail Run 1984 White Riesling, Mahre Vineyards, Yakima Valley, WA $7.50. Fruit-cocktail perfume. Well made. (AWC/Sept. '85) ★★★

Raymond 1985 Johannisberg Riesling, Selected Late Harvest, Napa Valley, CA $8.50. 11.5% Residual Sweetness. Spicy, Riesling aromas. Clean, citric flavors have a crisp finish. Very good balance and harmony of flavors. (AWC/Nov. '86) ★★★

Shenandoah Vineyards 1985 Riesling, t.b.a. (totally botrytis affected), Eldorado County, CA $16/375 ml. 24.0% Residual Sweetness. Deep, tawny amber color. Raisiny smells lead into thick, deep, apricot flavors. Intense. Much Botrytis. (AWC/Nov. '86) ★★★

Snoqualmie 1984 White Riesling, Late Harvest, Signature Reserve, Yakima Valley, WA $12.89. 9.0% Residual Sweetness. A fragrant aroma is more herbal than grapey. Luscious, ripe fruit flavors. (AWC/Nov. '86) ★★★

Staton Hills 1984 Johannisberg Riesling, Yakima Valley, WA $5.95. 1.9% Residual Sweetness. Intense, luscious nose with honey-like Botrytis. Opulent, complex fruit, but with a hot finish. (AWC/Nov. '86) ★★★

Stewart 1985 Johannisberg Riesling, Wahluke Slope, Columbia Valley, WA $6. 1.9% Residual Sweetness. Pretty, citrusy nose of medium intensity. A light-bodied, classy young wine that should age well. (AWC/Nov. '86) ★★★

V. Sattui 1985 Johannisberg Riesling, Dry, Napa Valley, CA $7.25. 0.6% Residual Sweetness. Clean, fresh-fruit nose with banana tones. Delicate finish. (AWC/Nov. '86) ★★★

Forgeron 1984 White Riesling, OR $6.25. Sweet grapefruit aroma. Lots of acid nicely balanced with residual sweetness. Delicate, floral hints. (JPN/Jan. '86) ★★1/2 (★★★1/2)

Yamhill Valley Vineyard 1985 Riesling, OR $6.50. Floral, musk aromas; grapefruity, tart Riesling character. Barely sweet at 2.2%. Should gain complexity with age. (JPN/May '86)★★1/2 (★★★1/2)

Adelsheim 1984 White Riesling, Yamhill County, OR $7. Shy aroma opens to ripe, Golden Delicious apple and sweet, floral-buttery fragrance. Good character and complexity. Not too sweet. Medium body, smooth. Firm, spicy finish. (JPN/Jan. '87) ★★1/2 (★★★)

Broich 1985 Riesling, ID $6. Spritzy. Rich varietal nose has aromas of hay, slight smoke, green apple, musk. Sweet and very acidic. Needs bottle age. (JPN/Jan. '87) ★★1/2 (★★★)

Elk Cove Vineyards 1984 Riesling, Estate Bottled, Willamette Valley, OR $6.75. Clean, lemony, light, off-dry, with hints of apple. Needs age to develop. (JPN/Jan. '87) ★★1/2 (★★★)

F. W. Langguth 1984 Late Harvest Riesling, WA $8. Spätlese style. Peachy, fresh, crisp. Needs bottle age. (JPN/May '86) ★★1/2 (★★★)

Glenora 1984 Johannisberg Riesling, Finger Lakes, NY $5.99. Shy nose. Nice, tangy acidity and bright, delicious fruit. Endless, spicy fruit finish. (RF/Mar. '86) ★★1/2 (★★★)

Ch. Ste. Michelle 1985 Johannisberg Riesling, WA $5.50. Delicate floral, musk, and sweet fruit aroma. Crisp, clean, slightly sweet. (JPN/Jan. '87) ★★1/2

Hinman 1984 Riesling, OR $7.35. Sweet, fruity, powdery aroma. Sweet and sour flavors. Good character and complexity. Light, acidic, bracing, clean. (JPN/Jan. '87) ★★1/2

Mirassou 1983 Johannisberg Riesling, Late Harvest, Monterey County, CA $8.50. Botrytis character evident in apricot and vaguely floral aroma. Sweetness (7.2%) balanced by acidity. Apricot and peach flavor has a long finish, not cloying. Good value. (S&PW/Jan. '86) ★★1/2

Ste. Chapelle 1984 Johannisberg Riesling, ID $6.25. Peach aroma, hint of flowers. Fairly sweet, nicely balanced. (JPN/Jan. '86) ★★1/2

Dr. Konstantin Frank 1982 Johannisberg Riesling, Finger Lakes, NY $5.99. Floral aroma has a citrus-like backnote and herbal overtone. Nice mouthful of fruit with light sweetness balanced by zesty acidity. Nice mouth feel. Long finish. Good value. (S&PW/May '86) ★★1/2

Wasson Bros. 1984 Riesling, Willamette Valley, OR $6.50. Forward, green apple character. Semi-sweet. Solid structure. (JPN/Jan. '87) ★★1/2

Spring Creek 1985 Riesling, ID $5. Spritzy. Citric flavors, slightly sweet, balanced by good acidity. Needs time. (JPN/

Jan. '87) ★★ (★★★)

Arbor Crest 1983 Johannisberg Riesling, Select Late Harvest, WA $8/375ml. Fruity aroma. Crisp, Riesling taste. Very sweet dessert wine. (JPN/May '86) ★★

Barboursville 1985 Riesling, Monticello, VA $6.50. 0.8% Residual Sweetness. Shy nose with a hint of spice. Refreshing, quaffable style. (AWC/Nov. '86) ★★

Buena Vista 1984 Johannisberg Riesling, Sonoma Valley—Carneros, CA $7.75. 1.4% Residual Sweetness. Intriguing, earthy and grassy elements in the nose. (AWC/Nov. '86) ★★

Buena Vista 1984 Johannisberg Riesling, Sonoma Valley—Carneros, CA $8.25. 3.8% Residual Sweetness. Forward nose with slight Botrytis complexity. Elegant, subtle fruit. Grainy, lemon finish. (AWC/Nov. '86) ★★

Byrd 1984 Johannisberg Riesling, Estate Bottled, Catoctin, MD $7.50. Lemony nose, typical Riesling character. Short, crisp, clean. (AWC/Nov. '85) ★★

Ch. Georges 1985 Riesling, Special Select, NY $6. 2.94% Residual Sweetness. Light, floral nose. Refreshing and easy to drink. (AWC/Nov. '86) ★★

Clos du Bois 1981 Johannisberg Riesling, Late Harvest, Individual Bunch Selected, Alexander Valley, CA $10/375 ml. Well made though sweetness crowds ripe Riesling flavors. (AWC/Sept. '85) ★★

Clos du Bois 1982 Johannisberg Riesling, Late Harvest, Alexander Valley, CA $15/375 ml. 13.5% Residual Sweetness. An aromatic nose has pungent notes. Plump, forward fruit flavors. Tangy, light style. (AWC/Nov. '86) ★★

Colorado Mountain 1985 Johannisberg Riesling, Mesa County, CO $6.50. 1.5% Residual Sweetness. Licorice or anise-like scents and flavors. Spicy and yet mellow on the palate. A bit short on acid. (AWC/Nov. '86) ★★

Columbia 1984 Johannisberg Riesling, Cellarmaster's Reserve, WA $8. Restrained, lemony, citrus nose. (AWC/Sept. '85) ★★

Debevc 1984 Johannisberg Riesling, Wagner Vineyards, NY (winery in OH) $6.95. Grapey. (AWC/Nov. '85) ★★

Elk Cove Vineyards 1984 Riesling, Dundee Hills Vineyard, OR $6.75. Spritzy. Sweet, powdery aroma has hints of cheese. Tart, almost sour, with a grassy character. Unflawed but atypical. (JPN/Jan. '87) ★★

F. W. Langguth 1983 Classic Riesling, WA $6.50. Flowery aroma. German style: light, fruity, slightly sweet. (JPN/May '86) ★★

F. W. Langguth 1983 Johannisberg Riesling, Special Release, Select Harvest, Columbia Valley, WA $9.50. Raspberry, lemon, and ginger. Clean, sweet, adequate acidity. (AWC/Sept. '85) ★★

F. W. Langguth 1984 Johannisberg Riesling, Select Harvest, Columbia Valley, WA $8.50. 8.5% Residual Sweetness. Toasty, syrupy nose. Ripe, sweet flavors have just enough acidity. (AWC/Nov. '86) ★★

Felton-Empire 1985 White Riesling, Santa Cruz Mountains, CA $7. 1.75% Residual Sweetness. Light, spicy nose. Racy acidity. Snappy and refreshing. (AWC/Nov. '86) ★★

Finger Lakes 1985 Johannisberg Riesling, Finger Lakes, NY $6.99. 1.1% Residual Sweetness. Citric nose. Refreshing, delicate, pineapple flavors. (AWC/Nov. '86) ★★

Finger Lakes Wine Cellars 1984 Johannisberg Riesling, Finger Lakes, NY $7.99. Clean; high acid balanced by residual sweetness gives an off-dry, peaches-in-honey flavor. (RF/Jan. '86) ★★

Glenora 1984 Johann Blanc, Finger Lakes, NY $5.49. Clean, light, easy drinking. Bone dry. (AWC/Nov. '85) ★★

Haywood 1984 White Riesling, Estate Bottled, Sonoma Valley, CA $7. Honeyed nose. Balanced, long, citric finish. (AWC/Nov. '85) ★★

Haywood 1985 White Riesling, Estate Bottled, Sonoma Valley, CA $7.50. 1.6% Residual Sweetness. Light, clean, fruity nose. Zingy, spicy fruit with a little bite in the finish. (AWC/Nov. '86) ★★

Hazlitt 1985 Johannisberg Riesling, Finger Lakes, NY $6. 2.5% Residual Sweetness. Weak nose, but very good depth of fruit flavor. Soft, short finish. (AWC/Nov. '86) ★★

Heron Hill 1984 Johannisberg Riesling, Estate Bottled, Finger Lakes, NY $6.99. 0.8% Residual Sweetness. Ripe grapefruit nose. Full apricot fruit does not quite follow through to the finish. Balanced. Ageable. (AWC/Nov. '86) ★★

Ivanhoe 1985 Johannisberg Riesling, TX $5.99. 2.6% Residual Sweetness. Shifting nose has suggestions of ripe melons and toast. A bit of spritz. Soft finish. (AWC/Nov. '86) ★★

J. Lohr 1985 Johannisberg Riesling, Late Harvest, Monterey County, CA $7.50/375 ml. 12.65% Residual Sweetness. Unusual, light straw color. Allspice nose. Spicy, sweet lemon flavors. (AWC/Nov. '86) ★★

J. Pedroncelli 1984 Johannisberg Riesling, Sonoma County, CA $5.50. Alcohol, butter, or smoke nose. Hot but not unpleasant finish. (AWC/Nov. '85) ★★

Jekel 1981 Riesling, Late Harvest, Estate Bottled, Monterey County, CA $10/375 ml. Restrained nose with a touch of orange and apricot. Very young.

Needs time. (AWC/Sept. '85) ★★

Jekel 1984 Johannisberg Riesling, Monterey, CA $6.75. Citrus, strawberries; soft, easy drinking. (AWC/Nov. '85) ★★

Jekel 1985 Johannisberg Riesling, Arroyo Seco, CA $6.75. 2.1% Residual Sweetness. Clean, fresh nose. Pleasant, easy drinking. (AWC/Nov. '86) ★★

Kendall-Jackson 1984 Johannisberg Riesling, Monterey County, CA $7. Pear-like flavors with high acidity; lemony finish. (AWC/Nov. '85) ★★

Knudsen-Erath 1985 White Riesling, Yamhill County, OR $5.45. 1.5% Residual Sweetness. Nice, fruit-salad nose and flavors of peaches, apricots, and bananas, but a little short. (AWC/Nov. '86) ★★

Latah Creek 1984 White Riesling, WA $5.49. (AWC/Nov. '85) ★★

Mark West Vineyards 1984 Johannisberg Riesling, Estate Bottled, Russian River Valley, CA $6.95. Citrus and apricot. Solid wine with food. (AWC/Nov. '85) ★★

Paul Thomas 1984 Johannisberg Riesling, Vintage Reserve, WA $7. Lively, lemon, grapefruit, and pineapple flavors. (AWC/Nov. '85) ★★

Paul Thomas 1985 Johannisberg Riesling, WA $7. 2.7% Residual Sweetness. Shy, lemony, apricot smells. Forceful sugars in lush varietal flavors. Tingle-crisp acidity. (AWC/Nov. '86) ★★

Rex Hill Vineyards 1984 Riesling, OR $6. Perfumy nose. Slightly sweet. A bit thin. Pleasantly quaffable. (JPN/Jan. '86) ★★

Rodney Strong 1985 Johannisberg Riesling, Claus Vineyard, Russian River Valley, CA $8. 1.90% Residual Sweetness. Deep golden color telegraphs Botrytis in the nose. Round, full, apricoty fruit, but low acidity and slightly harsh finish. (AWC/Nov. '86) ★★

Sokol Blosser 1985 White Ries-

ling, Select Harvest, Yamhill County, OR $10.50.** 7.0% Residual Sweetness. Cinammon-apple nose. Crisp, clean, citric flavors linger. (AWC/Nov. '86) ★★

Staton Hills 1985 White Riesling, Yakima Valley, WA $6.95. 6.0% Residual Sweetness. Alluring, honey, nut, and cinnamon nose. Pleasant, straightforward flavors. (AWC/Nov. '86) ★★

The Gainey Vineyard 1984 Johannisberg Riesling, Santa Barbara County, CA $6.50. Spicy, grapefruit nose. (AWC/Nov. '85) ★★

The Hogue Cellars 1984 Johannisberg Riesling, Yakima Valley, WA $5.49. Fragrant, lemony, spritzy, lively. (AWC/Nov. '85) ★★

Tualatin 1984 White Riesling, Willamette Valley, OR $7. Some sulfur in a reserved varietal aroma. Crisp, appley, apricot taste. Sweet apple finish is a bit cloying. (JPN/Jan. '87) ★★

Ventana 1985 White Riesling, Estate Bottled, Monterey, CA $7. 2.1% Residual Sweetness. Simple fruit nose is bothered by sweaty hints. Piquant, appealing layers of fruit. (AWC/Nov. '86) ★★

Widmer 1985 Johannisberg Riesling, Private Reserve, Finger Lakes, NY $5.99. 1.8% Residual Sweetness. Minty, perfumy, Chenin-Blanc-like nose. Citrusy, lemon-lime flavors. (AWC/Nov. '86) ★★

Worden's Washington Winery 1985 Johannisberg Riesling, WA $5.99. 2.6% Residual Sweetness. Fragrant, fresh nose. Loosely structured flavors of sweet, soft fruit. (AWC/Nov. '86) ★★

Mulhausen Riesling (nonvintage), OR $6.30. Nice fruit behind some stinkiness. Off-dry. Very well balanced. Needs time. (JPN/Jan. '87) ★1/2 (★★)

Alpine 1984 White Riesling, Estate Bottled, Willamette Valley, OR $7. Salt water and Botrytis aroma. Off-dry, vague flavors. (JPN/Jan. '87) ★1/2

Christian Brothers 1984 Riesling, Napa Valley, CA $8. Pineapple aroma. Fairly full bodied. Not too sweet. A bit low in acid. Full, warm finish. (JPN/Mar. '86) ★1/2

Hidden Springs 1983 White Riesling, Reserve, OR $7. Old, apple butter aroma. Slight chemical taste. Medium sweet with nice balance. (JPN/Jan. '87) ★1/2

Northwest Daily 1984 Johannisberg Riesling, Yakima Valley, WA $5. Slightly smoky aroma. Smooth, full bodied, slightly sweet. A pleasant sipper. Crisp finish. (JPN/May '86) ★1/2

Rex Hill Vineyards 1985 White Riesling, OR $7. Very sweet, powdery aroma. Slight spritz. Salty, semi-sweet taste with pleasant acidity. (JPN/Jan. '87) ★1/2

Veritas 1984 Riesling, OR $5. Good varietal aroma. Very light body. (JPN/Mar. '86) ★1/2

Hillcrest 1982 White Riesling, OR $6.25. Apricot, cheese, honey nose. Sour, watery, unfocused flavors. Smoky finish. (JPN/Jan. '87) ★

Stag's Leap Wine Cellars 1985 White Riesling, Napa-Sonoma, CA $6. Intense, floral-musk aroma. Decent, semi-sweet flavors without delicacy. (JPN/Jan. '87) ★

Garden Valley 1984 White Riesling, OR $7. Cheese and sulfur aroma. Sweet, a bit cloying, flat. (JPN/Jan. '87) 1/2

Pellier 1985 White Riesling, Willamette Valley, OR $7.35. Sulfur nose. Vague, appley aroma and taste. Medium body. Sweet and flabby. (JPN/Jan. '87) 1/2

Sokol Blosser White Riesling (nonvintage), Columbia Valley, WA $5.25. Decent fruit is masked by a medicinal quality. Good balance. Semi-sweet. Bittersweet, soapy finish. (JPN/Jan. '87) 1/2

Ch. Ste. Michelle 1982 White Riesling, Chateau Reserve, Late Harvest, Hahn Hill Vineyards, Hand Se-

lected Clusters, WA **$11.50.** 6.02% Residual Sweetness. (AWC/Nov. '86)

Covey Run 1985 Johannisberg Riesling, Yakima Valley, WA $6.98. 1.8% Residual Sweetness. Spicy fruit up front. Refreshingly tart, but with a bitter, candy-like finish. (AWC/Nov. '86)

Knudsen-Erath 1985 White Riesling, Vintage Select, Willamette Valley, OR $7.95. 3.2% Residual Sweetness. (AWC/Nov. '86)

The Hogue Cellars 1985 Johannisberg Riesling, Yakima Valley, WA $5.49. 1.7% Residual Sweetness. (AWC/Nov. '86)

Alba 1984 Riesling, NY (winery in NJ) $6.50. (AWC/Nov. '85)

Alba 1985 Riesling, Hunterdon County, NJ $6.50. 3.0% Residual Sweetness. (AWC/Nov. '86)

Alexander Valley Vineyards 1985 Johannisberg Riesling, Estate Bottled, Alexander Valley, CA $6. 1.5% Residual Sweetness. (AWC/Nov. '86)

Amity 1984 White Riesling, OR $7. (AWC/Nov. '86)

Amity 1985 White Riesling, OR $7.50. 1.0% Residual Sweetness. (AWC/Nov. '86)

Arbor Crest 1982 Johannisberg Riesling, Cameo Reserve, Selected Late Harvest, Stewart's Sunnyside Vineyard, WA $28/375 ml. (AWC/Sept. '85)

Arbor Crest 1984 Johannisberg Riesling, WA $5. 3.1% Residual Sweetness. (AWC/Nov. '86)

Arbor Crest 1984 White Riesling, WA $6.25. Clean, light. (AWC/Nov. '85)

Baldwin 1984 Riesling, Reserve, NY $6.99. Very closed; yields little varietal character. (AWC/Nov. '86)

Beringer 1984 Johannisberg Riesling, Napa Valley, CA $7.50. (AWC/Nov. '85)

Bridgehampton 1984 Riesling, The Hamptons, Long Island, NY $7.50. 5.0% Residual Sweetness. (AWC/Nov. '86)

Callaway 1984 White Riesling, Temecula, CA $6.25. (AWC/Nov. '86)

Callaway 1985 White Riesling, Temecula, CA $5.50. 1.45% Residual Sweetness. (AWC/Nov. '86)

Cascade Mountain (nonvintage) Riesling, NY $7. (AWC/Nov. '86)

Catoctin 1984 Johannisberg Riesling, MD $5.95. 0.5% Residual Sweetness. Neutral. (AWC/Nov. '86)

Ch. Benoit 1984 White Riesling, OR $6.95. 1.0% Residual Sweetness. (AWC/Nov. '86)

Ch. Diana 1984 Johannisberg Riesling, Late Harvest, Dawn Manning Selection, Santa Barbara, CA $8. 5.5% Residual Sweetness. Ripe nose of melon and almond. Ripe peachy flavors are overwhelmed by sweetness. (AWC/Nov. '86)

Ch. Grand Traverse 1983 Johannisberg Riesling, Late Harvest, MI $8.99. (AWC/Sept. '85)

Ch. Grand Traverse 1983 Johannisberg Riesling, Limited Bottling, Late Harvest Dry, MI $8.99. (AWC/ Nov. '85)

Ch. Grand Traverse 1984 Johannisberg Riesling, Semi-Dry, MI $7.99. 3.0% Residual Sweetness. (AWC/Nov. '86)

Ch. Morrisette 1984 Riesling, VA $7. (AWC/Nov. '85)

Ch. St. Jean 1985 Johannisberg Riesling, Sonoma County, CA $8.50. 1.9% Residual Sweetness. Oily or sweaty smells. (AWC/Nov. '86)

Ch. Ste. Michelle 1983 White Riesling, Limited Bottling, WA $6.15. (AWC/Nov. '85)

Ch. Ste. Michelle 1984 Johannisberg Riesling, WA $5.85. 1.8% Residual Sweetness. (AWC/Nov. '86)

Charles Krug 1983 Johannisberg

Riesling, Napa Valley, CA $6.50. (AWC/Nov. '85)

Cilurzo 1984 Johannisberg Riesling, Botrytised Late Harvest, Temecula, CA $30. 12.5% Residual Sweetness. (AWC/Nov. '86)

Clos du Bois 1985 Johannisberg Riesling, Early Harvest, Alexander Valley, CA $7.50. 1.75% Residual Sweetness. (AWC/Nov. '86)

Colony 1985 Johannisberg Riesling, Clegg Ranch, Knight's Valley, Sonoma County, CA $4.99. 1.8% Residual Sweetness. (AWC/Nov. '86)

Columbia 1983 Johannisberg Riesling, WA $6. (AWC/Nov. '85)

Columbia 1984 Johannisberg Riesling, Late Harvest, Red Willow Vineyards, WA $7/375 ml. 10.0% Residual Sweetness. Cardboard or oily smell. Rich flavors could use more depth. (AWC/Nov. '86)

Columbia 1985 Johannisberg Riesling, Cellarmaster's Reserve, WA $7. 7.0% Residual Sweetness. (AWC/Nov. '86)

Commonwealth 1983 Riesling, MA $7.95. (AWC/Nov. '85)

Commonwealth 1984 Riesling, MA $7.95. (AWC/Nov. '85)

Debevc 1985 Johannisberg Riesling, Grand River Valley, OH $6.95. 2.8% Residual Sweetness. (AWC/Nov. '86)

Domain San Martin 1981 Johannisberg Riesling, Late Harvest, Central Coast, CA $7.99. Strange, raisiny smells. (AWC/Sept. '85)

Domain San Martin 1983 Johannisberg Riesling, Central Coast, CA $5.50. Ripe, shows a little Botrytis. Dry with good body. (AWC/Nov. '85)

Domain San Martin 1984 Johannisberg Riesling, Soft, Central Coast, CA $3.99. (AWC/Nov. '85)

Domain San Martin 1985 Johannis-

berg Riesling, Central Coast, CA $5.50. 1.4% Residual Sweetness. Simple, pleasant, refreshing. (AWC/Nov. '86)

Durney 1984 Johannisberg Riesling, Estate Bottled, Carmel Valley, CA $6.50. 1.55% Residual Sweetness. (AWC/Nov. '86)

Elk Cove Vineyards 1985 Riesling, Estate Bottled, Willamette Valley, OR $6.75. 1.5% Residual Sweetness. (AWC/Nov. '86)

Elk Run Vineyards 1985 Riesling, Classic Eastern, American, MD $5.99. 1.0% Residual Sweetness. (AWC/ Nov. '86)

Ernest & Julio Gallo 1984 Johannisberg Riesling, Limited Release, CA $3.50. 0.63% Residual Sweetness. (AWC/Nov. '86)

Estrella River Winery 1984 Johannisberg Riesling, Estate Bottled, Paso Robles, CA $6. (AWC/Nov. '85)

F. W. Langguth 1983 Johannisberg Riesling, Special Release, Anders Gyving Vineyard, WA $5.99. Cloying honey and pineapple bouquet. (AWC/Nov. '85)

Fetzer 1984 Johannisberg Riesling, CA $6. (AWC/Nov. '85)

Firelands 1985 Johannisberg Riesling, Lake Erie, OH $5.95. 1.01% Residual Sweetness. (AWC/Nov. '86)

Forgeron 1985 White Riesling, OR $6.50. 2.5% Residual Sweetness. (AWC/ Nov. '86)

Franciscan 1983 Johannisberg Riesling, Estate Bottled, Napa Valley, CA $6.50. (AWC/Nov. '85)

Freemark Abbey 1985 Johannisberg Riesling, Napa Valley, CA $7.25. 2.4% Residual Sweetness. (AWC/ Nov. '86)

Giumarra 1985 Johannisberg Riesling, Proprietor's Reserve, Central Coast, CA $4.19. 1.8% Residual Sweetness. (AWC/Nov. '86)

Glenora 1985 Johann Blanc, Finger Lakes, NY $5.69. 0.6% Residual Sweetness. (AWC/Nov. '86)

Glenora 1985 Johannisberg Riesling, Finger Lakes, NY $5.99. 1.5% Residual Sweetness. (AWC/Nov. '86)

Glenora 1985 Johannisberg Riesling, Springledge Vineyard, Finger Lakes, NY $6.99. 4.0% Residual Sweetness. (AWC/Nov. '86)

Hermann J. Wiemer 1984 Johannisberg Riesling, Late Harvest, Finger Lakes, NY $9.99. 3.5% Residual Sweetness. Flowery nose. Nice, light fruit flavors. (AWC/Nov. '86)

Hidden Cellars 1984 Johannisberg Riesling, Late Harvest, Potter Valley, Mendocino County, CA $7.50. (AWC/Nov. '85)

Inglenook 1984 Johannisberg Riesling, Estate Bottled, Napa Valley, CA $6.50. 1.2% Residual Sweetness. (AWC/Nov. '86)

Joseph Phelps 1984 Johannisberg Riesling, Early Harvest, Napa Valley, CA $7.50. (AWC/Nov. '86)

Knapp 1985 Johannisberg Riesling, Finger Lakes, NY $6.95. 2.0% Residual Sweetness. A fragrant, melony nose seems a bit candyish. Low acid makes the sugar stand out. (AWC/Nov. '86)

Knudsen Erath 1984 White Riesling, Yamhill County, OR $6. Cheesy, bacterial aroma and taste. Sweet, low in acid. Cloying, watery finish. (JPN/Jan. '87)

Latah Creek 1985 Johannisberg Riesling, WA $5.75. 2.1% Residual Sweetness. (AWC/Nov. '86)

Latah Creek 1985 White Riesling, Late Harvest, WA $10.99. 7.5% Residual Sweetness. (AWC/Nov. '86)

Llano Estacado 1985 Johannisberg Riesling, TX $8. 2.7% Residual Sweetness. Appley smells. Funky, unpleasant character. (AWC/Nov. '86)

Louis Facelli 1984 Johannisberg Riesling, Dry, WA $5.99. (AWC/Nov. '86)

Lynfred Johannisberg Riesling (nonvintage), Bottled in 1985, Private Reserve, Limited Edition, CA (winery in IL) $9.50. Soft, slight candy flavors. (AWC/Nov. '85)

Lynfred Johannisberg Riesling (nonvintage), Bottled in 1985, Select Harvest, American (winery in IL) $19.50. (AWC/Sept. '85)

Mark West Vineyards 1985 Johannisberg Riesling, Estate Bottled, Russian River Valley, CA $6.95. 0.7% Residual Sweetness. (AWC/Nov. '86)

McGregor 1984 Johannisberg Riesling, Finger Lakes, NY $7.50. (AWC/Nov. '85)

Meier's 1985 Johannisberg Riesling, Isle St. George, OH $4.99. 1.0% Residual Sweetness. (AWC/Nov. '86)

Meredyth 1984 Riesling, VA $7.50. (AWC/Nov. '85)

Mirassou 1984 Johannisberg Riesling, Monterey County, CA $6.50. (AWC/Nov. '86)

Mission Mountain Winery 1984 White Riesling, Columbia Valley, WA (winery in MT) $5. (AWC/Nov. '85)

Mission Mountain Winery 1985 Johannisberg Riesling, Columbia Valley, WA (winery in MT) $4.99. 1.9% Residual Sweetness. (AWC/Nov. '86)

Monterey 1985 Johannisberg Riesling, Monterey County, CA $6. 1.45% Residual Sweetness. (AWC/Nov. '86)

Montdomaine 1984 White Riesling, Semi-dry, VA $6. 1.5% Residual Sweetness. (AWC/Nov. '86)

Napa Creek Winery 1984 Johannisberg Riesling, Napa Valley, CA $6.50. (AWC/Nov. '86)

Navarro 1984 White Riesling, An-

derson Valley, Mendocino, CA
$6.85. 2.8% Residual Sweetness. Ripe, floral nose, but dull, unvarietal flavors. (AWC/Nov. '86)

Oak Knoll 1985 White Riesling, OR $6.50. 1.5% Residual Sweetness. (AWC/Nov. '86)

Obester 1984 Johannisberg Riesling, Monterey County, CA $6.95. (AWC/Nov. '86)

Otter Spring (Heron Hill) 1983 Johannisberg Riesling, Estate Bottled, Free Run, Finger Lakes, NY $8.99. (AWC/Nov. '85)

Paul Masson 1983 Johannisberg Riesling, Monterey County, CA $5.99. (AWC/Nov. '86)

Paul Masson 1985 Johannisberg Riesling, Monterey County, CA $5.99. 1.5% Residual Sweetness. (AWC/Nov. '86)

Peconic Bay Vineyards 1984 White Riesling, North Fork, Long Island, NY $7.49. (AWC/Nov. '85)

Pindar 1984 Johannisberg Riesling, Green Label, Long Island, NY $7.99. 3.0% Residual Sweetness. (AWC/Nov. '86)

Pindar 1984 Johannisberg Riesling, Long Island, NY $6.99. 1.5% Residual Sweetness. Candied, non-varietal nose. Flat, dull flavors. (AWC/Nov. '86)

Plane's Cayuga Vineyard 1984 Johannisberg Riesling, Finger Lakes, NY $6.99. (AWC/Nov. '85)

Plane's Cayuga Vineyard 1985 Johannisberg Riesling, Dry, Finger Lakes, NY $6.99. 0.75% Residual Sweetness. (AWC/Nov. '86)

Preston Wine Cellars 1982 Johannisberg Riesling, WA $5.40. (AWC/Nov. '85)

Prince Michel 1985 White Riesling, VA $7. 1.5% Residual Sweetness. (AWC/Nov. '86)

Pucci 1984 Johannisberg Riesling, WA $5.75 (AWC/Nov. '85)

Quail Run 1984 Johannisberg Riesling, Whiskey Canyon Vineyard, Yakima Valley, WA (AWC/Nov. '85)

Quail Run 1984 Johannisberg Riesling, Yakima Valley, WA $6.51. (AWC/Nov. '86)

Raymond 1984 Johannisberg Riesling, Napa Valley, CA $6. (AWC/Nov. '86)

Rodney Strong 1984 Johannisberg Riesling, Le Baron Vineyard, Late Harvest, Russian River Valley, CA $9/375 ml. 6.7% Residual Sweetness. (AWC/Nov. '86)

Rodney Strong 1984 Johannisberg Riesling, Le Baron Vineyard, Russian River Valley, CA $8. 2.0% Residual Sweetness. (AWC/Nov. '86)

Rustridge 1985 Johannisberg Riesling, Estate Bottled, Napa Valley, CA $8.70. 1.9% Residual Sweetness. Spicy, Rheingau-style nose, but strange, moldy flavors. (AWC/Nov. '86)

Rutherford Vintners 1984 Johannisberg Riesling, Napa Valley, CA $7.50. 2.0% Residual Sweetness. Pungent, honeyed, Botrytis smells, but flabby; low acid. (AWC/Nov. '86)

Saddle Mountain (Langguth Winery) 1984 Johannisberg Riesling, WA $6.99. 6.0% Residual Sweetness. Disturbing, petroleum smells. (AWC/Nov. '86)

Sakonnet 1984 White Riesling, Southeastern New England, winery in RI $6.99. (AWC/Nov. '85)

Salishan 1985 Dry White Riesling, WA $6. 0.05% Residual Sweetness. (AWC/Nov. '86)

San Dominique 1983 Johannisberg Riesling, AZ $6.27. (AWC/Nov. '85)

Sebastiani 1983 Johannisberg Riesling, Sonoma County, CA $6.65. (AWC/Nov. '86)

Sebastiani 1985 Johannisberg Riesling, Sonoma County, CA $6.65. 1.0% Residual Sweetness. (AWC/Nov. '86)

Shafer Vineyard Cellars 1983 Riesling, Dry, Willamette Valley, OR $7. Clean, no defects, but lacks pizazz. (AWC/Nov. '85)

Shafer Vineyard Cellars 1984 Riesling, Estate Bottled, Willamette Valley, OR $6.75. 1.0% Residual Sweetness. Lightweight. Lemony. (AWC/Nov. '86)

Smith-Madrone 1984 Johannisberg Riesling, Napa Valley, CA $7.25. (AWC/Nov. '85)

Snoqualmie 1984 Johannisberg Riesling, Yakima Valley, WA $5.99. Petroleum nose. (AWC/Nov. '85)

Sokol Blosser 1985 Oregon White Riesling, Yamhill County, OR $6.95. 2.0% Residual Sweetness. (AWC/Nov. '86)

Souverain 1984 Johannisberg Riesling, Mendocino County, CA $5. 1.3% Residual Sweetness. (AWC/Nov. '86)

Stag's Leap Wine Cellars 1984 White Riesling, Birkmyer Vineyards, Napa Valley, CA $7.50. Light, delicate, slightly green flavors. (AWC/Nov. '86)

Ste. Chapelle 1984 Johannisberg Riesling, Special Harvest, W. F. Dakota Ranch, ID $9.39. (AWC/Sept. '85)

Ste. Chapelle 1985 Johannisberg Riesling, 10th Anniversary, ID $5.79. 2.6% Residual Sweetness. Off nose. (AWC/Nov. '86)

Tepusquet 1984 Johannisberg Riesling, Santa Maria Valley, CA $3.35. (AWC/Nov. '85)

Tucker 1984 Johannisberg Riesling, Estate Bottled, Yakima Valley, WA $5.25. Zesty, cinnamon nose. (AWC/Nov. '85)

Ventana 1984 White Riesling, Monterey, CA $6. (AWC/Nov. '85)

Walker Valley 1984 Riesling, Semi-Dry, NY $5.99. Oxidized. (AWC/Nov. '85)

Weibel 1984 Johannisberg Riesling, Mendocino County, CA $5. Candyish nose. Thin and short. (AWC/Nov. '86)

Wente Bros. 1983 Johannisberg Riesling, Monterey, CA $3.90. Green apple nose. (AWC/Nov. '85)

Wente Bros. 1984 Johannisberg Riesling, Monterey, CA $3.60. 1.94% Residual Sweetness. (AWC/Nov. '86)

Whitehall Lane 1984 Johannisberg Riesling, Special Select, Late Harvest, Napa Valley, CA $9/375 ml. (AWC/Sept. '85)

Wolfe 1984 Riesling, Monterey County, CA $6.50. (AWC/Nov. '86)

Worden 1984 Johannisberg Riesling, WA $5.99. 2.4% Residual Sweetness. A petrol scent mars an otherwise pleasant quaffing wine. (AWC/Nov. '86)

Zaca Mesa 1985 Johannisberg Riesling, Santa Barbara County, CA $7. 2.19% Residual Sweetness. Musty. (AWC/Nov. '86)

FRENCH

Domaine Weinbach 1984 Riesling, Reserve, Clos Des Capucins, Alsace $10.99. Spicy nose. Fresh, lively, packed with opulent fruit. (CC/Mar. '86) ★★★★

Trimbach 1983 Riesling, Alsace $5.99. Rather delicate, elegant structure and firm acidity. (CC/Mar. '86) ★★★ (★★★1/4)

Dopff 1983 Riesling, Reserve, Alsace $6.50. Complex, tropical-fruit aromas and flavors. Full, round, very dry. (CC/Mar. '86) ★★★

Klug 1983 Riesling, Reserve, Alsace $6.99. Simple, agreeable. (CC/Mar. '86) ★★

Preiss-Henny Ch. de Mittelwihr

1983 Riesling, Alsace $5.59. Subtle, flowery, varietal nose. Very dry, medium bodied. Slight, refreshing spritz. Apricot note in crisp finish. (CC/Mar. '86) ★★

Klug 1983 Riesling, Alsace $4.99. Quite dry, with a subtle, flowery nose with earthy undertones. Simple, lemony flavors. (CC/Mar. '86) ★1/2

SAUVIGNON BLANC

Nearly all American Sauvignon Blancs are produced in California. Once used to produce sweet, heavy wines generically labeled Sauterne, the variety is now made into dry white varietals, a change first made by Concannon Vineyards in the Livermore Valley.

The major white grape of Bordeaux (notably in Graves and Sauternes) and the upper Loire Valley (Sancerre and Pouilly-Fumé), Sauvignon Blanc fits comfortably into California's climatic range. It thrives in areas somewhat warmer than those best suited to Chardonnay. Climatic factors seem to have a significant effect on this varietal's characteristic scent and flavor often described as grassy, weedy, or herbaceous, reminiscent of fresh-mown hay and bell pepper.

In recent years, Sauvignon Blanc has threatened to unseat Chardonnay as the fashionable varietal among American white wine drinkers. More wineries have been making it and paying more attention to how to make it. Some choose to highlight the grape's grassiness, some downplay or finesse it in various ways, primarily by vineyard site selection, vine training, blending with other varieties, and the use of wooden cooperage. Since the early 1970s, Sauvignons showing the prominent influence of aging in wood have been marketed as Fumé Blanc, echoing the style of French Pouilly-Fumé. Most Sauvignon Blancs are 100% varietals, but recently more wineries have begun blending in Semillon, another grape native to Bordeaux, to give the wine more finesse and complexity.

Beringer 1983 Fume Blanc, Private Reserve, Sonoma County, CA $12.50. Rich and full bodied as a Chardonnay. 100% Sauvignon Blanc, but easy to imagine the presence of some Semillon. (JDM/ Jan. '86) ★★★★

Charis 1984 Sauvignon Blanc, Dry Creek Valley, Sonoma County, CA $6.50. Emphasis on fruit, without a hint of grassiness. A tingle of spritz adds to already lively mouth-feel. (JDM/May '86) ★★★★

Parducci 1984 Sauvignon Blanc, Mendocino County, CA $5.60. No wood present. Fruit is the major statement. Good varietal character without overt grassiness. (JDM/Jan.'86) ★★★★

J. Rochioli 1984 Sauvignon Blanc, Sonoma, CA $8. Intense varietal character, but no grassy smell. Great fruit, great middle, subtle oak. (JDM/Jan. '86) ★★★1/2 (★★★★)

Arbor Crest 1985 Sauvignon Blanc, Columbia Valley, WA $7.50. Clean, assertive, pine and herbal nose. Refreshing, herbal taste. Good acidity but smooth, with a trace of residual sweetness. Smoky-oaky finish. (JPN/Jan. '87) ★★★1/2

David S. Stare (Dry Creek) 1983 Soleil Sauvignon Blanc, Late Harvest, Dry Creek Valley, CA $9/ 375ml. Complex bouquet shows Botrytis, some varietal notes, hints of berries and spice. Rich, thick, sweet, luscious, with the acid to balance. Enormous length. Very young and impressive. (S&PW/Jan. '86) ★★★1/2

Hogue Cellars 1985 Fume Blanc (Dry Sauvignon Blanc), WA $6. Assertive, herbaceous aroma. Clean, herbal, grapefruit flavors. Fresh, citric finish. Good with clams, artichokes. (JPN/May '86) ★★★1/2

Quivira 1984 Sauvignon Blanc, Sonoma, CA $8. Herbal, but mostly forward, fig-like fruit. Half was barrel-fermented for richness and softness. Fruity, rich, refreshing crispness. (JDM/Jan.'86) ★★★1/2

Rutherford Hill 1983 Sauvignon Blanc, Napa Valley, CA $7.50. Not grassy, superbly balanced. 8% Semillon tones down herbaceousness. (JDM/Jan. '86)

★★★1/2

St. Vrain 1984 Sauvignon Blanc, Alexander Valley, CA $7.50. Full flavored but not heavy handed, with subtle, herbal note. Great fruit-acid balance, very long finish. (JDM/Jan.'86) ★★★1/2

Ventana 1985 Sauvignon Blanc, Monterey, CA $7.50. Very rich but not woody or oaky. (JDM/May '86) ★★★1/2

Arbor Crest 1984 Sauvignon Blanc, WA $9. Herbal, grassy, smoky nose. Nice fruit. Understated style goes well with food. Medium body, good balance. (JPN/May '86) ★★★

Ch. Ste. Michelle 1983 Fume Blanc, WA $8.99. Refined aroma of oak and varietal grassiness. Well balanced, firm, full of flavor. Long finish. Has class. (S&PW/Jan. '86) ★★★

Christian Brothers 1985 Fume Blanc, Napa Valley, CA $7. Flowery nose. Some smoke in medium-bodied, crisp, grapefruity flavors with an illusion of sweetness. Refreshing. (JPN/Jan. '87) ★★★

Creston Manor 1984 Sauvignon Blanc, San Luis Obispo, CA $8. No overt grassiness. Semillon adds a layer of complexity. Crisp acidity. (JDM/May '86) ★★★

Dry Creek 1984 Fume Blanc, Sonoma, CA $8.50. Herbal, but toned down. Great fruit, great balance, with a touch of oak. (JDM/Jan. '86) ★★★

Hogue Cellars 1984 Fume Blanc, WA $6. Herbal nose. Explosively fruity, somewhat grassy. Light, lovely balance. (JPN/Jan. '86) ★★★

Liberty School 1985 Sauvignon Blanc, Lot 3, CA $5.50. Dry, with no trace of grassiness. Flavor of ripe, Texas grapefruit. (JDM /May '86) ★★★

Monticello 1982 Sauvignon Blanc, Napa Valley, CA $8.25. Slightly grassy aroma leads to forward varietal flavors showing more herbaceousness. Stylish, balanced, aggressive. Steely, flinty finish. (JDM/Jan./ 86) ★★★

Robert Mondavi 1981 Sauvignon Blanc, Botrytised, Napa Valley, CA $25/375 ml. Smoke and herb aroma. Moderately sweet, fairly grassy, very smokey taste. Interesting austerity. High alcohol, burnt sugar finish. (JPN/Jan. '87) ★★★

Robert Pepi 1983 Sauvignon Blanc, Napa Valley, CA $7. Attractive, herbaceous nose. Understated style. Medium body. Well balanced. (JPN/May '86) ★★★

Stag's Leap Wine Cellars 1984 Sauvignon Blanc, Napa Valley, CA $8.50. Fresh, herbal, crisp, and clean. Great balance underplays substantial (13%) alcohol. (JPN/Jan. '87) ★★★

Weinstock Cellars 1984 Sauvignon Blanc, Sonoma, CA $5. No-oak style, multi-dimensional fruit. Perfect fruit-acid balance. Relatively long finish for a young wine. Not grassy. Kosher. (JDM/Jan. '86) ★★★

Arbor Crest 1983 Sauvignon Blanc, WA $9.25. Subtle, maraschino cherry perfume underscored by sweet hay and grassy nuances. Rich, bright flavors. (CC/ Jan. '86) ★★3/4

Adler Fels 1984 Fume Blanc, Sonoma, CA $8.50. Bold intense flavor, leaning more to grapefruit than grass. Flinty, crisp, clean finish. (JDM/Jan. '86) ★★1/2

Beringer 1983 Fume Blanc, Sonoma County, CA $8. Plenty of that Sauvignon Blanc herbaceousness in the aroma and taste. Traditional Fume Blanc style. (JDM/Jan. '86) ★★1/2

Chinook 1983 Sauvignon Blanc, WA $9. Medium-light body. Delicate, herbaceous aroma and flavor. Nice with grilled white fish. (JPN/May '86) ★★1/2

Christian Brothers 1984 Fume Blanc (Dry Sauvignon Blanc), Napa Valley, CA $8. Clean, herbaceous aroma has pineapple notes. A hint of pears in the flavor. Nicely balanced, but the finish is a bit hot. (JPN/Mar. '86) ★★1/2

De Loach 1983 Fume Blanc, Russian River Valley, CA $8.50. Oak and restrained varietal grassiness in the aroma. Dry, clean, well balanced, smooth, with a slight weedy note to the flavor. Finish is a bit light. (S&PW/Jan. '86) ★★1/2

Flora Springs 1983 Sauvignon Blanc, Napa Valley, CA $10.29. Understated, varietal grassiness overlaid with a nice touch of oak. Tasty, with smooth texture and some length. (S&PW/Mar. '86) ★★1/2

Iron Horse 1984 Fume Blanc, Alexander Valley, CA $8.75. Herbaceousness with added notes of grapefruit. Very lively and spritely. (JDM/May '86) ★★1/2

Napa Cellars 1984 Sauvignon Blanc, Napa Valley, CA $7.50. Lively, sprightly, citrusy style that just plain feels good in the mouth. Hint of oak. (JDM/Jan.'86) ★★1/2

Preston Vineyards & Winery 1984 Sauvignon Blanc, Reserve, Dry Creek Valley, CA $9. Refined, restrained, varietal aroma. A lot of flavor, smooth center, well balanced. Long finish. (S&PW/Jan. '86) ★★1/2

The Christian Brothers 1984 Fume Blanc (Dry Sauvignon Blanc), Napa Valley, CA $8. Clean, herbaceous aroma becomes pineappley. Hint of pears in the mouth. Nicely balanced. (JPN/Mar. '86) ★★1/2

Valfleur 1984 Sauvignon Blanc, Alexander Valley, CA $7. Austere and crisp. Lean and somewhat herbaceous, with a pleasantly tart finish. (JDM/May '86) ★★1/2

White Oak 1984 Sauvignon Blanc, Sonoma County, CA $7.50. Delicate, slightly herbaceous, with some ripe grapefruit quality. (JDM/May '86) ★★1/2

Murphy-Goode 1985 Fume Blanc, Alexander Valley, CA $7. Understated, varietal grassiness on the nose. A mouthful of lush fruit with green, grassy flavor in the background. Well balanced. Young. (S&PW/May '86) ★★ (★★3/4)

Byron 1984 Sauvignon Blanc, Santa Barbara, CA $7.50. Solid varietal aroma and flavors; not overly grassy. Lively acidity. (JDM/Jan.'86) ★★ (★★1/2)

Bandiera 1983 Dry Sauvignon Blanc, Mendocino County, CA $5. Understated varietal grassiness in the aroma. Soft, fruity, clean, and balanced. Has character. Good value. (S&PW/Jan. '86) ★★

Bandiera 1983 Fume Blanc, Mendocino County, CA $5. More grassy than Bandiera's '83 Sauvignon Blanc. A suggestion of sweetness (although it is dry). Fruity and balanced. Good value. (S&PW/Jan. '86) ★★

Gallo 1983 Sauvignon Blanc, Reserve Cellar, CA $4. Good varietal character without being overly grassy. Fairly austere, dry, pleasant. Good value. (JPN/Mar. '86) ★★

McDowell Valley 1983 Fume Blanc, Reserve, McDowell Valley, CA $12.79. Characteristic varietal grassiness with a suggestion of menthol. Fruity flavor with a nice touch of oak for texture and complexity. (S&PW/Mar. '86) ★★

Preston Wine Cellars 1982 Fume Blanc, WA $7.75. Dry, smoky aroma. Decent fruit. Fairly crisp. (JPN/May '86) ★★

Preston Vineyards 1984 Cuvee de Fume, Dry Sauvignon Blanc, Dry Creek Valley, CA $7. Grassy aroma. Fairly dry and soft, with nice flavor. Could use more firmness. (S&PW/Jan. '86) ★★

Rodney Strong 1984 Fume Blanc (Dry Sauvignon Blanc), Charlotte's Home Vineyard, Alexander Valley, Sonoma County, CA $8.50. Fresh, herbal in the nose and mouth. Medium bodied. Subtle. A bit low in acid. (JPN/Jan. '87) ★★

Sebastiani 1984 Sauvignon Blanc, Sonoma County, CA $7. Lemongrass and oak aromas. Herbal flavor with a bit of weedy-woody harshness. (JPN/Mar. '86) ★★

Waterbrook Winery 1985 Sauvignon Blanc, WA $9. French oak in nose and mouth. Very crisp, good fruit. (JPN/May '86) ★★

Ch. St. Jean 1984 Fume Blanc, Sonoma County, CA $8.75. Restrained, varietal aroma has an oaky component. Soft, round, flavorful. Full bodied and balanced. Moderately long finish. (S&PW/May '86) ★3/4

Gallo 1983 Sauvignon Blanc, CA $3.50. Plenty of fruit, well balanced for immediate enjoyment. (JDM/Jan. '86) ★1/2

Columbia River Cellars 1983 Sauvignon Blanc, WA $5.75. Aroma and flavors verge on ponderous, but there are no flaws. Some residual sweetness. (JPN/May '86) ★

WHITE BURGUNDY

The French province of Burgundy produces three times more red wine than white, but the whites are just as available in the North American market and often more affordable. Virtually all of the wines exported are made from the Chardonnay grape.

The austere, crisp, bright flavors of French Chablis reflect their origin in the cool, northern part of the province. The Côte de Beaune, in the heart of the region, produces the great, golden Burgundies considered by many to be the finest dry white wines in the world. They come from select vineyards around the villages of Chassagne-Montrachet, Puligny-Montrachet, Meursault, and Aloxe-Corton — names that appear on the labels of very fine wines from surrounding vineyards.

South of the Côte de Beaune lie the districts of the Chalonnaise and Mâcon. The most famous wine — Pouilly-Fuissé — is almost always overpriced, but many of its sister wines are reviewed below as some of the better, affordable white wines from Burgundy. Simpler than the great Chablis or Beaune wines, they can be fine, food-oriented Chardonnays.

Latour-Giraud 1984 Meursault $16.99. Stunning bouquet. Loads of mellow vanilla-oak backed by lush fruit. Excellent depth, amazing length; intense butterscotch. Perfectly balanced, beautifully made. (CC/Mar. '86) ★★★★

Moillard 1982 Montrachet $40. A bit too much alcohol on the nose at first, but bouquet is very well-developed. Good fruit, gorgeous, round yet delicate body with lovely, vanilla flavor. (DM/Jan. '86) ★★★1/2

Cave de Lugny 1984 Mâcon-Lugny, Les Charmes $6. Fresh pineapple notes, fruity aroma. Bright, buoyant flavors, nicely balanced by lively acidity. (CC/Jan. '86) ★★★

Cuvée Madame Cottin 1983 Bourgogne $9.99. Touch of oak underscores Chardonnay fruit that hints of figs and fresh, ripe pineapple. Delicious, butterscotch, and lemony notes in lingering finish. (CC/Mar. '86) ★★★

Jacques Berger 1984 Ch. de Mercey, Bourgogne Hautes Côte de Beaune $10.99. Delightful, flowery perfume with pineapple overtones. Generously fruited, medium-light-bodied, dry. (CC/Mar. '86) ★★★

Moillard 1984 Chassagne-Montrachet $23. Very closed. Fresh, slightly floral and lipstick flavors. Steely middle. (JPN/Jan. '87) ★★★

Olivier Leflaive 1984 Bourgogne $9. Intensely perfumed, with candy apple and pineapple nuances. Loaded with ripe fruit, richly flavored. Crisp acidity. (CC/Jan. '86) ★★★

Sylvain Fessy 1984 Saint-Véran $8. Elegant, harmonious, with delicate, toasty aromas and bright, lively flavors. Crisp acidity gives a tangy edge to a silky texture. (CC/Jan. '86) ★★★

Felix Besson 1984 Chablis $8.99. Distinctive, Chardonnay-aged-on-its-lees bouquet. Nicely balanced with crisp acidity. Pleasant, flinty, pineapple finish. (CC/Mar. '86) ★★3/4

Prosper Maufoux 1983 Ch. de Viré, Mâcon-Viré $8. Medium to full bodied, dry, wonderfully supple and full of character. Lush, tropical-fruit aromas and flavors. (CC/Mar. '86) ★★3/4

Joseph Drouhin 1983 Chassagne-Montrachet $18. Some fruit, an overabundance of alcohol, and a hint of apples. Not an aperitif. Still very young, almost a little green. (DM/Jan. '86) ★★1/2

Joseph Drouhin 1984 Mâcon-Villages $8.50. Floral nose with melon and banana undertones. Light bodied, but good flavors and lively acidity keep it dancing. (CC/Jan. '86) ★★1/2

Joseph Drouhin 1984 Chardonnay, Laforêt, Bourgogne $7. Mild, flowery perfume laced with earth. Fat, fleshy; fair complexity and delicate, pineapple notes. (CC/Jan. '86) ★★1/2

Labouré-Roi 1984 Chardonnay, Vin de Pays D'oc $6. Fairly rich, tropical-fruit, subtle hint of spearmint. Bright, refreshing, tangy acidity. (CC/Mar. '86) ★★1/2

Prosper Maufoux 1983 Montagny $9.69. Flinty nose. Slightly tangy, very dry, accented by light agreeable lemon flavors. (CC/Mar. '86) ★★1/2

M. Vincent 1983 Saint-Véran $8. Intense aromas and flavors packed with buttery Chardonnay fruit, vanilla and pineapple. Full, fleshy, but balanced by tart acidity. High alcohol gives a hot finish. (CC/Jan. '86) ★★ (★★★)

Bichot 1984 Saint-Véran $8. Generous, pineapple aromas. Acidity is crisp, vibrant. A hint of licorice. Dominated from start to finish by copious varietal fruit. (CC/Jan. '86) ★★

Georges DuBoeuf 1984 Saint-Véran $7.99. Nose suggests pears. Lemony notes in the finish. Full flavor, firm acidity. (CC/Mar. '86) ★★

Jaboulet-Vercherre 1983 Bâtard-Montrachet $40. Lightweight. Fruit is not only hidden but possibly not even there. Wait five years and hope. (DM/Jan. '86) ★★

Jean-Pierre Meulien 1983 Bourgogne $8.99. True varietal aromas and flavors. Subtle, toasty nuances. Full-bodied. (CC/Mar. '86) ★★

Labouré-Roi 1983 Les Cles du Roi, Chardonnay, Bourgogne $8. Light, tropical-fruit aromas and flavors. Dry, simple, good acidity. (CC/Mar. '86) ★★

Louis Jadot 1984 Mâcon Blanc-Villages, La Fontaine $7.50. Attractive nose scented with pear blossoms and earth. Fat, fleshy flavors soothe raspy alcohol nip in the finish. (CC/Jan. '86) ★★

M. Delacroix 1984 Mâcon-Villages, Les Granges $5.99. Silky, racy. Tropical fruit bouquet and flavors of pineapple, banana, and pear. Good acidity. (CC/Mar. '86) ★★

Moillard 1983 Rully $10. Closed aroma of straw flowers. Crisp, with a straw and lipstick taste. Smooth finish. (JPN/Jan. '87) ★★

Moreau 1983 Chardonnay, La Couronne, Réserve du Maître, Bourgogne $9.50. Bright, fruity, flowery aromas of pear, vanilla, and sweet, exotic spices. Slightly weighty and a bit low in acidity. (CC/Jan. '86) ★★

Prosper Maufoux 1984 Mâcon-Villages $7.50. Charming scents of fruit and flowers. Restrained flavors hint of licorice. Tangy finish. (CC/Jan. '86) ★1/2 (★★)

Moreau 1983 Chardonnay, Bourgogne $7. Clean, ripe fruity nose laced with butter and vanilla. Flavors not quite as intense, with nice, pineapple note in finish. Low acidity causes flat impression. (CC/Jan. '86) ★1/2

Paul Sapin 1984 Mâcon-Villages, Cépage Chardonnay $6.50. Fresh, Juicy Fruit gum aromas. Firm acidity, light, buttery notes in the finish. (CC/Jan. '86) ★ (★1/2)

Bichot 1984 Chardonnay, Le Bourgogne Bichot $6. Mild but persistent, eggy odor. Silky texture. Fine, tangy acidity. Subtle, licorice flavors. (CC/Jan. '86) ★

J. J. Vincent 1984 Mâcon-Villages $7. Chardonnay aromas highlighted by mellow, Bartlett pear. Tart, tangy acidity, yet lacks crispness. Simple fruit flavors. (CC/Jan. '86) ★

Michel Nathan 1984 Saint-Véran $8. Earthy character dominates, but a few minutes of aeration bring out delicate, flowery undertones. Slightly tart, lemony notes. (CC/Jan. '86) ★

Prosper Maufoux 1983 Mâcon-Villages $7.50. Intense, butterscotch aromas and flavors. Acidity is adequate. Bitter note in the finish. (CC/Jan. '86) ★

Sylvain Fessy 1984 Mâcon Fessy, Mâcon-Villages $5.50. Distinctive, herbaceous, buttery nose. Clean, fresh, and full, but ends abruptly. Acidity is adequate. (CC/Jan. '86) ★

Pierre Blancher 1984 Mâcon-Villages $6. Initial, sulfurous odor fades, leaving a light-toasty aroma with earthy undertones. Thin and restrained, acidic flavors. (CC/Jan. '86) (★)

B. de Monthélie 1982 Bourgogne Blanc, Saint-Romain $7.60. Artificial banana-pineapple candy nose. Dull, flat, bitter. Very poor quality. (CC/Mar. '86)

Bichot 1984 Mâcon-Villages $6.50. Sharply acidic, thin, with simple fruit. Flavors mildly akin to rubbing alcohol. (CC/Jan. '86)

Bourgogne de l'Armorial 1983 $5.29. Overripe-fruit aroma of bananas and canned pineapple. Dry, medium-full-bodied. (CC/Mar. '86)

Georges Burrier 1984 Mâcon-Fuissé $5. Pleasantly fruity nose. Acid is extremely high. Candyish, dull flavors. (CC/Jan. '86)

Jean Bedin 1984 Mâcon-Villages, La Grande Chatelaine $5.99. Flavors and texture are insipid. Flat, dull, bland. (CC/Mar. '86)

Robert Sarrau 1984 Mâcon-Villages $6. Perfumy, tropical fruit aromas, but lemony acidity is too tart. (CC/Jan. '86)

PINK WINES

ABBREVIATIONS & SYMBOLS

RATINGS

★★★★—Like extremely or Platinum Medal
★★★1/2—Like very strongly or Gold Medal
★★★—Like strongly or Silver Medal
★★—Like slightly or Bronze Medal
★—Neither like nor dislike, a useful wine
(★)—Estimated peak score with aging
No Star—A wine with no star is a wine that won no medal in competition or a wine that the reviewer disliked.

WHO WROTE THE DESCRIPTIONS

AWC—American Wine Competition Judges
BC—Bordeaux Classic Judges
JB—John Binder
CC—Carole Collier
RF—Richard Figiel
CG—Craig Goldwyn
JDM—Jerry D. Mead
DM—Denman Moody Jr.
JPN—Judy Peterson-Nedry
CR—Christina Reynolds
S&PW—Sheldon & Pauline Wasserman

PRICES. Prices are typical of those in major metropolitan markets for standard, 750-ml bottles *at the time the review was written* (note the date following the descriptions). The prices of some wines are likely to rise as time passes. Prices may also vary *significantly* from state to state and store to store.

AVAILABILITY. Some wines may be hard to find because they are produced in small quantities, and distribution methods often make wines that are bestsellers in one city unavailable in another. Even large stores can't carry more than a fraction of the thousands of wines sold in the US and Canada, so many merchants are happy to order wines for you. If can't find wines you want in your area, try to shop when you're in other major cities.

PINK WINES

Rosé, Blush, and Blanc de Noir are all names for pink wines of various shades and hues. Most pink wines are produced by limiting the time the clear juice that is pressed from dark grapes is kept in contact with the dark skins. The longer the juice is on the skins the darker the color. Some pink wines are produced by blending white and red wines, and a few are even charcoal filtered to lighten the color.

In the wake of the white wine boom, many of the paler wines are called Blanc de Noir because the juices are separated from the skins immediately, the way white wines are made, but the resulting wine is rarely white.

Zinfandel has become the favorite variety for this style of wine, usually marketed as White Zinfandel. Even Cabernet Sauvignon has been used for Blanc de Noir.

All these wines generally have some residual sweetness. The best are fresh, crisp, fruity quaffs, good for lunches and aperitifs.

Buena Vista 1985 Sonoma Steelhead Run, CA $5.50. Light, delicate, very crisp. Subtle but bright, cherry smell and taste. (JDM/May '86) ★★★
Heitz 1985 Grignolino Rosé, Napa Valley, CA $5. Fresh spice and rose petal aroma and flavor. Dry, appealingly crisp. (JPN/Jan. '87) ★★★
Simi 1984 Rosé of Cabernet Sauvignon, North Coast, CA $7. Delicate, refreshing fruit aroma and flavor, with threshhold sweetness. (JPN/Mar. '86) ★★★
Tualatin 1985 Pinot Noir Blanc, Estate Bottled, OR $5.50. Delicate, fruity aroma. Fresh varietal character. Excellent balance. Crisp, almost dry. (JPN/May '86) ★★★
Forgeron 1984 Rosé of Pinot Noir, OR $5. Nice, varietal nose and flavor, notes

of strawberry. Tartness masks residual sweetness. (JPN/Jan.'86) ★★1/2

Forgeron 1985 White Pinot Noir, OR $6.75. Good Pinot Noir aroma, flavor. Crisp, refreshing, slightly sweet. (JPN/May '86) ★★1/2

Spring Creek 1985 Rosé of Cabernet Sauvignon, WA $5. Slight asparagus behind pleasant varietal fruit. Clean, acidic, slight residual sweetness. (JPN/Jan. '87) ★★1/2

Sterling 1985 Cabernet Sauvignon Blanc, Napa Valley, CA $6.25. Clean, fresh, appealing aroma has charm. Lively and well balanced, with a touch of sugar. Fairly nice finish. (S&PW/Mar. '86) ★★1/2

The Christian Brothers (nonvintage) Premium Rosé CA $5. Lively, spicy. Simple, delicious quaff. (JPN/Mar. '86) ★★1/2

Worden's Washington Winery 1985 Gamay Beaujolais Blush, Willamette Valley, OR $5. Peach aroma, flavor. Slight spritz. Fairly sweet; high acid to balance. Off-dry, delicate flavors. A lovely sipper. (JPN/May '86) ★★1/2

Worden's Washington Winery 1985 Gamay Beaujolais Rosé, WA $5. Cranberry color. Dry, fruity aroma. Cranberry-like taste. Crisp, refreshing. (JPN/May '86)★★1/2

Alpine 1985 Pinot Noir Blanc, Estate Bottled, OR $6.50. Yeasty aroma. Some varietal character. Delicate Pinot Noir taste. Very crisp. Semi-sweet. (JPN/May '86) ★★

Arbor Crest 1984 Jardin des Fleurs, WA $6.50. Mostly Merlot. Aromatic, fruity, crisp. A bit sweet. (JPN/May '86) ★★

Columbia Crest 1985 Blush, Vineyard Reserve, Columbia Valley, WA $5. Proprietary blend from Chateau Ste. Michelle. Pale copper color from Grenache. Grapey in aroma and taste. Medium sweet, fruity, smooth. (JPN/Jan. '87) ★★

Pastel (Mirassou) (nonvintage) $5.50. The addition of juice infuses very intense fruit flavors and reduces the alcohol to about 7%. Juice-like, perhaps a little too sweet. (JDM/May '86) ★★

Preston Wine Cellars 1982 Pinot Noir Blanc, WA $6.75. Heavy Pinot Noir aroma and pronounced varietal flavor. Spritzy. Good acidity. Dry. (JPN/May '86) ★★

Rex Hill 1984 Pinot Noir Blanc, OR $5. Fresh, peachy, light, clean; a bit thin. (JPN/Jan. '86) ★★

Sakonnet 1985 Eye of the Storm, Southeastern New England Blush Table Wine, winery in RI $4.50. Refined, strawberry fruit. Residual sweetness offset by high acidity and spritz. (RF/May '86) ★★

The Monterey Vineyard 1984 White Zinfandel, Monterey County, CA $4.50. Fresh, fruity aroma and flavor. Moderate sugar balanced by good acidity. Perhaps the best '84 blush wine we've tasted. (S&PW) ★★

Eberle 1985 Cabernet Sauvignon Blanc, Paso Robles, CA $5. Purplish blush. Slight vegetable quality along with reasonable fruit. Smooth, unflawed, but boringly sweet. (JPN/Jan. '87) ★

Tepusquet 1985 White Cabernet Sauvignon, Paso Robles, CA $5. Sweet, vegetal character dominates. (JPN/Jan. '87) 1/2

SPARKLING WINES

ABBREVIATIONS & SYMBOLS

RATINGS

★★★★—Like extremely or Platinum Medal
★★★1/2—Like very strongly or Gold Medal
★★★—Like strongly or Silver Medal
★★—Like slightly or Bronze Medal
★—Neither like nor dislike, a useful wine
(★)—Estimated peak score with aging
No Star—A wine with no star is a wine that won no medal in competition or a wine that the reviewer disliked.

WHO WROTE THE DESCRIPTIONS

AWC—American Wine Competition Judges
BC—Bordeaux Classic Judges
JB—John Binder
CC—Carole Collier
RF—Richard Figiel
CG—Craig Goldwyn
JDM—Jerry D. Mead
DM—Denman Moody Jr.
JPN—Judy Peterson-Nedry
CR—Christina Reynolds
S&PW—Sheldon & Pauline Wasserman

PRICES. Prices are typical of those in major metropolitan markets for standard, 750-ml bottles *at the time the review was written* (note the date following the descriptions). The prices of some wines are likely to rise as time passes. Prices may also vary *significantly* from state to state and store to store.

AVAILABILITY. Some wines may be hard to find because they are produced in small quantities, and distribution methods often make wines that are bestsellers in one city unavailable in another. Even large stores can't carry more than a fraction of the thousands of wines sold in the US and Canada, so many merchants are happy to order wines for you. If can't find wines you want in your area, try to shop when you're in other major cities.

SPARKLING WINES

Although sparkling wines are made in many French regions, the best and most famous are made within the region about 90 miles northeast of Paris called Champagne. The most northerly wine district in France, Champagne turned a liability into an asset more than two centuries ago. When the grapes wouldn't ripen reliably, sugar was added to produce wines with sufficient alcohol to keep them from spoiling. Occasionally, in the cool limestone cellars, the yeast went dormant before the fermentation was complete. As the cellars warmed in spring, the fermentation began again in the bottles, the world's original sparkling wine was born.

Since then, Champagne production has become refined to an expensive, precise method, meticulously regulated, and very profitable. The grapes used are Chardonnay, Pinot Meunier, and Pinot Noir, grown in carefully rated vineyards. In sharp contrast to other French vineyard districts, Champagne acreage has expanded dramatically in the last 15 years. Some observers are concerned that young vines on less-desirable sites are diluting the quality of many Champagnes, and strong market demand is pressuring the producers to shorten aging periods.

Têtes de Cuvée (top-of-the-line wines) and Champagne Rosés have proliferated on the North American market over the past couple of years. Wines from these two fashionable categories account for most of the reviews of French Champagnes below.

Although many American wineries make wine called Champagne, true Champagne comes only from the Champagne region in France. American sparkling wines, as they are more accurately called, are getting better and more numerous. Not long ago they were made only by large wineries. Today sparkling wines come from both large and small wineries, and many of the wines are made in the classic French Champagne method, identified on their labels by the terms "Methode Champenoise" or "Fermented in *This* Bottle." This time-consuming, labor-intensive production regimen yields the best and the most expensive sparkling wines. But even at their top end, American sparklers rarely scale the heights of price tags on French Champagne. The American wines offer increasingly attractive alternatives.

The great strides in American sparkling wine production and the growing American market for these wines have not escaped the attention of foreign producers. Several have set up California subsidiaries: Champagne producer Moët & Chandon has built Domaine Chandon in Napa Valley, Piper-Heidsieck has built Piper-Sonoma in Sonoma County, G.H. Mumm recently opened Domaine Mumm in Napa Valley, Taittinger has planted vineyards in the Carneros district and will open a winery soon, Michel Tribaut has built Tribaut de Romery in San Leandro, and Spain's Freixenet has opened Gloria Ferrer in Sonoma.

Unlike French Champagne, American sparkling wines can be made from any grape variety. Pinot Blanc, French Colombard, Seyval Blanc, and Riesling are among the grapes that turn up in cuvées, and they can be very good, but the best wines are those made from the classic Champagne varieties Chardonnay, Pinot Noir, and Pinot Meunier.

AMERICAN SPARKLING

Quail Run 1983 Brut, Methode Champenoise, Yakima Valley, WA $14.95. Very fine bead. Delicate, fresh, outstanding. (JPN/Jan. '86) ★★★★

Shadow Creek 1982 Blanc de Blanc, Sonoma County, CA $15.50. Dry, lively, with austere fruit. Elegant. (JPN/Mar. '86) ★★★★

Michel Tribaut (nonvintage) Brut,

CA $12.50. Made from Monterey County fruit: 75% Pinot Noir, 25% Chardonnay. Rich, complex, toasty. (JDM/May '86) ★★★1/2

Shadow Creek 1982 Blanc de Noir, Robert Young Vineyard, Sonoma County, CA $14. Tart, lively, with layers of complexity and a slightly toasty finish. (JPN/Mar. '86) ★★★1/2

Arterberry 1984 Sparkling White Riesling, OR $11. Citrus and green apple nose. Good mousse, very fine bubbles; refreshing and delicate. Finishes clean. (JPN/Mar. '86) ★★★

Arterberry (nonvintage) Sparkling Apple Cider, Carbonated, OR $5.50. Crisp, clean, complex apple flavors. Sweet, good acidity, only 7.5% alcohol. (JPN/Jan. '86) ★★★

Ch. Benoit (nonvintage) Brut, OR $12. Fresh grape aromas. Very tart, austere, light, delicate. (JPN/Jan. '86) ★★★

Ch. Ste. Michelle 1978 Blanc de Noirs, Brut, Methode Champenoise, WA $22.50. Steady stream of tiny bubbles. Light, bread-like, yeasty aroma. Lively acidity, well-balanced, dry, round, almost creamy in texture. Medium bodied. (S&PW/Mar. '86) ★★★

Gloria Ferrer (nonvintage) Brut, Sonoma County, CA $12. Full-bodied style, with Pinot Noir prominent. Pleasantly toasty, yeasty, nicely balanced between richness and crisp acidity. (JDM/May '86) ★★★

Mirassou 1982 Champagne, Au Natural, Monterey County, CA $12.50. Steady stream of tiny bubbles. Light, bread-like, yeast aroma with a vanilla note. Firm, crisp, dry, fresh, austere, and lively. Good value. Methode champenoise. (S&PW/Mar. '86) ★★★

Piper-Sonoma 1980 Tete de Cuvee, Sonoma County, CA $25. Explosive bubbles. Appley nose. Delicate but rich, yeasty flavor. (JPN/Jan. '87) ★★★

Scharffenberger 1983 Brut Rosé, Mendocino County, CA $15. Considerable, relatively complex fruit. Shows some austerity. Pinpoint fine effervescence. (JDM/ May '86) ★★★

Scharffenberger (nonvintage) Brut, Cuvee #2, Mendocino County, CA $15. Tart, austere, lively, and fresh. (JPN/ Jan. '86) ★★★

Gold Seal (nonvintage) Blanc de Noirs, American (winery in NY) $11.99. Yeasty, a little dusty. Plenty of sweetish, Pinot Noir fruit and rugged earthiness. (RF/Mar. '86) ★★1/2

Piper-Sonoma (nonvintage) Brut, Sonoma County, CA $10. Very light, coppery blush. Lively bubbles. Closed aroma. Clean, crisp, delicate, Pinot Noir flavor. Good value. (JPN/Jan. '87) ★★1/2

Shadow Creek 1982 Brut, Sonoma County, CA $14. Very tart, with a fine bead. Green-fruit taste dominates. (JPN/Mar. '86) ★★1/2

Shadow Creek (nonvintage) Brut, Sonoma County, CA $12. Clean, lively. (JPN/Mar. '86) ★★1/2

Tijessling (nonvintage) Brut, Mendocino County, CA $12. Medium-light body. Clean, lively aroma and flavor. (JPN/ Mar. '86) ★★1/2

Arterberry 1982 Red Hills Brut, OR $14. Slightly toasty and appley. Medium-light body. Bracing. (JPN/Mar. /86) ★★

Weibel (nonvintage) White Zinfandel Champagne, CA $6. Only slightly sweet, with nice, restrained fruit. (JPN/Mar. '86) ★★

Knudsen Erath (nonvintage) Brut, OR $15. Slightly weedy aroma. Rich, mature flavor. (JPN/Mar. '86) ★1/2

Woodbury (nonvintage) Spumante, NY $7.99. Good, clean, Muscat flavor. Simple, direct, fun. (RF/Mar. '86) ★1/2

FRENCH CHAMPAGNE
WHITE

Piper-Heidsieck 1976 Rare, Champagne $61.33. Superbly crafted. Lively, fast rising, pinpoint bead. Elegant, refined bouquet. Delicate and rich in nose and flavor. Enormously long finish. Sublime. Everything in perfect harmony. Sheer perfection. (S&PW/ Nov. '86) ★★★★

Bollinger 1973 Année Rare, R.D. (disgorged 26 Nov. 1984), Champagne $74.48. Bouquet is the epitome of Champagne: deep, rich, classic. Full bodied, full of flavor, lively. Superbly balanced. Enormous length. (S&PW/Nov. '86) ★★★1/2

Bollinger 1975 R.D., Champagne $50.28. Tiny bead, swift and steady stream. Complex bouquet has mellowness from age. Full bodied, richly flavored, creamy center. Very long, dry, refreshing finish. (S&PW/ Nov. '86) ★★★1/2

Bollinger 1975 Tradition R.D. (Recently Disgorged), Champagne $30. Exceptional bouquet from lengthy aging on the yeast. Depth and complexity indicate Pinot Noir. Excellent. (DM/Jan. '86) ★★★1/2

Bollinger 1979 Vieilles Vignes Française, Champagne $99.99. Fast-rising pinpoint perlage. Incredibly rich bouquet, toasty notes. Dry, firm, full-bodied, creamy. Smooth texture, superb balance, enormously long finish. (S&PW/Nov. '86) ★★★1/2

Krug 1979 Champagne $65.79. Deep, rich bouquet. Superbly balanced, richly flavored. Elegant, stylish. (S&PW/Nov. '86) ★★★1/2

Krug (nonvintage) Grande Cuvée, Champagne $53.99. Rich, intense aroma with characteristic yeasty overlay. Full body, creamy texture, with a lightness that is the hallmark of fine bubbly. Very long, clean finish. (S&PW/Nov. '86) ★★★1/2

Taittinger 1978 Collection Brut, Champagne $50. Fast-rising, pinpoint mousse. Lovely, complex bouquet, clean and pure. Elegant, stylish, creamy texture. Long finish. (S&PW/Nov. '86) ★★★1/2

Georges Goulet 1979 Crémant Blanc de Blancs, Champagne $17.50. Steady stream of pinpoint bubbles. Rich, complex, toasty aroma. Light-bodied, well-balanced, toasty flavor, smooth-textured; a lot of style and class. (S&PW/Nov. '86) ★★★

Gosset 1973 Grand Millesime, Champagne $39.95. Lovely, rich bouquet. Creamy textured, full bodied, with delicacy. Some oxidation beginning to creep in, but still displays breed. (S&PW/Nov. '86) ★★★

Louis Roederer (nonvintage) Cour Royal Brut, Champagne $23.75. Lovely, classic bouquet. Richly flavored, firm acidity. Very long. Fine quality. One of the best and most reliable of the genre. (S&PW/Nov. '86) ★★★

Mumm (nonvintage) Crémant de Cramant, Blanc de Blancs, Champagne $42.69. Delicacy and style; dry, light, firm, well balanced. Lingering, lively finish. (S&PW/Nov. '86) ★★★

Pol Roger 1979 Cuvée Sir Winston Churchill, Champagne $49.50. Lovely champagne bouquet. Richly flavored, elegant, stylish. Should improve in another year or two. Very long finish. (S&PW/Nov. '86) ★★★

Taittinger 1979 Comtes de Champagne, Blanc de Blancs, Champagne $60. Still young. Elegance and breed quite evident. Delicate. Long finish. (S&PW/Nov. '86) ★★★

Veuve Clicquot 1978 Brut, Champagne $33.95. Rich, intense bouquet with vanilla, toasty notes. Creamy texture. Richly flavored, superbly balanced. Very long finish. (S&PW/Nov. '86) ★★★

Veuve Clicquot 1979 La Grande Dame, Champagne $62.82. Rich, classic aroma, with some intensity. Full flavored, well balanced, almost creamy texture. (S&PW/Nov. '86) ★★★

Veuve Clicquot (nonvintage) Brut, Champagne $30. Fresh, green-apple aroma and taste. Tart, clean, austere in a fruity rather than flinty style. (JPN/Jan. '87) ★★★

Bollinger 1979 Grande Année, Champagne $29.83. Lively stream of tiny bubbles. Light, refined aroma, some complexity. Quite dry, lively. Underlying richness and strength. Long, dry, firm finish. (S&PW/Nov. '86) ★★3/4 (★★★)

Deutz 1979 Cuvée Williams Deutz, Champagne $41.12. Lively, pinpoint bead. Rich, classic bouquet. Fairly full bodied, good structure, smooth texture. Fairly long finish. Can improve, nice now. (S&PW/Nov. '86) ★★3/4

Henriot 1976 Cuvée Baccarat, Champagne $57.49. Lively mousse. Light, fresh-bread-like, yeast aroma. Soft, round, smooth, some elegance. Age beginning to creep in with a touch of maderization. (S&PW/Nov. '86) ★★3/4

Moët & Chandon 1978 Dom Pérignon, Champagne $60.29. One bottle was corked. A second bottle had elegance and style. Smooth texture, long finish; high price. (S&PW/Nov. '86) ★★3/4

Piper-Heidsieck 1979 Brut Sauvage, Champagne $42. Lively mousse. Fresh-bread-like, yeast aroma. Dry, firm, a bit austere. Real character, some length. (S&PW/Nov. '86) ★★3/4

Deutz (nonvintage) Brut, Champagne $23.90. Lively mousse. Classic bouquet. Fuller style, dry, smooth texture, balanced. Fairly long finish. (S&PW/Nov. '86) ★★1/2

Georges Goulet 1979 Cuvée du Centenaire, Champagne $46.88. Steady stream of tiny bubbles. Fresh, fruity, lightly yeasted aroma. Light body, lively, smooth. Firm, dry, moderately long finish. Some style. (S&PW/Nov. '86) ★★1/2

Laurent Perrier 1978 Grand Siècle, Champagne $56.24. Elegant, well balanced, lively acidity, could use more length. Nice but doesn't measure up to its lofty price. (S&PW/Nov. '86) ★★1/2

Laurent Perrier (nonvintage) Ultra Brut, Champagne $28.24. Lovely nose, some yeast. Dry, firm, lively, well balanced. Well made; good Champagne character. Long, clean finish. (S&PW/Nov. '86) ★★1/2

Mumm 1976 René Lalou, Champagne $53.98. Lovely, rich aroma. A lot of character, though acid a tad low. (S&PW/Nov. '86) ★★1/2

Mumm 1979 René Lalou, Champagne $55.49. Fast-rising, tiny bubbles. Delicate, fresh-bread-like, yeast aroma. Light, fresh, clean, balanced. Nice palate picker-upper. Rather high price. (S&PW/Nov. '86) ★★1/2

Perrier-Jouet 1979 Fleur de Champagne, Champagne $55. Lively, pinpoint bead. Elegant, stylish bouquet with depth and complexity. Fairly dry, well balanced. Long, refreshing finish. (S&PW/Nov. '86) ★★1/2

Taittinger (nonvintage) Brut, La Française, Champagne $25.50. Lovely, fresh aroma; typical fresh-bread component. Smooth, almost creamy texture. Balanced. Fairly long finish. (S&PW/Nov. '86) ★★1/2

Barancourt (nonvintage) Bouzy Brut, Reserve, Champagne $19.49. Lively mousse. Toasty, yeasty aroma. Quite dry. Full bodied, balanced. Lively finish. (S&PW/Nov. '86) ★★

Bollinger (nonvintage) Brut, Champagne $21.15. Steady stream of pinpoint bubbles. Full, intense aroma. Bottle-aged character. Smooth textured, full bodied, dry, firm, quite nice. Moderately long finish. (S&PW/Nov. '86) ★★

Charles Lafitte (nonvintage) Brut, Champagne $15. Light, balanced, fresh, clean, some character and length. Very nice. Fair value. (S&PW/Nov. '86) ★★

Guy Larmandier (nonvintage) Cramant Grand Cru Blanc de Blancs, Champagne $19.99. Lively bead. Lovely, fresh-bread-like, yeast aroma. Light, fresh, clean, balanced. Some length. (S&PW/Nov. '86) ★★

Mailly (nonvintage) Brut, Champagne $19. Dry, fruity, clean. (S&PW/Nov. '86) ★★

Masse (nonvintage) Brut, Champagne $14.99. Light, fresh-bread-like, yeast aroma. Medium dry for a Brut. Good character. Fairly long finish. (S&PW/Nov. '86) ★★

Masse (nonvintage) Extra Dry, Champagne $14.18. Fresh aroma. Drier style in the genre. Flavorful, medium bodied, balanced. (S&PW/Nov. '86) ★★

Pol Roger 1979 Brut, Champagne $29. Fresh-bread-like, yeast aroma. Fairly sweet for a Brut. Well balanced, somewhat light for this house. Real Champagne character. (S&PW/Nov. '86) ★★

Pommery 1980 Cuvée Spéciale Louise Pommery, Champagne $49.99. Fairly one-dimensional aroma, fresh-bread-like, yeast overlay. Light bodied, some flavor. Lacks richness and depth. Not bad but grossly overpriced. (S&PW/Nov. '86) ★★

P. Louis Martin (nonvintage) Bouzy Brut, Champagne $14.99. Fairly lively mousse. Some vanilla in the aroma. Good body. Clean, balanced, quite nice. (S&PW/Nov. '86) ★1/2

Perrier-Jouet (nonvintage) Brut, Champagne $21.99. Tiny bead rises steadily. Light, fresh yeast aroma. Lighter, somewhat sweeter style. Balanced, clean, some length. (S&PW/Nov. '86) ★1/2

Piper-Heidsieck 1979 Brut, Champagne $31.50. Lively stream of tiny bubbles. Light, fresh-bread-like, yeast aroma. Moderate sweetness for the genre, with underlying firmness. Light-bodied. Finishes somewhat firm. (S&PW/Nov. '86) ★1/2

Pommery 1981 Brut Royal, Champagne $29.99. Fresh bread aroma. Quite dry, light bodied, fruity. Some firmness. Short, lively finish. (S&PW/Nov. '86) ★1/2

De Ste Marceaux (nonvintage) Blanc de Blancs, Champagne $17.25. Fresh, clean, balanced, fruity, but without much character. (S&PW/Nov. '86) ★

Georges Goulet (nonvintage) Extra Quality Brut, Champagne $15. Steady stream of tiny bubbles. Fresh aroma with a bread-like nuance. Somewhat sweeter style Brut. Light-to-medium body, soft texture. Could use more length. (S&PW/Nov. '86) ★

Jacquesson (nonvintage) Perfection Brut, Champagne $14.99. Lively mousse. Light, characteristic aroma. A bit light, moderate sweetness, balanced. (S&PW/ Nov. '86) ★

Leclerc-Briant (nonvintage) Blanc de Noirs, Champagne $17.25. Light, bread-yeast aroma. Fairly nice acid. A bit pedestrian. (S&PW/Nov. '86) ★

Moët & Chandon (nonvintage) Brut Imperial, Champagne $23.99. Clean, fresh, fruity aroma and palate. Moderately sweet for a Brut. Good example of the genre. (S&PW/Nov. '86) ★

Mumm 1979 Cordon Rouge Brut, Champagne $29.99. Fast-rising, tiny bubbles. Fresh-bread-like, yeast aroma. Light, fruity style; lacks some zip. (S&PW/Nov. '86) ★

Mumm (nonvintage) Cordon Rouge Brut, Champagne $24.69. Sweeter style, fruity, soft, round, easy. (S&PW/Nov. '86) ★

Piper-Heidsieck (nonvintage) Brut, Champagne $25.50. Lively perlage.

Fresh, fruity, clean aroma. Light bodied, fruity, vague toasty note. Reasonably well balanced. (S&PW/Nov. '86) ★

Piper-Heidsieck (nonvintage) Extra Dry, Champagne $23.75. Fairly lively bead. Light, clean, fresh-bread-like, yeast aroma. Moderate sweetness for the style. Fruity, agreeable, simple. (S&PW/Nov. '86) ★

Alexandre Bonnet (nonvintage) Brut, Champagne $13.99. Lively, fast-rising bead. Fresh-bread-like, yeast aroma. Shows age on the palate. Could use more acid. One dimensional. (S&PW/Nov. '86) 1/2

Le Brun (nonvintage) Brut, Champagne $15.99. Light-bodied, fruity, rather dull, without charm. (S&PW/Nov. '86) 1/2

Pommery (nonvintage) Brut Royale, Champagne $22.99. Light, fresh-bread-like, yeast aroma. Light, lively, fruity. A bit short. Lively. (S&PW/Nov. '86) 1/2

Pommery (nonvintage) Extra Dry, Champagne $22.29. Very little of interest. Agreeable at best, though a bit coarse. (S&PW/Nov. '86) 1/2

Barancourt (nonvintage) Bouzy Brut, Champagne $24.75. Oxidized. Shallow. Short. (S&PW/Nov. '86)

Beaumet 1979 Brut, Champagne $14.99. Lively mousse. It's all downhill from there: tired, dull, old. (S&PW/Nov. '86)

Bricout (nonvintage) Brut Carte Or, Champagne $14.99. Good mousse. Stinky. Dull, flat. (S&PW/Nov. '86)

De Castellane 1980 Blanc de Blancs, Champagne $24.89. Bread, yeast aroma. Very light, quite short. (S&PW/Nov. '86)

Jacquart (nonvintage) Brut, Champagne $17.49. Steady stream of tiny bubbles. Light, toasty aroma. Overly soft, sweeter style Brut; rather low acid. Pleasant but a bit coarse, lacks definition. (S&PW/Nov. '86)

Jacquart (nonvintage) Extra Dry, Champagne $15.99. Large, lazy bubbles. Fruity, dull, a bit heavy handed. Pricey for the quality. (S&PW/Nov. '86)

Laurent Perrier 1973 Grand Siècle, Champagne $56.24. Some oxidation painfully evident from the aroma through a somewhat bitter finish. Fading fast. (S&PW/Nov. '86)

Le Brun (nonvintage) Carte Blanche Demi Sec, Champagne $14.99. Old, tired. Never amounted to much. (S&PW/Nov. '86)

Leclerc-Briant (nonvintage) Brut, Cuvée La Liberté, Champagne $17.75. Off note mars the aroma; unclean. Dull and mediocre. (S&PW/Nov. '86)

Maurice Laurent (nonvintage) Brut, Champagne $13.99. Rather flat, dull, tired. (S&PW/Nov. '86)

Philippe Flaurent (nonvintage) Brut, 1er Cru, Champagne $12. Light, fruity, fresh. Lacks acid and length. Drinkable, no more. (S&PW/Nov. '86)

FRENCH CHAMPAGNE ROSÉ

Besserat de Bellefon (nonvintage) Crémant, Rosé, Brut, Champagne $30. Sprightly effervescence lavishes elegance across the palate. Supple fruit. Crisp. Dry. (CC/Jan. '86) ★★★★

Billecart-Salmon (nonvintage) Rosé, Brut, Champagne $30. Expansive bouquet of mellow, toasty spice introduces complex flavors. Lively bubbles, firm acidity give a refreshing edge to a long, silky smooth finish. (CC/Jan. '86) ★★★★

Taittinger 1976 Comtes de Champagne, Rosé, Brut, Champagne $68. Delicate, spicy-fruit aromas carry through and magnify in the mouth. Superb. (CC/Jan.'86) ★★★★

Veuve Clicquot Ponsardin 1979 Rosé, Brut, Champagne $26. Typical Clicquot style. Intensely perfumed; aromas of ripe raspberries, cassis, exotic spices. Multifaceted flavors, generously dispersed by tiny, power-packed bubbles. (CC/Jan. '86) ★★★★

Krug (nonvintage) Rosé, Brut, Champagne $65. Frothy mousse of extremely fine bubbles introduces complex nose with distinctive earthiness. Pinot Noir aromas and flavors are bright, well defined. (CC/Jan. '86) ★★★ (★★★1/2)

Charbaut 1976 Certificate Rosé, Brut, Champagne $58. Full-blown, berryish fruit laced from nose to finish with delicate, green apple. Rich, creamy style, nicely offset by ample acidity, energetic, tiny bubbles. (CC/Jan. '86) ★★★

Gosset (nonvintage) Rosé, Brut, Champagne $22. Rich fruit; lush, ripe flavors are straightforward. Subtle sweetness nicely balanced by acidity. (CC/Jan. '86) ★★★

Laurent Perrier (nonvintage) Cuvée Rosé, Brut, Champagne $30. Lavish fruit aromas have delicate, yeasty highlights. Fine bubbles have good impact, delivering lots of fruit flavors that linger nicely. Acidity is crisp. Dry style. (CC/Jan. '86) ★★★

Moët & Chandon 1973 Dom Pérignon Rosé, Brut, Champagne $75. Delicate perfume of vanilla, spices, Rubrum lilies, needs a few minutes aeration. Medium intense flavors. Mousse is a tad soft, but firm acidity gives vibrancy. Green-apple accents in a dry finish. (CC/Jan. '86) ★★★

Piper-Heidsieck 1976 Rosé, Brut, Champagne $31. Toasty, complex. Vivacious mousse. Nicely balanced, with lingering, light toasty finish. (CC/Jan. '86) ★★★

Pol Roger 1975 Rosé, Brut, Champagne $26. Delicate fruit and toast. Very dry, crisp; long finish. (CC/Jan. '86) ★★★

Roederer (nonvintage) Rosé, Brut, Champagne $32. Very fine bubbles reveal elegant melange of aroma and flavor. Fresh, bracing. (CC/Jan. '86) ★★★

Charbaut (nonvintage) Rosé, Brut, Champagne $22. Packed with lush fruit.

Cherry-berry perfume, mildly candyish, leads to subtle, sweet aftertaste. Rich, bright, lively. (CC/Jan. '86) ★★3/4

Bollinger 1979 Grande Année Rosé, Brut, Champagne $35. Mild, toasty aromas. Direct fruit flavors. Fine, frothy mousse. Not powerful or complex, but still lively, elegant, dry. (CC/Jan. '86) ★★1/2 (★★★)

Bollinger 1981 Rosé, Champagne $37.99. Typical Bollinger depth on the nose. Somewhat austere, perhaps too serious for the genre. (S&PW/Nov. '86) ★★1/2

Moët & Chandon 1980 Rosé, Brut, Champagne $32. Fresh, restrained aromas lead to simple, pleasant, fruit flavors. Youthful, delicate, soft, easy-to-drink. (CC/Jan. '86) ★★

Piper-Heidsieck 1979 Rosé, Champagne $37.50. Lively mousse. Fresh-bread aroma also recalls berries. Fairly sweet, fruity, light-bodied. Lovely acid to balance. (S&PW/Nov. '86) ★★

Ruinart Père et Fils 1976 Dom Ruinart Rosé, Brut, Champagne $35. Berry-like perfume, almost candyish. Moderately complex, finishes dry. (CC/Jan. '86) ★★

De Castellane (nonvintage) Rosé, Brut, Champagne $24. Fresh, ripe Pinot Noir nose with just a candyish hint. Simple, fruity. Fine, lively mousse underscores crisp acidity. (CC/Jan. '86) ★1/2

Ayala (nonvintage) Rosé, Brut, Champagne $24. Complex aromas and flavors include a mild earthiness layered with grass and tobacco. Tart, moderately long. Astringent finish. (CC/Jan. '86) ★

Jacquesson (nonvintage) Rosé, Brut, Champagne $17. Toast and smoke aromas almost overwhelm a rich, fleshy wine. Bracing acidity and insistent, tiny bubbles. (CC/Jan. '86) ★

Nicolas Feuillatte (nonvintage) Rosé, Brut, Champagne $18. Aroma and flavor rather simple, verging on bland. Lively mousse reveals a hint of caramel in the finish. (CC/Jan. '86) ★

Perrier Jouet (nonvintage) Blanson de Champagne, Champagne $28. Fat, fleshy texture incongruous with delicate aromas and mild, appley flavors. Bubbles are exceedingly tiny, squelched by weighty fullness; leaves a flat finish. (CC/Jan. '86) ★

Pommery (nonvintage) Rosé, Champagne $29.99. Fruity aroma. Rather unimpressive. (S&PW/Nov. '86) 3/4

Albert Le Brun (nonvintage) Rosé, Brut, Champagne $15. Guava and tropical fruit aromas; candy-like scent. Similar flavors leave bitter, metallic finish. (CC/Jan.'86)

Charles Heidsieck 1976 Rosé, Champagne $29.99. Color has a copper cast. Some maderization beneath a toasty aroma. Somewhat tired. (S&PW/Nov. '86)

Lanson (nonvintage) Rosé, Brut, Champagne $25. Well endowed with lively, tiny bubbles and a crisp acid edge. Unappealing, earthy notes and bitterness. (CC/Jan. '86)

Mailly (nonvintage) Rosé, Champagne $23.50. Some oxidation apparent. A bit heavy and dull. Getting on in age. (S&PW/Nov. '86)

Mumm 1979 Rosé, Brut, Champagne $30. Aroma and flavors of green, unripe fruit. Well-made, dry, quite crisp. (CC/Jan.'86)

FORTIFIED WINES

ABBREVIATIONS & SYMBOLS

RATINGS

★★★★—Like extremely or Platinum Medal
★★★1/2—Like very strongly or Gold Medal
★★★—Like strongly or Silver Medal
★★—Like slightly or Bronze Medal
★—Neither like nor dislike, a useful wine
(★)—Estimated peak score with aging
No Star—A wine with no star is a wine that won no medal in competition or a wine that the reviewer disliked.

WHO WROTE THE DESCRIPTIONS

AWC—American Wine Competition Judges
BC—Bordeaux Classic Judges
JB—John Binder
CC—Carole Collier
RF—Richard Figiel
CG—Craig Goldwyn
JDM—Jerry D. Mead
DM—Denman Moody Jr.
JPN—Judy Peterson-Nedry
CR—Christina Reynolds
S&PW—Sheldon & Pauline Wasserman

PRICES. Prices are typical of those in major metropolitan markets for standard, 750-ml bottles *at the time the review was written* (note the date following the descriptions). The prices of some wines are likely to rise as time passes. Prices may also vary *significantly* from state to state and store to store.

AVAILABILITY. Some wines may be hard to find because they are produced in small quantities, and distribution methods often make wines that are bestsellers in one city unavailable in another. Even large stores can't carry more than a fraction of the thousands of wines sold in the US and Canada, so many merchants are happy to order wines for you. If can't find wines you want in your area, try to shop when you're in other major cities.

FORTIFIED WINES

There is a special breed of wine, fortified wine, that is different from all other wine. Fortified wines have been fortified with the addition of raw, unaged grape brandy, raising the alcohol level from the normal 10-13%, for most table wines, to 17-21%. The additional alcohol helps preserve the wines longer than any other type, and adds flavor and complexity.

The best-known types of fortifieds are Sherry, Madeira, and Port. Sherry originated in the Jerez region of Spain, and is made in several styles. *Fino* sherry is dry, delicate, nutlike in flavor, and best served chilled, when young and fresh. *Manzanilla* is similar, with a slightly salty character. Fino and Manzanilla get their unique aroma from a special surface yeast called *flor*. *Amontillado* is fuller and richer. *Oloroso* is fuller still, and *cream sherry* is rich, sweet, and concentrated. *Palo Cortado* is full-flavored, like an Oloroso, but has the light, delicate, nutty nose of a fino. Sherry is almost never vintage-dated because the wines are blended from several vintages in a process called *solera*.

Madeiras come from the tiny Portuguese island of Madeira about 600 miles off the coast of Morocco. *Sercial* is light, pale, almost dry, and usually served chilled. *Verdelho* is fuller, *bual* is fuller still, and *malmsey* is full, rich, and sweet. *Rainwater* is a medium-bodied blend. Some Madeiras bear a "vintage" date, but even dated Madeiras are usually blended from several vintages.

Porto is the official, Portuguese name of Port made in Portugal. Most Port is made from red grapes, and ranges in color from bright ruby when young, to pale tawny when older, although there are several lovely white Ports made. Most Ports are blends of several vintages, but in the best years they are bottled with the harvest date and the bottling date on the label. *Vintage Ports* are very slow to age, and usually require 15 years to begin to mellow. *Late Bottled Vintage Ports* are wines that have spent more time in the barrel than traditional vintage Ports, and are softer, lighter, and easier to drink when young. *Port "of the vintage"* is blended from several vintages, beginning with the vintage on the label. *Ruby Port* is a blend of young, barrel-aged Port. *Tawny Port* is usually older.

Ports are usually served at room temperature (some people chill their tawnies), and the older Vintage Ports usually require decanting to separate the clear wine from the heavy crust deposited in the bottle.

Most Ports are made in the town of Oporto by large wineries called *bodegas*, but there has been a recent trend toward small producers "estate bottling" their wines. Port has been enjoying the attentiveness of wine buyers lately, and has become quite popular with collectors.

The wines reviewed below are all Ports, with the exception of one noteworthy American sherry at the end.

PORT

Taylor Fladgate (nonvintage) 20 Year Old Tawny $31.99. Lovely, complex bouquet with characteristic vanilla and nut nuances. Smooth, harmonious, complete. Superb. The finish lingers and lingers. (S&PW/Jan. '87) ★★★★

Burmester (nonvintage) Tordiz Tinto Adamado, Ultra Reserva $44.99. Over 40 years old. Intensely concentrated bouquet and flavor, like a liqueur. Smooth and rich. A lot of class and style. A Tawny Port for meditation. (S&PW/Jan. '87) ★★★1/2

Adriano Ramos Pintos 1927 Late Bottled Vintage Port $150. Bouquet displays a lot of fruit with components that recall nuts, vanilla, flowers; surprisingly fresh. Sweet, smooth, almost velvety mouth feel. Very long finish. A lot of charcter, class, elegance. (S&PW/Jan. '87) ★★★1/4

Adriano Ramos Pintos 1937 Port $72.99. Bottled in 1984. Intense vanilla, nuts, dried-fruit, and floral bouquet. Soft, nutty flavor. Smooth texture. Very long finish; some delicacy. (S&PW/Jan. '87) ★★★1/4

Niepoort 1963 Colheita $30. Bottled in 1984. Intense, complex bouquet with nuances of vanilla, nuts, flowers, vague honey and quince notes. Sweet, smooth, rich, with an almost lush flavor and licorice note. Very long, complex finish. (S&PW/Jan. '87) ★★★1/4

Offley 1951 Baron Forrester Reserve $40.29. Bottled in 1985. Penetrating bouquet has hints of flowers, pecans, vanilla. Smooth, silky, mellow, sweet, mouthfilling. Long finish has a bit of a bite that adds interest. (S&PW/Jan. '87) ★★★1/4

Ferreira (nonvintage) Duque de Bragança, 20 Year Old Tawny $20.99. Moderately intense, nutty aroma. Sweet, smooth, velvety, harmonious. Long finish. A sweeter-style Tawny with real style and class. (S&PW/Jan. '87) ★★★

Fonseca (nonvintage) Bin 27 $12. Richly fruited aroma with nuances of cherry, chocolate, nuts. Lush fruit flavors, sweet, full bodied, with some tannin. Very long finish. Loads of class. A best buy. (S&PW/Jan. '87) ★★★

Graham (nonvintage) Emperor, 20 Year Old Tawny $29.88. Intense, nutty aroma with a vanilla overlay. Sweet, almost lush flavor has a nutty component. Smooth and harmonious, with real style. Long finish. Loads of character. (S&PW/Jan. '87) ★★★

Niepoort 1966 Colheita $23.50. Bottled in 1984. Nuts and vanilla up front on the nose with dried apricots in the back. Sweet, smooth, and round, some firmness. Long, dry, almost firm finish. A lot of class and well worth the price. (S&PW/Jan. '87) ★★★

Noval (nonvintage) Reserva da Quinta $29.99. 20 years old. Delicate bouquet has hints of vanilla, flowers, nuts. Lovely, balanced, with characteristic, Noval gentleness. (S&PW/Jan. '87) ★★★

Offley 1963 Baron Forrester Reserve $30.79. Bottled in 1985. Vanilla, walnut, pecan aroma. Sweet, smooth, nutty flavor. Long finish. Classic Port. (S&PW/Jan. '87) ★★★

Taylor Fladgate 1978 Late Bottled Vintage Port $13.75. Fairly rich, fruity aroma with a spicy, chocolate overlay. Full bodied, smooth, fruity; in a drier style. Has evolved nicely and rounded out. Harmonious. Lingering finish. Excellent value. (S&PW/Jan. '87) ★★★

Adriano Ramos Pintos (nonvintage) Quinta do Bom Retiro, 20 Year Old Tawny $24.99. Lovely, rich, intense aroma with characteristic vanilla and nut components; vaguely floral. Smooth and harmonious, rich and complete. (S&PW/Jan. '87) ★★3/4

Niepoort (nonvintage) VV $100. Rich, penetrating bouquet has notes of vanilla, nuts, some sharpness (volatile acidity); more like Madeira than Port. Smooth, soft, velvety. Long finish has slight harshness. Interesting. (S&PW/Jan. '87) ★★3/4

Kopke 1977 Colheita $7.50. Bottled in 1985. Interesting bouquet combines walnuts and fruit. Sweet and fruity with vanilla and nut flavors. Well balanced. A lot of character. Outstanding value. (S&PW/Jan. '87) ★★1/2

Niepoort 1934 Colheita $134.99. Interesting, complex bouquet. Many nuances of flavor under vanilla and caramel components, smooth and concentrated. (S&PW/Jan. '87) ★★1/2

Niepoort 1970 Colheita $19.99. Bottled in 1984. Nutty with a vanilla-and-caramel overlay. Smooth. Lingering finish. Stylish. (S&PW/Jan. '87) ★★1/2

Noval 1964 $35. Lovely bouquet has delicacy and a light, floral note. Smooth and balanced. Has style and class. (S&PW/Jan. '87) ★★1/2

Offley (nonvintage) Baron Forrester, 20 Year Old Tawny $28.89. Bottled in 1985. Lovely bouquet recalls walnuts. Sweet and smooth with a velvety texture. Loads of flavor and class in a sweeter style. (S&PW/Jan. '87) ★★1/2

Quarles Harris 1979 Late Bottled Vintage Port $16.99. Bottled in 1985. Classic, peppery, cherry aroma. Sweet, soft, gentle style; full flavored and supple. Well balanced. Long, peppery, spicy finish. (S&PW/Jan. '87) ★★1/2

Taylor Fladgate (nonvintage) 10 Year Old Tawny $16.99. Dried fruit, vanilla, and nut aroma. Well balanced, smooth. Some complexity. Fairly long aftertaste. (S&PW/Jan. '87) ★★1/2

Warre's 1986 Grand Reserve $17.75. Bottled in 1984. Complex aroma of nuts, vanilla, dried fruit, apricots. Relatively dry. Fairly rich. Long, dry, firm finish with a chocolate note. (S&PW/Jan. '87) ★★1/2

Ferreira (nonvintage) Dona Antonia Personal Reserve $7.99. Walnut, cherry aroma. Flavor of ripe fruit and nuts. Smooth texture. Fairly long finish recalls nuts and vanilla. Good value. (S&PW/Jan. '87) ★★1/4

Offley (nonvintage) Baron Forrester, Quinta Reserve $14.49. Fairly intense, walnut, vanilla aroma. Nutty flavor: sweet, smooth, round, and soft. Some length and grip. (S&PW/Jan. '87) ★★1/4

Warre's 1965 Grand Reserve $21.49. Fragrant bouquet recalls walnuts and vanilla. Well balanced, smooth, somewhat drier style. Moderately long finish is a tad hot. (S&PW/Jan. '87) ★★1/4

Adriano Ramos Pintos 1982 Late Bottled Vintage Port $10.99. Bottled in September 1986. Cherry, peppery, grapey aroma carries over on the palate. Smooth textured. Moderately rich. (S&PW/Jan. '87) ★★

Adriano Ramos Pintos (nonvintage) Quinta da Ervamoira, 10 Year Old Tawny $13.75. A melange of nut aromas with a vanilla overlay. Sweet and smooth, with flavors of fruit and nuts. A tad hot at the end. A nice sipper. (S&PW/Jan. '87) ★★

Croft 1978 Late Bottled Vintage Port $15. Bottled in 1984. Moderately intense, cherry aroma hints of spice. Richly flavored, cherry-like, drier style. Moderate length. (S&PW/Jan. '87) ★★

Ferreira (nonvintage) Ruby Superior $5.99. Peppery, cherry aroma. Sweet and fruity, with an alcoholic bite. Almost chewy texture. (S&PW/Jan. '87) ★★

Noval 1937 Colheita $150 (estimated). Vaguely vanilla aroma with a fruit component and a hint of flowers; a slight harshness intrudes. Sweet but beginning to dry out toward the back. Age is setting in though it still has flavor and interest. (S&PW/Jan. '87) ★★

Noval 1941 $75. Bottled in 1986. Ethereal scent shows some age with a touch of sharpness (volatile acidity). Flavors are quite interesting. Somewhat edgy, especially toward the end. (S&PW/Jan. '87) ★★

Noval (nonvintage) Trinity House, Choice Reserve $14.99. 10 years old. Walnuts, pecans, and vanilla define the aroma. Smooth, round flavor with some complexity. Somewhat spirity at the end. (S&PW/Jan. '87) ★★

Taylor Fladgate 1981 Late Bottled Vintage Port $12.99. Rich, fruity aroma, fairly straightforward. Peppery, spicy, chocolate-like nuances on the palate. Nice for current drinking though somewhat firm at the end. (S&PW/Jan. '87) ★★

Warre's (nonvintage) Nimrod $14.49. 15-20 years old. Nuts, flowers, and vanilla aroma. Dried fruit flavor. Smooth, firm, well balanced. Long, firm finish. (S&PW/Jan. '87) ★★

Delaforce (nonvintage) His Eminence's Choice Reserve Tawny $13.19. 16 years old. Walnut, vanilla aroma. Smooth-textured and sweet, with a lingering finish. (S&PW/Jan. '87) ★3/4

Dow's (nonvintage) Boardroom $12.25. Vanilla and walnuts on the nose and palate. Smooth and easy. (S&PW/Jan. '87) ★3/4

Ferreira 1980 Late Bottled Vintage Port $10.99. Bottled in 1985. Light, plummy aroma with a nut-like backnote. Sweet and fruity with a licorice component; on the light side. Some firmness at the end. (S&PW/Jan. '87) ★3/4

Ferreira (nonvintage) Quinta do Porto, 10 Year Old Tawny $11.99. Nutty aroma. On the sweet side. Light bodied. Smooth. Firm finish. (S&PW/Jan. '87) ★3/4

Niepoort 1960 Colheita $39.99. Complex aroma hints of vanilla, flowers, nuts. Fairly sweet and concentrated. Smooth. Rather short. (S&PW/Jan. '87) ★3/4

Noval 1981 Late Bottled Vintage Port $12.99. Bottled in 1986. Small but nice nose. Fairly dry. Some firmness across the palate and at the end. (S&PW/Jan. '87) ★3/4

Noval (nonvintage) LB $10.99. Intense aroma suggests cherries. Nice fruit flavors. A sophisticated Ruby Port; deeper, richer and more complex than Noval's Old Coronation. (S&PW/Jan. '87) ★3/4

Offley (nonvintage) Baron Forrester, 10 Year Old Tawny $19.49. Bottled in 1985. Aroma of vanilla and nuts. Fairly sweet. On the light side. More fruit than nuts in the flavor. Long, sweet aftertaste. (S&PW/Jan. '87) ★3/4

Offley Boa Vista 1980 Late Bottled Vintage Port $12.49. Bottled in 1985. Cherryish, spicy aroma. Sweet, fruity, full-flavored within a light frame. Some heat at the end. Enjoyable for current consumption. (S&PW/Jan. '87) ★3/4

Robertson (nonvintage) Imperial, 20 Year Old Tawny $29.95. Walnut and vanilla aroma. Sweet. Somewhat simple for its age but most agreeable. (S&PW/Jan. '87) ★3/4

Sandeman (nonvintage) Royal Tawny $13.49. 12 years old. Floral, vanilla aroma. Smooth and sweet, with backbone and length. (S&PW/Jan. '87) ★3/4

Taylor Fladgate (nonvintage) Special Tawny $8.99. Aroma has some complexity. Smooth and flavorful. Some character. (S&PW/Jan. '87) ★3/4

Warre's (nonvintage) Ruby $7.49. Fresh, spicy, cherry aroma; some complexity. Fruity but still in a drier style. (S&PW/Jan. '87) ★3/4

Adriano Ramos Pintos (nonvintage) Quinta Urtiga, Vintage Character $11.99. Fresh, cherry-like aroma with chocolate and cherry components. Sweet, rich flavors have licorice and chocolate notes. Smooth. Alcohol in the finish. (S&PW/Jan. '87) ★1/2

Cockburn (nonvintage) Special Reserve $11.99. Straightforward, fruity aroma. Round, fruity flavors with a firm finish. (S&PW/Jan. '87) ★1/2

Croft 1980 Late Bottled Vintage Port $15. Bottled in 1985. Peppery, fruity aroma displays a cherry-like component. Balanced, fruity, sweet. Nice for current drinking. (S&PW/Jan. '87) ★1/2

Delaforce 1979 Late Bottled Vintage Port $17.09. Bottled in 1985. Fresh, moderately intense, peppery-cherry aroma vaguely recalls nuts. Sweet, smooth, fresh. On the lighter side. Firm, dry finish. (S&PW/Jan. '87) ★1/2

Hutcheson 1974 Colheita $11.76. Bottled in 1985. Walnut and vanilla aroma. Smooth entry. Round and sweet, with a walnut flavor. (S&PW/Jan. '87) ★1/2

Noval (nonvintage) Old Coronation $7.49. Peppery, spicy, fruity aroma has some complexity. Sweet, fruity, with some firmness. (S&PW/Jan. '87) ★1/2

Offley 1968 Baron Forrester Reserve $23.99. Bottled in 1986. Refined, vanilla and walnut aroma. Sweet style with a soft center; lacks some concentration but agreeable. Firm finish with a slight alcoholic bite. (S&PW/Jan. '87) ★1/2

Sandeman (nonvintage) Founders Reserve $12.49. 7 years old. Aroma hints of dried fruit, vanilla, nuts. Fruity flavor with dried-fruit component. (S&PW/Jan. '87) ★1/2

Smith Woodhouse (nonvintage) Old Lodge, Finest Rare Tawny $11.89. Nutty and vanilla aroma with a dried fruit component. Sweet, smooth, nutty, somewhat simple flavors. (S&PW/Jan. '87) ★1/2

Taylor Fladgate (nonvintage) Special Ruby $8.99. Fruity aroma and flavor with some character. A very good example of the genre. (S&PW/Jan. '87) ★1/2

Warre's 1957 Grand Reserve $29.99. Bottled in 1984. Somewhat restrained bouquet of vanilla and nuts with a floral backnote. Nutty, chocolate flavor. Moderately long finish recalls chocolate. (S&PW/Jan. '87) ★1/2

Warre's (nonvintage) Warrior $11.99. Fruity, peppery, cherry aroma with spicy notes. Medium-to-full bodied, moderate sweetness, nice fruit, rich flavor. Long, chocolatey finish. (S&PW/Jan. '87) ★1/2

Kopke (nonvintage) Varsity Ruby $5.49. Fruity, spicy aroma has a licorice note. Sweet and fruity, with a bit of a bite at the end. (S&PW/Jan. '87) ★1/4

Niepoort (nonvintage) Tawny $5.99. Bottled in 1985. Nutty, vanilla aroma. Sweet, simple, on the light side. Nice flavor hints of dried fruit. (S&PW/Jan. '87) ★1/4

Smith Woodhouse (nonvintage)

Fine Tawny $6.75. Aroma recalls dried fruit, nuts, vanilla. Sweet, simple, agreeable. (S&PW/Jan. '87) ★1/4

Adriano Ramos Pintos (nonvintage) Ruby $6.99. Fresh, fruity aroma recalls cherries and chocolate. Fruity, round, smooth. (S&PW/Jan. '87) ★

Borges 1977 Colheita, Quinta do Junco $9.99. Bottled in 1985. Walnut aroma. Medium sweet, smooth, nutty flavor. Simple. (S&PW/Jan. '87) ★

Borges (nonvintage) Ruby $5.99. Peppery, fruity aroma. Sweet, simple, balanced. (S&PW/Jan. '87) ★

Cockburn 1978 Late Bottled Vintage Port $9.99. Fruity aroma, vanilla overlay. Fairly rich flavor with good concentration, some grip. (S&PW/Jan. '87) ★

Cockburn (nonvintage) Cadima Choice Tawny $10.99. 7-9 years old. Dried-fruit aroma and flavor, sweet and easy. (S&PW/Jan. '87) ★

Croft (nonvintage) Distinction, 10 Year Old Tawny $11. Fruit-and-nut aroma. Surprisingly fruity for a Tawny. Somewhat simple but agreeable. (S&PW/Jan. '87) ★

Dow 1981 Late Bottled Vintage Port $8.25. Lovely, fruity aroma with a vanilla overlay. Dry, firm style. Short finish. (S&PW/Jan. '87) ★

Ferreira (nonvintage) Tawny $5.99. A simple, fruity, good example of the genre. (S&PW/Jan. '87) ★

Feuerheerd (nonvintage) Casino Ruby $5.99. Peppery, spicy, cherry aroma. Rich, sweet, fruity. (S&PW/Jan. '87) ★

Graham (nonvintage) Prince Regent's, 10 Year Old Tawny $12.99. Caramel, vanilla, butterscotch aroma. Sweet, full bodied, soft. Not a lot of character but nice. (S&PW/Jan. '87) ★

Hutcheson 1937 Colheita $61.50. Bottled in 1985. Nuts, vanilla, and caramel aromas marred by a touch of sharpness (volatile acidity). Beginning to fade but still has character and interest. (S&PW/Jan. '87) ★

Hutcheson 1947 Colheita $40.64. Bottled in 1985. Nuts-and-vanilla aroma with age apparent. Sweet and concentrated, like a liqueur. Harsh edges detract but still interesting. (S&PW/Jan. '87) ★

Hutcheson 1975 Colheita $11.63. Bottled in 1985. Walnut scents up front, dried fruit in the back. Sweet and smooth. A touch of bitterness at the end. (S&PW/Jan. '87) ★

Hutcheson 1977 Colheita $10.49. Bottled in 1985. Chocolate and vanilla aroma. Dried fruit and vanilla flavor. Lacks depth but nice. (S&PW/Jan. '87) ★

Kopke 1977 Colheita $7.99. Bottled in 1986. Lovely nose of vanilla and dried fruit. Smooth but simple, even a bit pedestrian. Perhaps bottle age will help. (S&PW/Jan. '87) ★

Kopke 1980 Late Bottled Vintage Port $11.50. Peppery, spicy aroma. Soft and fruity, on the simple side. A bit light but most agreeable. A tad hot at the end. (S&PW/Jan. '87) ★

Niepoort (nonvintage) Ruby $5.99. Intensely fruited aroma suggests dried apricots. Sweet. Some firmness. (S&PW/Jan. '87) ★

Ramos Pintos (nonvintage) Tawny $6.99. Fruity aroma and flavor. (S&PW/Jan. '87) ★

Robertson (nonvintage) No. 1 Game Bird Tawny $6.99. Fruity, simple aroma. Agreeable flavor. (S&PW/Jan. '87) ★

Sandeman (nonvintage) Fine Ruby $6.99. Dried-fruit aroma hints of vanilla and plums. Sweet, fruity, simple. Firm finish. (S&PW/Jan. '87) ★

Smith Woodhouse (nonvintage) Old Priory, Superb Fine Reserve $9.89. Youthful, black-pepper, cherry aroma. Sweet, fruity, soft. Lacks some depth but nice. (S&PW/Jan. '87) ★

Smith Woodhouse (nonvintage) Ru-

by **$6.75.** Peppery, cherry aroma. Simple, fruity, agreeable. (S&PW/Jan. '87) ★

Warre's 1974 Late Bottled Vintage Port $16.99. Bottled in 1978. Fairly deep red, more Ruby than Tawny. Small, fruity aroma. Somewhat flat on the palate, with cherry notes, some smoothness; alcohol at the end. (S&PW/Jan. '87) ★

Borges (nonvintage) Tawny $5.99. Fruity, youthful aroma. Sweet, smooth, simple, agreeable. (S&PW/Jan. '87) 3/4

Delaforce (nonvintage) Ruby $8.15. Grapey, sweet, straightforward. (S&PW/Jan. '87) 3/4

Feuerheerd 1965 Casino Wood Port $17.99. Bottled in 1985. Vanilla and walnut aroma, vaguely peach-like. Fairly sweet for the genre. Smooth, nutty flavor. Hot, alcoholic finish. Fairly nice but lacks depth. (S&PW/Jan. '87) 3/4

Hutcheson 1957 Colheita $27.38. Bottled in 1985. Nutty aromas up front, dried-fruit background. Intense entry but falls off at the end. (S&PW/Jan. '87) 3/4

Offley (nonvintage) Duke of Oporto, Ruby $8.99. Dried fruit and peppery aroma. Sweet, with a dried-fruit flavor. Somewhat bitter at the end. (S&PW/Jan. '87) 3/4

Robertson (nonvintage) Ruby $8.69. Straightforward, grapey, peppery aroma. Simple, fruit flavors. (S&PW/Jan. '87) 3/4

Hutcheson 1965 Colheita $17.50. Bottled in 1985. Dried apricot and vanilla aromas. Some smoothness but thinning out toward the back. Not much to it. (S&PW/Jan. '87) 1/2

Kopke (nonvintage) Tourist, Tawny $5.49. Dried fruit, vanilla, and vaguely nutty aroma. Sweet, dried-fruit flavor. A bit hot at the end. (S&PW/Jan. '87) 1/2

Offley (nonvintage) Duke of Oporto, Rich Tawny $8.99. Light nose of vanilla and fruit. Unbalanced, with alcohol intruding. Quite sweet, fruity, simple. Somewhat rough finish. (S&PW/Jan. '87) 1/2

Sandeman (nonvintage) Fine Tawny $6.99. Light aroma with some fruit evident. Drier than Sandeman's Ruby and less interesting. (S&PW/Jan. '87) 1/2

Warre's 1962 Grand Reserve $25.75. Bottled in 1985. Aroma has a nutty nuance; alcohol intrudes. Nice flavor suggests nuts. Unbalanced, with harsh edges and a rough finish. (S&PW/Jan. '87) 1/2

AMERICAN SHERRY

Angelo Papagni Finest Hour Cream Sherry, 1971 Solera, CA $9. Intense, concentrated bouquet of pecans, vanilla, vaguely of flowers; superb and complex. Velvety mouth feel with fine balance. Richly flavored, sweet, intense. Very long finish. (S&PW/Mar. '87) ★★★1/2

INDEX

INDEX to all 2,138 wines

A

B

C

F

G

H

K

M

P

S

W

N O T E S

Subscribe now to